The greater of the
and part still remains
in cultivation for a
divided, it might form part
Union Farm
Field No 1 120
2 129
3 121
4 120
5 110
6 116
7 125
Meadow ... 42
25 .. 67
Clover lots 20 925
3 52
4 54
5 65
6 80
7 74
Clover lots 20 476
Dogue R. Farm
Field No 1 70
2 74
3 74
4 71
5 75
6 73
7 80
Meadow .. 38
18
12
10
36 .. 114
Clover lots ... 18 649
River Farm
Field No 1 120
2 120
3 125
4 132
5 132
6 130
7 120
Pasture 212
Orchards do ... 84
Clover lots ... 32 1207
Union Farm ... 928
Dogue Run Do ... 649
In the 4 farms 3260
December 1793
W
E
Road to Alexandria &c &c
Scale
100
200
300
400
E
No 7
No 5
River Farm
No 6
No 4
Orchards
Grass lots
Barn
No 1
C
No 2
Common Pasture
No 3
D

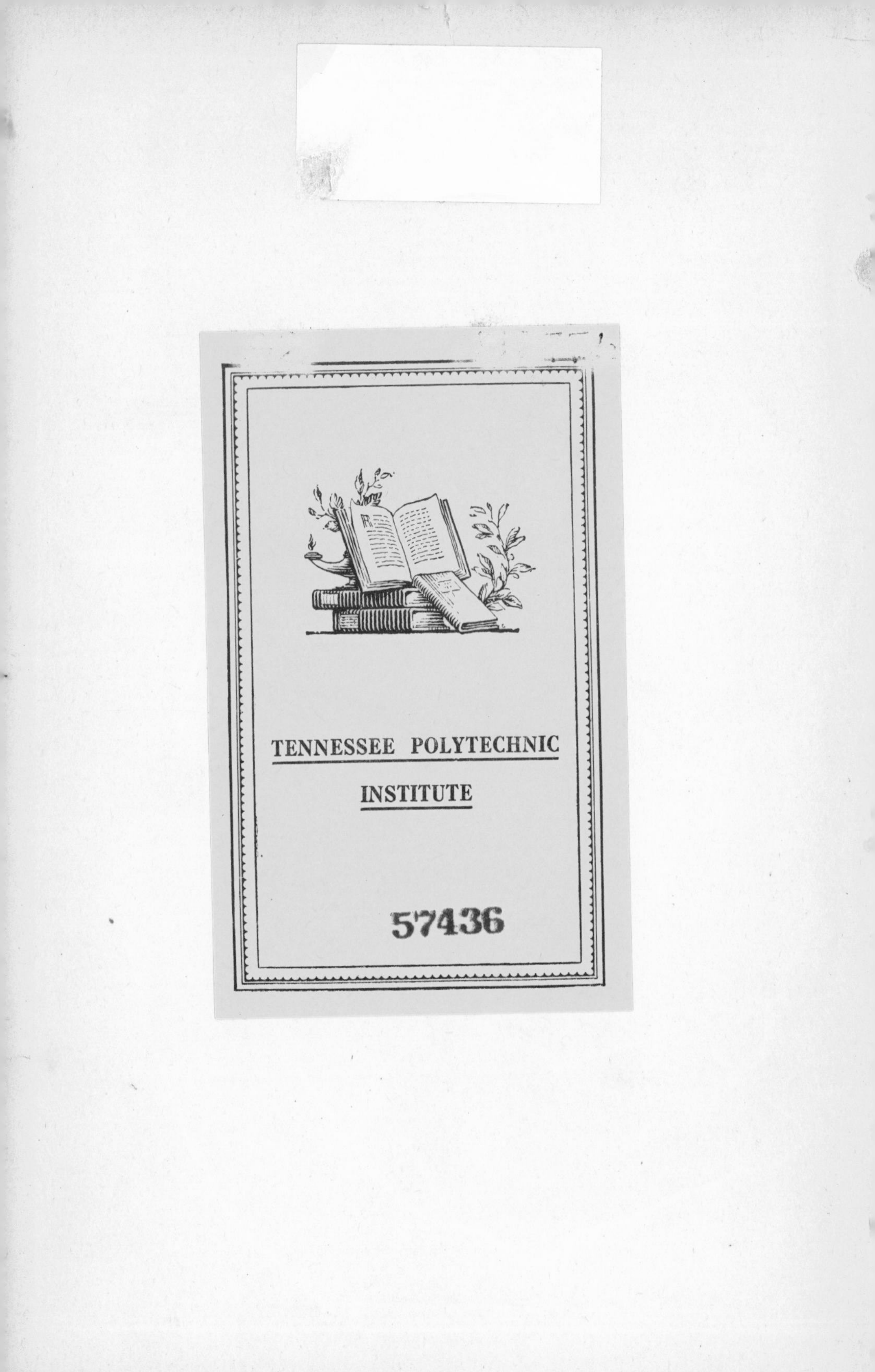
TENNESSEE POLYTECHNIC
INSTITUTE
57436

Courtesy Virginia State Chamber of Commerce

Mount Vernon—East Front

WASHINGTON AND HIS NEIGHBORS

WASHINGTON

and His Neighbors

By

CHARLES W. STETSON

GARRETT AND MASSIE, INCORPORATED
RICHMOND, VIRGINIA

LIBRARY OF CONGRESS CATALOG CARD NUMBER 55-11155
MANUFACTURED IN THE UNITED STATES OF AMERICA

To

my wife

Margaret Olcott Stetson

Foreword

Most lives of Washington, from Marshall's to Woodrow Wilson's, deal primarily with his public career, his services in the French and Indian War, the Revolutionary War, his wise guidance of the young Republic during his presidency, his inflexible integrity, his sound judgment, his constancy in adversity. These were the achievements and qualities that gave him fame in his lifetime and have received the praise of historians ever since. The lofty obelisk on the bank of the Potomac was reared in memory of the Father of his Country and not in honor of a Virginia planter. It is true Washington's sense of nationality grew as he advanced in years and public honors. In his will he describes himself as: "I George Washington of Mount Vernon, a citizen of the United States, and lately President of the same," but he never forgot that he was a Virginian. His ancestors had lived in the colony for a century. Most of his relatives were living in that state when he made his will, and he never forgot that he lived in Fairfax County. His home, he once wrote, "was like a well resorted tavern," but the visitors, the ones he enjoyed seeing and entertaining, were mostly his neighbors of Fairfax, and most of the homes he visited were Fairfax homes. After his term of office ended he served on juries, voted there and took an active interest in local affairs. He loved Fairfax as Jefferson loved Albemarle. On his way home an address was presented to him on behalf of the citizens of Alexandria and its neighborhood; a public dinner was tendered him at Gadsby's Tavern. In his reply he said: "For the affectionate and flattering manner in which you have been pleased to express your regrets on the occasion of my relinquishing public employment, and for your congratulations on my return to my long forsaken residence at Mount Vernon, I pray you to accept my warmest acknowledgments, and the assurance of the additional pleasure I shall derive from the prospect of spending the remainder of my days in ease and tranquility among you; employed in rural pursuits, and in the exercise of Domestic and other duties."

For all his voluminous correspondence, Washington was reticent about his private life. He wrote to his intimate friend Dr. Craik "I will frankly declare to you, my Dr. Doctor, that any memoirs of my life, distinct and unconnected with the general history of the war, would rather hurt my feelings than tickle my pride whilst I lived. I had rather glide gently down the stream of life, leaving to posterity to think and say what they please of me, than by any act of mine to have vanity or ostentation imputed to me."

This book is an attempt to depict some aspects of Washington's private life, but the author is conscious that it can be only partially successful. There are depths of hidden personality that no words can reveal. In Anna Karenina, Tolstoi makes Levin say: "I shall always feel a certain barrier between the Holy of Holies of my inmost soul, and the souls of others, even my wife's."

CHARLES W. STETSON

Contents

List of Illustrations

WASHINGTON AND HIS NEIGHBORS

Chapter 1

Ancestry and Early Life

In response to a request for genealogical information, Washington wrote to Sir Isaac Heard in 1792: "This is a subject to which I confess I have paid very little attention. My time has been so much occupied in the busy and active scenes of life from an early period of it that but a small portion of it could have been devoted to researches of this nature, even if my inclination or particular circumstances should have promoted the inquiry."[1] He enclosed in his reply all the information he possessed about his great-grandfather John Washington, the immigrant, and his descendants. He knew that John Washington had a brother Lawrence, who also came to Virginia about the same time. He promised to make inquiry about his descendants. He went to considerable trouble to gather such information about that branch by letters to Hannah Fairfax Washington, widow of Warner Washington. When he received Sir Isaac's letter, he was sixty years old—an age at which many persons who have not theretofore concerned themselves about their forebears, begin to be interested in the subject. He was President of the United States and must have realized that his ancestry was of interest to many of his English and American admirers, and perhaps to posterity. It is evident from his reply to Sir Isaac that he then knew nothing about his English ancestry.

In a general work of this sort it is not desirable to trace Washington's ancestry further back than to Lawrence Washington, Rector

[1]Washington, George, *Writings of Washington*, J. C. Fitzpatrick, Editor (hereinafter cited *Writings*), Vol. 32, p. 31. The information Washington furnished is printed in Vol. 32, p. 26.

of Purleigh, born in 1602. The Washingtons owned Sulgrave Manor for about eighty years. Their grant originated in a priory forfeited in 1539. The Washingtons had parted with the Manor before the time of the Rector of Purleigh.

In the first World War many American visitors became interested in the restoration and preservation of Sulgrave Manor. A corporation was formed by English and American admirers of Washington, the funds being equally furnished by British and Americans. A competent guide resides on the premises to give information to strangers and others. The future of the Manor is assured. It is the mecca of thousands of American tourists each year.

The Washington family of Virginia was descended from this Lawrence Washington, a graduate of Oxford University, a fellow of Brasenose College, who took holy orders and obtained the good living of Purleigh. He was a royalist during the Civil War and was ejected by the Puritan Parliament on the apparently trumped-up charge, "that he was a common frequenter of alehouses, not only himself sitting dayly tippling there . . . but hath often been drunk,"—"a charge indignantly denied by the royalists, who asserted that he was a worthy Pious man . . . always a very Modest, Sober Person."[2]

This Lawrence Washington had two sons, John and Lawrence. Both emigrated to Virginia, but separately, John coming first in 1657, as mate in the *Sea Horse* of London. Virginia was the natural refuge for royalists when the King's cause went down in defeat. Its governor, Sir William Berkeley, welcomed them. Henry Norwood's Voyage to Virginia tells of his fellow royalist exiles that he found at "Captain Wormly's" house on the York River—"Sir Thomas Lundsford, Sir Henry Chickley, Sir Philip Honeywood and Colonel Hammond, feasting and carousing." John Washington settled on the Potomac River in the newly formed county of Westmoreland. He was young, vigorous, without financial resources. He had no time for "feasting and carousing." He found

[2]Ford, Paul Leicester. *True George Washington* (hereinafter cited as Ford), p. 16.

Martha Washington
Portrait by Gilbert Stuart

George Washington
Portrait by Gilbert Stuart

Courtesy Virginia State Chamber of Commerce

Wakefield (Pages 4 and 5)

his neighbors friendly, among them, Nathaniel Pope, a Marylander who had come to Virginia and patented land there on a tidal inlet which was named after him. John Washington married Pope's daughter Ann and began patenting land on his own account. He rose in importance; became Justice of the County Court, a Burgess, and Vestryman of a parish that was presently named after him. He built his home on Bridges Creek. By his wife Ann Pope he left three children who survived him, Lawrence, John and Ann. After the death of his first wife he married Anne Brett, a widow. There was no issue by their marriage.

For our present purpose the most significant act of Colonel John Washington was his patent in connection with Secretary Nicholas Spencer, in 1669, of five thousand acres of escheated land, lying in the freshes of the Potomac between Dogue Run and Little Hunting Creek; this was the future Mount Vernon. John Washington died in 1677. His will divided his lands between his three children, Lawrence, John, and Ann. Lawrence received his father's share in the five thousand acres patented by Spencer and Washington and also the land at Bridges Creek.[3]

The family vault in which are interred the bodies of Colonel John Washington, his wife Ann and other members of the family is situated on Bridges Creek about a mile northwest of the present Wakefield. Colonel John Washington never owned the land on which that mansion stands. He did own a seven hundred acre tract nearby which had been given him and his first wife by her father, Colonel Pope.

Lawrence Washington, John Washington's older son, was a Justice of the Peace, a Burgess and Sheriff of Westmoreland County. He married Mildred, daughter of Augustine Warner, of Gloucester County, who was Speaker of the House of Burgesses, and a member of the Council of the Colony.[4] His marriage gave him wealth and

[3]Much of the information given here is contained in a folder issued by the National Park Service on George Washington's Birthplace.

[4]Warner Hall, the estate of Augustine Warner, is near the Severn River, a tributary of Mobjack Bay. All the house except one wing was burned early in the nineteenth century. It has been rebuilt and restored to its originial appearance. It is interesting to note that Augustine Warner was the ancestor of both George Washington and Robert E. Lee.

improved his social status. He died in 1698 in his thirty-eighth year and was buried in the family vault at Bridges Creek. He left sons, John and Augustine, and a daughter Mildred. His connection with the building at Mount Vernon will be discussed later. He devised to his daughter, who married Roger Gregory, his twenty-five hundred acres of the Little Hunting Creek plantation, which they deeded to Mildred's brother Augustine.

Augustine Washington was born at Bridges Creek in 1694. His son George, made an entry in the family Bible in his round schoolboy handwriting that "Augustine Washington was born at Bridges Creek in 1694 and married Mary Ball the sixth day of March 1730/31. Augustine Washington departed this Life ye 12th of April 1743 Aged 49 years." He was educated at Appleby School in England. He married Jane Butler and had issue by her of two sons, Lawrence and Augustine, and a daughter Jane. His second marriage was to Mary Ball, daughter of Captain Joseph Ball of Epping Forest. He had an interest in the Accokeek iron mines in Stafford County. He removed, with family then consisting of his wife and his three children, George, Betty and Samuel, to his land in the freshes of the Potomac (the future Mount Vernon) before November 18, 1735,[5] and left there in 1739 to make his home on his Ferry Farm on the Rappahannock River, near Fredericksburg, his reason probably being his desire to provide a home for his son Lawrence when he married Ann Fairfax.

"In 1718 Augustine Washington bought from Joseph Abbington 150 acres of land on Popes Creek a mile east of the Bridges Creek house." The available evidence shows he was living on this land before February 1726. His son George was born and spent the first three years of his life in this house, later called Wakefield. When Augustine left this house he put his second son Augustine in charge and subsequently devised it to him. This son lived there

[5]The evidence of this statement is the following entry in the Vestry Book of Truro Parish: 1735. Nov. 18th. "Augustine Washington, gent. being this day sworn one of the members of this Vestry, took his place therein accordingly."—Quoted in *History of Truro Parish* by Philip Slaughter. Edited by Edward L. Goodwin (Philadelphia, G. W. Jacobs & Co., 1907). According to law, only a resident of the parish could serve on the Vestry.

until his death in 1762. The farm then passed to his son, William Augustine, who was living there when it was accidentally burned during the Revolutionary War.[6] The site of the house and adjoining land was acquired in 1928 by The Wakefield National Memorial Association, which conveyed it to the United States in 1931. There is no reliable evidence of the appearance of the original house. The folder issued by the National Park Service has this to say: "The structure that was erected therefore represents generally a Virginia plantation house of the first half of the eighteenth century." Colonel Burgess Ball (1749-1800) is reported to have said that the original house resembled Providence Forge in New Kent County, which is a smaller building than the restored Wakefield.

Augustine Washington's will gave his eldest son Lawrence the largest part of his estate and confirmed his title to the plantation on Little Hunting Creek which had already been conveyed to him;[7] to George he gave the Ferry Farm. His body, at his request, was buried in the family graveyard on Bridges Creek.[8]

But for his untimely death, he probably would have given George a good education.

Lawrence Washington was born in 1718 and was thus fourteen years older than his half brother George. He was educated at Appleby School in England. He seems to have been managing his Epsewasson plantation (as Mount Vernon was then called) before his father's death. Some time later he took George to live there with him. Lawrence was ambitious and secured an appointment as Adjutant General of Northern Virginia. It was probably from that office that he gained the title of "Major." In 1744 he became a burgess from Fairfax County. He was an active member of the Ohio Company, which sought to gain control of the western lands before the French should get them. He was already launched on a promising career.

In 1739 England declared war on Spain. An expedition against

[6]Much of this information is contained in a folder issued on George Washington's Birthplace by the National Park Service.

[7]Deed recorded in the General Court of the Colony on October 23, 1740.

[8]Folder on George Washington's Birthplace issued by the National Park Service.

Cartagena was planned. The southern colonies of North America were called upon to furnish a contingent. The war was unpopular and conscription had to be resorted to in order to obtain soldiers. Lawrence Washington was commissioned a captain, and the Virginia and Maryland contingents finally sailed from Annapolis under command of Lieutenant Governor Gooch, to Jamaica where they were met by an army and a fleet. The latter was under the command of Admiral Vernon. The expedition failed miserably. On his return Lawrence named his estate Mount Vernon in honor of the Admiral.

On the neck below Mount Vernon at Belvoir lived the Honorable William Fairfax, the most influential man in that part of Virginia.

Lawrence spent much time at Belvoir and fell in love with the daughter of the house, Ann. They were married in August 1743. The death of three infants saddened their early married years and an additional shadow soon darkened their lives. Lawrence developed a racking cough. It was hoped that a sea voyage to Barbadoes would improve his health, and it was arranged that George should accompany him. George kept a diary of the trip, mutilated fragments of which survive. The greater part of it is like a ship's log giving weather, etc. From the items dealing with his personal affairs the following have been selected:

1751

"November 17th. Was strongly attacked with the small Pox: sent for Dr. Lanahan whose attendance was very constant till my recovery, and going out which was not 'till thursday the 12th of December.

"December 12th. Went to town visited Majr. Clarke's Family (who kindly visited me in my illness and contributed all they cou'd in sendg. me the necessary's required in ye disorder) . . . .

"December 22d. Took my leave of my Br. Majr. Clarke &ca. and Imbar (ked) in the Industry Captn. John Saund (ers) for Virginia. . . ."[9]

[9] *Diaries*, Vol. 1, p. 25, 27.

"Lawrence Washington's health did not improve. . . . It was arranged that George should return to Virginia; that Lawrence should go to Bermuda, and after a time, if his health improved, George would bring Mrs. Lawrence Washington out to him. The experiment failed, his health did not improve and George did not return to Bermuda. Lawrence's strength gradually failed, and he returned to Virginia from Bermuda in 1752 and died at Mount Vernon on July 26th of that year. (Toner)"[10]

His will dated June 20th 1752 is recorded in the Fairfax Will Book. It devised to his wife a life estate in all his land in the Parish of Truro in the County of Fairfax: to his daughter Sarah all lands in Virginia and Maryland not otherwise disposed of. "But if it please God my said daughter should die without issue . . . 2d. I give and bequeath to my brother George and his heirs all my lands in Fairfax County."[11] Other lands were bequeathed to his brothers Samuel, John and Charles, and £150 to his sister Bettie Lewis.

"4th. My will is also that upon the death of my said brothers, George, Samuel, John, and Charles without lawful issue, such lands as was given to them or any of them, in case of my daughter's demise as aforesaid, to become the property and right of my brother, Augustine and his heirs."[11]

The daughter, Sarah, died before December 10, 1754, as shown by a memorandum of agreement on the devise of Lawrence's slaves quoted by Freeman in his *George Washington*, Vol. 2, page 3.

At that time Lawrence's widow, Ann, had already remarried. Her second husband was Colonel George Lee of Mount Pleasant, Westmoreland County, where he and his wife were then living. As Ann Lee was no longer residing at Mount Vernon, she and her husband leased the mansion and farm to Washington for her life.[12] On her death he became the owner, subject to the provisions of Lawrence's will.

---

[10]*Ibid.*, p. 26-27, Editor's note.

[11]Fairfax County Will Book A no. 1, pt. 2, p. 540.

[12]Fairfax County, D. B. C no. 1, p. 822.

That Washington knew that his title to Mount Vernon, or so much of it as passed to him by Lawrence's will, might be defeasible, if he left no issue, is evident from an entry in his cash book and ledger:

"1755. Jany 11 Cash by Mr. Mercer[13] for his opinion
of the devise of my brothers negroes £ 1 . 1 . 6
By ditto on his opinion on the devise
of Mount Vernon tract to me[14] £ 1 . 1 . 6"

When Washington married he looked forward to having issue. That hope had hardly disappeared when he was named Commander in Chief of the American Army, and he became absorbed in the cares and activities of the American Revolution. He seems to have forgotten the clause in question. If when he drew his will he had remembered it, he could easily have gotten a release from the descendants of Augustine Washington. He devised all the land he had acquired from Lawrence, and more besides, to his nephew, Bushrod Washington, who was not a descendant of Augustine. The will, however, named William Augustine Washington, Elizabeth Spottswood, Jane Thornton, the heirs of Anne Ashton; "son and daughters of my deceased brother Augustine Washington," among his residuary legatees. These persons became the owners of so much of the Mount Vernon estate as had belonged to Lawrence Washington. They could not be deprived of their title by the will of George Washington. But each of them received an interest in Washington's estate (actually one-twenty-third each)

[13]John Mercer of Marlborough (1704-1768) was an emigrant from Ireland. He was a planter, a lawyer, and the author of a compilation of the laws of Virginia, known as Mercer's Abridgement. His plantation was on the Potomac at the end of the peninsula formed by Potomac and Aquia Creeks. The place still bears the name of Marlborough Point. His two older sons, George and James, (as heirs of their father), sold land on Four Mile Run to Washington. He speculated in frontier lands. One of his largest patents was at the head of the Bull Run Mountains, and included the site of the village of Aldie, where his grandson, Charles Fenton Mercer, built a house still standing in a grove in the center of the village. John Mercer was the first of many who named Washington as executor of their wills. The sales of Mercer's Loudoun lands involved Washington in much correspondence with John Mercer's son, James. The estate was not completely settled as late as 1782. (See Washington's letter to Lund Washington in *Writings,* v. 25, p. 470.)

[14]Ledgers A-60. (*Washington Papers,* Library of Congress).

by the residuary clause. The law put them to an election—either to retain their rights under Lawrence's will, or to surrender their portions of Washington's residuary estate. They stated that an injustice had been done them, but that they did not care to upset their uncle's will. Bushrod Washington also knew it, as is shown by a memorandum on election among his papers.

As Washington's will was holographic (wholly in his handwriting) it was effective for lands in Virginia and Kentucky, but did not pass title to lands he owned in Maryland, Pennsylvania, New York, or in that part of the District of Columbia formerly in Maryland. This did not affect the election, as the heirs of Augustine Washington acquired title by descent and not by the will.

George Washington was born on February 11 (old style), 1732, at his father's plantation on Popes Creek. He was baptized, presumably by the Reverend Roderick McCullough, rector of Washington Parish.[15] His sponsors were Mr. Beverley Whiting, Capt. Christopher Brooks, and his Aunt Mildred Gregory.[16] As already noted, Augustine Washington removed with his family to his Hunting Creek plantation in 1735. The unreliable Parson Weems in his *Life of Washington* wrote: "The first place of education was a little 'old fields school' kept by one of his father's tenants named Hobby." This statement cannot be true as the boy left the neighborhood when between three and four years old. There was little opportunity for study at the new home on Little Hunting Creek. The family moved from there to Ferry Farm on the opposite side of the Rappahannock from Fredericksburg, when George was seven years old. The Reverend James Mayre kept a school in Fredericksburg which tradition says young Washington attended. This is probable though it would have meant ferrying the river twice a day—not a difficult matter. His education was meager and little is known about it, but he early acquired his round legible handwriting. The rules of capitalization were not firmly fixed in

---

[15]Douglas Southall Freeman. *George Washington,* Vol. 1, p. 47.

[16]Torrence, Clayton. "A Virginia Lady of Quality and Her Possessions," *Virginia Magazine of History and Biography,* Jan. 1948, p. 48.

Washington's youth, and he continued to use capitals for common as well as proper nouns, even though the custom was changing. In his will he wrote, "Crops," "Negroes," "Bank Stock," "Education." His spelling was always uncertain, as is shown by his private letters, which had not the benefit of the revision given his military and state papers by his secretaries.

Some of his school exercises have survived and are now in the Library of Congress. They include drafts of business papers, leases, conveyances, promissory notes, bills of exchange and the like. The best known and most interesting is "Rules of Civility and Decent Behavior" which he probably copied from the "Young Man's Companion," a book he is known to have possessed. A few of these rules are reproduced:

> "Labor to keep alive in your breast that little spark of Cllestial fire called conscience.
>
> Be not hasty to believe flying reports to the disparagement of any.
>
> Speak not evil of the absent, for it is unjust."

Is it fanciful to see the influence of this last precept in a sentence Washington wrote later in life: "I never say anything of a Man that I have the slightest scruple in saying to him"?

The most characteristic of these records, however, are those dealing with arithmetic, multiplication, decimals, interest, passing on into trigonometry and finally into surveying "where the problems are much more practical and advanced." There is a plot of a survey—probably a school exercise.[17]

Surveying required a knowledge of trigonometry, of linear measurements on the ground to obtain the desired angles and triangles, the use of a special kind of telescope and the ability to use Gunther's chain. It is improbable he learned all this without an instructor. We do not know who this instructor was. A natural supposition would be that he was James Genn, registered surveyor of Prince

[17] *Writings,* Vol. 1, pp. 1-3 (notes).

William County, under whom he worked for Lord Fairfax in the Shenandoah Valley.

But before George's future was determined, a new career was suggested when he was fifteen years old—that of joining the merchant marine plying between England and Virginia, and of joining it not as a mate or officer, but as a common sailor. How did such a strange idea present itself to persons having an interest in his future?[18] George's father was dead. It was apparently Lawrence's idea. He had been an officer in the expedition against Cartagena and had been impressed with the possibilities of a career at sea. George had no prospects in Virginia. The bulk of his father's estate had passed to the two older sons by his first marriage. Lawrence enlisted the support of his father-in-law, William Fairfax, a member of the Council for the colony and one of the most powerful men in Virginia. William Fairfax's influence might procure a commission for George in the Royal Navy. It was necessary to get the consent of his mother, who was also his guardian. She did not like the prospect of being separated from her son, and wrote to her brother, Joseph Ball, then residing in England for advice. In due time she received a letter from him opposing the project. It read in part: "Dear Sister: I understand that you are advised and have some thoughts of putting your son George to sea. I think he had better be put a prentice to a tinker, for a common sailor before the mast has by no means the common liberty of the subject; for they will press him from a ship where he has fifty shillings a month and make him take three-and-twenty, and cut and slash him like a negro, or rather like a dog . . .

Your loving brother,

Joseph Ball."

The plan was dropped and it was well for the future of our country that it was, but George's future was still unsettled.

By the terms of his father's will George owned the Ferry Farm

---

[18]Freeman's *George Washington,* Vol. 1, p. 194.

in King George County on the Rappahannock below Fredericksburg. It was necessary that he earn his living, and surveying came again into his mind.

Surveying is now a specialized career. High school and college students may take courses in it and do a little practical work as a part of their studies. In Washington's youth, however, surveying was something of a polite art. Young gentlemen of fortune, like George William Fairfax, might find the knowledge useful on their own estates. It was about this time (1747) that Washington changed his residence from the Ferry Farm to Mount Vernon. After his father's death he spent more and more of his time at the homes of his two elder brothers. This was fortunate for they were educated men, leaders in their respective neighborhoods in Westmoreland and Fairfax. Lawrence, as we have seen, had married the daughter of William Fairfax. His son, George William Fairfax, became a lifelong friend of Washington. The talk he heard at his brother's home and at the Fairfax home turned on happenings at Williamsburg, at London and in the world at large. It was at Mount Vernon that his real education began.

Washington was now sixteen years old. He had surveyed the Mount Vernon tract for his brother Lawrence. He was known to be accurate and careful. So when Lord Fairfax applied to William Fairfax to recommend a competent man to survey his tracts on the Shenandoah River and the South Branch of the Potomac, he recommended James Genn, and young Washington as an assistant. With them he sent his son, George William Fairfax.

George was not yet a licensed surveyor. He could work only under direction of such. Genn was the official surveyor of Prince William County. The College of William and Mary was by its charter authorized to appoint a surveyor for each county. Washington was appointed the official surveyor for Culpeper County in July 1749.[19]

Fairfax and Washington set out on March 11th, 1748 and were

[19]*Ibid.*, p. 234.

joined at Neaval's Ordinary by James Genn. They then proceeded to Winchester by Ashby's Gap. The spot where the party crossed the Alexandria-Warrenton Road is marked by a Virginia Highway marker.

After crossing the Blue Ridge at Ashby's Gap[20] they ferried the Shenandoah at Capt. Ashby's ferry. Turning south they visited his "Lordships Quarter"—Lord Fairfax was still at Belvoir and had not then established himself at Greenway Court, but Washington was struck by the "Sugar Trees" and the richness of the land, which he no doubt contrasted with the Fairfax County land. The party then went on to Capt. Hite's[21] near Frederick Town (now Winchester). The next day the surveyors went down the river to lay off some lands on Cates Marsh and Long Branch.[22]

At Capt. Bennington's, George had an experience which is best described in his own words:

"Tuesday 15th We set out early with Intent to Run round ye sd. Land but being taken in a Rain and it Increasing very fast obliged us to return it clearing about one oClock and our time being too Precious to Loose we a second time ventur'd out and Worked hard till Night and then return'd to Penningtons we got our Supper and was lighted into a Room and I not being so good a Woodsman as ye rest of my Company striped myself very orderly and went in to ye Bed as they called it when to my Surprise I found it to be nothing but a Little Straw—Matted together without Sheets or any thing else but only one thread Bear blanket with double its Weight of Vermin such as Lice Fleas &c I was glad to get up (as soon as y. Light was carried from us) I put on my cloths

[20]They approached the Gap by the road leading from the present railway station of Delaplane to Paris at the foot of the Gap. Captain John Ashby, who kept the ferry, where the Winchester road still crosses, was the eldest son of Thomas Ashby for whom the Gap was named. Diaries, Vol. 1, p. 4.

[21]Jost Hite in 1732 brought sixteen German families from Pennsylvania and settled near the Opequon Creek, taking grants from the Virginia authorities, who did not, at that time, recognize Lord Fairfax's claim to the Shenandoah Valley. There was subsequent litigation between Fairfax and Hite, in which the latter was victorious.

[22]Cates and Long Branch were two small streams which flow from the foothills of North Mountain to the Shenandoah. (Toner) *Diaries,* Vol. 1, p. 5.

and Lay as my Companions. Had we not been very tired I am sure we should not have slep'd much that night I made a Promise not to Sleep so from that time forward chusing rather to sleep in y. open Air before a fire as will appear hereafter."[23]

"Wednesday 16th We set out early and finish'd about one oClock and then Travell'd up to Frederick Town where our Baggage come to us we cleaned ourselves (to get Rid of y. Game we had catched y. Night before) and took a Review of y. Town and thence return'd to our Lodgings where we had a good Dinner Prepar'd for us Wine and Rum Punch in Plenty and a good Feather Bed with clean Sheets which was a very agreeable regale."[24]

The party started for the South Branch of the Potomac where the principal part of the work was to be done, and on the 21st of March, travelling the "worst road ever trod by Man or Beast," reached "Collo Cresaps,"[25] where they were delayed by two days of rain.

"Wednesday 23rd Rain'd till about two oClock and Clear'd when we were agreeably surpris'd at y. sight of thirty odd Indians coming from War with only one Scalp We had some Liquor with us of which we gave them Part it elevating there Spirits put them in y. Humour of Dauncing of whom we had a War Daunce there manner of Dauncing is as follows Viz They clear a Large Circle and make a Great Fire in y. middle then seats themselves around it y. Speaker makes a grand speech telling them in what Manner they are to Daunce after he has finished y. best Dauncer jumps up as one awaked out of a Sleep and runs and Jumps about y. Ring in a most comical Manner he is followed by y. Rest then begins there Musicians to Play ye. Musick is a Pot half (full) of Water with a Deerskin Streched over it as tight as it can and a goard with

[23]*Diaries,* Vol. 1, p. 5.

[24]*Ibid.,* p. 6.

[25]Colonel Thomas Cresap lived a few miles above the junction of the North and South Branches of the Potomac on the Maryland side; his place was known as "Cresaps" and also as "Old Town." He was an Indian trader and an outstanding frontiersman. He seems to have taken little or no part in the French and Indian War. He lived to a great age. *Diaries,* Vol. 1, p. 401.

some Shott in it to Rattle and a Piece of an horses Tail tied to it to make it look fine y. one keeps Rattling and y. other Drumming all y. while y. others is Dauncing."[26]

In the course of their journey they swam their horses across the Potomac to get pasturage and got to Patterson's Creek, a few miles below Will's Creek (later Cumberland). "They traveld up ye Creek to Solomon Hedges Esqr one of his Majestys Justices of ye. Pease for ye County of Frederick where we camped when we came to Supper there was neither a Cloth upon ye. Table nor a knife to eat with but as good luck would have it we had knives of (our) own."[27]

They then started back east to the South Branch where large sized lots, really farms, as one of 500 acres is mentioned, were surveyed. This work took a week.

At the mouth of the South Branch of the Potomac, Washington found a considerable population where he says "our work was attended by a great Company of People Men Women and Children that attended us through ye Woods as we went showing their Antick tricks I really think they seemed to be as Ignorant a Set of People as the Indians they would never speak English but when spoken to they speak all Dutch."[28] In returning they crossed the Great Cacapehon; the next day dined in Winchester and lodged at Capt. Hite's. The surveying had taken a month. Washington had been as far west as Patterson's Creek, had surveyed there, had gone fifty miles up the South Branch of the Potomac and surveyed on the Shenandoah River. He knew the roads or trails to Fort Cumberland. At the time all this land was in Frederick County; in 1753 the west part was formed into Hampshire County with its courthouse at Romney. He knew not only the land but the people. In spite of their uncouth ways he knew, or at least later knew, the sturdy determined character of these frontier

[26] *Ibid.*, p. 7.
[27] *Ibid.*, p. 8.
[28] *Ibid.*, pp. 9-10.

farmers and traders, many of whom were to serve under him in the war that was close at hand. It gave him a most valuable experience of life in the wilds.

In returning to the lowlands the party spent the night at Wm. West's Ordinary in Fairfax (later Loudoun) County, eighteen miles from the top of the Ridge.[29]

[29]West's Ordinary was kept successively for three generations of Wests by William, Charles and Thomas West. It stood near the head of the Bull Run Mountains not far from the present village of Aldie, at the junction of the Carolina Road (which ran from Leesburg south through Haymarket) and the Colchester Road (mistakenly called the Braddock Road). The William West of the text was probably the brother of Hugh West whose land was taken for Alexandria and who was one of the trustees of that town. The ordinary was pulled down some twenty years ago. Like most Virginia ordinaries it was a large story and a half frame building with a covered porch extending across its front. When the writer saw it, it was lived in by a tenant family; the woman resident told him "old man Braddock built this house." Fairfax Harrison's *Landmarks of Old Prince William* contains a note (page 138) on the Wests of Fairfax.

Chapter 2

Washington in the French and Indian War

The plan of this book precludes any extensive discussion of Washington's public career. The fame he gained as Colonel of the provincial troops in the French and Indian War made him the best known American soldier and led to his appointment as Commander-in-Chief of the American Army in the Revolution, and that in turn led to the Presidency. A short account of his services in this War seems necessary.

The conflicting claims of the French and English to the Ohio Valley caused Governor Dinwiddie to send an envoy to warn the French that they were trespassing on land claimed by Virginia and particularly by the Ohio Company. The French were first on the ground with detachments of troops to back up their claim. The disputed territory was full of their hunters and traders. They were winning the Indian tribes of the region. No time was to be lost. The Governor selected young Major Washington to deliver a letter of protest. He knew the frontier country and was used to its rough life. With him went Christopher Gist, an Indian trader, employed by the Ohio Company. Gist was to pilot the party, which included among others, Jacob Van Braam as interpreter.

On December 12th 1753, Washington arrived at Fort Le Boeuf and delivered the Governor's letter to the French commandant, received his reply and started for Williamsburg. He had left his horses several miles behind and was accompanied only by Gist. After three days travelling on foot, hampered by snow and threatened by hostile Indians, they reached the Allegheny River where they had a dangerous experience.

"The next day (December 28) we continued travelling till quite dark, and got to the River (Allegheny) about two Miles above *Shannapins* . . . The Ice was driving in vast Quantities . . . There was no way of getting over but on a Raft; Which we set about with but one poor Hatchet, and finished just after Sun-setting. This was a whole Day's Work. Then set off; But before we were Half Way over we were jammed in the Ice, in such a Manner that we expected every Moment our Raft to sink, and ourselves to perish. I put-out my setting Pole to try to stop the Raft, that the Ice might pass by; when the Rapidity of the Stream threw it with so much Violence against the Pole, that it jerked me out into ten Feet Water: but I fortunately saved myself by catching hold of one of the Raft Logs. Notwithstanding all our efforts we could not get the Raft to either Shore; but were obliged, as we were near an Island to quit our Raft and make to it.

"The Cold was so extremely severe, that Mr. Gist had all his Fingers, and some of his Toes frozen; but the water was shut up so hard, that we found no Difficulty in getting-off the Island, on the Ice, in the Morning, and went to Mr. Frazier's. . .

"As we intended to take Horses here, and it required some Time to find them I went-up about three Miles to the Mouth of *Yaughyaughane* to visit Queen *Aliquippa,*[1] who had expressed great Concerns that we passed her in going to the Fort. I made her a Present of a Matchcoat and a Bottle of Rum; which latter was thought much the best Present of the Two."[2]

The Virginia Assembly authorized the enlistment of a regiment to occupy the forks of the Ohio, or drive the French away if they had seized it. The story of Washington's defeat and surrender of Fort Necessity is well known, and need not be repeated here.

The British government resolved to send a fleet and an army to Virginia to finish the job the colonials had failed to accomplish. General Braddock,[3] with two regiments under the command of

[1]"Queen Aliquippa, of the Delaware Nation. She lived on the site of the present McKeesport, Pennsylanvia."—Editor's note.

[2]*Diaries,* Vol. 1, pp. 65-66.

[3]Braddock was then about sixty years of age and had been in the army forty-five years, and had learned the routine of Army life, but had seen little fighting.—Freeman, Vol. 2, p. 15.

Courtesy Virginia State C

Carlyle House (Pages 19 and 168)

Th...as Fairfax (1693-1781), Sixth Lord Fairfax of Ca...eron, Proprietor of the Northern Neck
(Pages 34 to 39)

(From the original now in Alexandria-Washington Lodge, A. F. & A. M., Alexandria, Virginia. Reproduced through the courtesy of the Curator of the Lodge.)

Col. Sir Peter Halkett and Col. Thomas Dunbar, respectively, arrived off Alexandria in March 1755. It was a great day for the little town. Braddock called a conference of the governors of five of the colonies, which met in John Carlyle's handsome house.

Washington accepted the offer of General Braddock to serve on his staff, and was thus present at the battle of the Monongahela. His vivid account of the defeat is given in a letter to his mother.

"(Fort Cumberland, July 18, 1755).

"Honour'd Mad'm: As I doubt not but you have heard of our defeat, and perhaps have it represented in a worse light (if possible) than it deserves; I have taken this earliest oppertunity to give you some acct. of the Engagement, as it happen'd within 7 miles of the French Fort, on Wednesday the 9th. Inst.

"We March'd on to that place with't any considerable loss, having only now and then a stragler pick'd up by the French Scoutg. Ind'nd. When we came there, we were attack'd by a Body of French and Indns. whose number, (I am certain) did not exceed 300 Men; our's consisted of abt. 1,300 well arm'd Troops; chiefly of the English soldiers, who were struck with such a panick, that they behav'd with more cowardice than it is possible to conceive; The Officers behav'd Gallantly in order to encourage their Men, for which they suffer'd greatly; there being near 60 kill'd and wounded; a large proportion out of the number we had! The Virginia Troops shew'd a good deal of Bravery, and were near all kill'd; for I believe out of 3 Companys that were there, there is scarce 30 Men left alive; Capt. Peyrouny and all his Officer's down to a Corporal was kill'd; Capt. Polson shar'd near as hard a Fate; for only one of his was left: In short the dastardly behaviour of those they call regular's expos'd all others that were inclin'd to do their duty to almost certain death; and at last, in dispight of all the efforts of the Officer's to the Contrary, they broke and run as Sheep pursued by dogs; and it was impossible to rally them.

"The Genl. was wounded; of w'ch he died 3 Days after; Sir

Peter Halket was kill'd in the Field where died many other brave Officer's; I luckily escap'd with't a wound, tho' I had four Bullets through my Coat, and two Horses shot under me; Captns. Orme and Morris two of the Genls. Aids de Camp, were wounded early in the Engagem't. which render'd the duty hard upon me, as I was the only person then left to distribute the Genl's Orders which I was scarely able to do, as I was not half recover'd from a violent illness, that confin'd me to my Bed, and a Waggon, for above 10 Days; I am still in a weak and Feeble cond'n; which induces me to halt here, 2 or 3 Days in hopes of recov'g. a little Strength, to enable me to proceed homewards; . . ." .[4]

It had been proposed that he assume command of the troops Virginia was raising to defend the frontier. At this juncture his mother intervened. She had his letter telling her of the terrible casualties the Virginians had suffered in the recent battle, and of his narrow escape. He must not expose himself to such risks again. She had saved him when a boy from an unsuitable career at sea; she would save him again. But Washington was now a man and he replied shortly, but firmly:

"Mount Vernon, August 14, 1755.

"Honor'd Madam: If it is in my power to avoid going to the Ohio again, I shall, but if the Command is press'd upon me by the genl. voice of the Country, and offer'd upon such terms as can't be objected against, it wou'd reflect eternal dishonour upon me to refuse it; and that, I am sure must, or ought, to give you greater cause of uneasiness than my going in an honourable Com'd.; for upon no other terms I will accept of it if I do at all; at present I have no proposals or any mention made abt. it only from private hands. I am etc."[5]

Although Washington always addressed his mother as "Honored Madam," she had little influence on his life. His ideals had been formed by his associations with his brother Lawrence and with the Fairfaxes of Belvoir.

---

[4]*Writings,* Vol. 1, pp. 150-152.
[5]*Ibid.,* p. 159.

In the dark days that followed Braddock's defeat the Indian allies of the French began murderous attacks on the inhabitants of Frederick and Augusta counties. Cabins and farms were abandoned, numbers of the frightened farmers taking refuge east of the Blue Ridge.

On September 17, 1755, Washington was appointed by Governor Dinwiddie "Colonel of the Virginia Regiment and commander in chief of all the Forces that now are, or shall be raised, etc. etc."[6]

A vivid account of the situation Washington faced is given in the Journal of Captain Charles Lewis of Fredericksburg, which was privately published by his descendant, H. Latane Lewis. Captain Lewis was born at Warner Hall in Gloucester County. He started from Fredericksburg on October 10, 1755 as a member of a detachment under command of Major Andrew Lewis. When the party arrived at the "Little Cape Capon," they were joined by "the Hon. Colonel George Washington and Captain George Mercer A.D.C." He found the country between Winchester and Cumberland thinly sown with houses and farms, mostly deserted, leaving "corn, wheat and pasturage." At Cumberland he was shown the Fort: "It is a quadrangular fort with four bastions, about one hundred feet in the square, has eleven four-pounders and two smaller mounted. It is situated on the north side of the Potomac, in Maryland, on a hill, very pleasant, more so I think than advantegous, has a romantic prospect from the mountains and is very healthy." He saw many evidences of Indian barbarity: "This evening Captain Spottswood went, with a soldier to the plantation of one Williams, where the houses were burned by savages. The body of a woman layed near one of the houses, her head being scalped, and, also a small boy and a young man." On another occasion:—"In this last command I may with the greatest truth aver that I saw the most horrid, shocking sight I ever yet behold. At a house adjoining the corn field in which our soldiers were employed in gathering corn we saw the bodies of three different

[6]*Ibid.*, Vol. 1, p. 175.

people, who were first massacred, then scalped, and afterwards thrown into a fire. These bodies were not yet quite consumed, but the flesh was on many parts of them. We saw the clothes of these people yet bloody and the stakes, the instruments of their death, still bloody and their brains sticking to them."

The massacres that Captain Lewis narrated took place far west of the Shenandoah Valley, but the series of forts could not prevent the Indians from slipping through. The Assembly failed to provide the two thousand men Washington estimated as necessary to man the existing and projected forts.[7] He was ceaselessly travelling from one fort to another, and to Williamsburg for conferences with the Governor and prominent members of the Assembly. On one occasion he was recalled from Fredericksburg by "an express sent from Colonel Stephen, informing him that a body of Indians had fallen on the inhabitants, killed many of them, destroyed and burnt many of their houses." This danger to Virginia was over after General Forbes captured Fort Duquesne in 1758, and Washington felt free to resign his command.

[7]For Washington's plan for the forts, their location and the number of men needed to garrison them, see *Writings,* Vol. 1, p. 490.

Chapter 3

George Mercer

One of Washington's earliest friends, and his intimate companion during the French and Indian War was George Mercer. He was the eldest son of John Mercer of Marlborough.[1] On the outbreak of hostilities with France in 1754 George Mercer became a lieutenant in the First Virginia Regiment commanded by Washington and was among those who surrendered at Fort Necessity. Later he served in the campaign of General Braddock. He was appointed aide-de-camp to Washington with rank of Captain. Subsequently he was made a lieutenant colonel. After Braddock's defeat he shared with Washington the defense of the Virginia frontier from the destructive Indian raids. While in command at Fort Cumberland, Washington's authority was disputed by Captain Dagworthy, commander of the Maryland troops, on the ground that he held a commission from the King and was not therefore subject to the orders of Washington whose commission was derived from the Governor of Virginia. This was an intolerable situation and Washington decided to appeal to Governor Shirley who had command of the colonial forces. This required the long journey to Boston. He chose Mercer as his travelling companion. Shirley decided the dispute in Washington's favor. With the capture of Fort Duquesne, both Washington and Mercer resigned their commissions. In 1761 they were both elected to the House of Burgesses, representing Frederick County.

Mercer built a house at the Frederick Warm Springs (later

[1]For a note on John Mercer, see Footnote 13, Chapter I.

Bath, now Berkeley Springs, West Virginia), which Washington rented for two seasons.[2] In 1763 he went to England in connection with the affairs of the Ohio Company. As it turned out it was a most unfortunate trip for him, financially and politically. While there he penned a graphic description of the personal appearance of his former commander:

"Although distrusting my ability to give an adequate account of the personal appearance of Col. George Washington, late Commander of the Virginia Provincial troops, I shall, as you request, attempt the portraiture. He may be described as being straight as an Indian, measuring six feet two inches in his stockings, and weighing 175 pounds when he took his seat in the House of Burgesses in 1759. His frame is padded with well-developed muscles, indicating great strength. His bones and joints are large, as are his feet and hands.

"He is wide shouldered, but has not a deep or round chest; is neat waisted, but is broad across the hips, and has rather long legs and arms. His head is well shaped though not large, but is gracefully poised on a superb neck. A large and straight rather than prominent nose; blue-gray penetrating eyes, which are widely separated and overhung by a heavy brow. His face is long rather than broad, with high round cheek bones, and terminates in a good firm chin. He has a clear though rather a colorless pale skin, which burns with the sun. A pleasing, benevolent, though a commanding countenance, dark brown hair, which he wears in a cue.

"His mouth is large and generally firmly closed, but which from time to time discloses some defective teeth. His features are regular and placid, with all the muscles of his face under perfect control, though flexible and expressive of deep feeling when moved by emotions. In conversation he looks you full in the face, is deliberate, deferential and engaging. His voice is agreeable rather than strong. His demeanor at all times composed and dignified. His movements

[2] *Writings,* Vol. 3, p. 53.

and gestures are graceful, his walk majestic, and he is a splendid horseman."[8]

While Mercer was still abroad the Stamp Act was passed by Parliament in 1765 and he was appointed chief distributor of stamps for Maryland, Virginia and North Carolina. The colonials then in England had no idea of the fierce opposition the act would arouse in the Colonies. Franklin had opposed the act before a committee of the House of Commons, but when the act was passed, he secured a collectorship for a friend.

Kate Mason Rowland in her *George Mason* gives a vivid account of Mercer's arrival in Virginia:

"In the meantime Colonel George Mercer . . . arrived at Hampton in the odious character of a stamp distributor. It was evident that he did not realize the condition of affairs, or he would not have put himself in such a false position. A soldier by profession and not a politician, he had not entered into the merits of the case, and as he was coming over to America on business of his own, or in the interest of the Ohio Company, he undertook at the request of the Stamp Office Commissioners to carry over with him the stamps intended for three of the colonies. He was confronted by an excited mob at Hampton and only protected from violence through the influence of prominent gentlemen of the town. At Williamsburg he was met by several members of the General Court then in session, and required to say if he intended to enter on the duties of the office. They went with him to the coffee-house where the Governor, most of the Council, and the other gentlemen were assembled, and here a crowd collected outside and could only be dispersed when it was known that Colonel Mercer would give an answer the next day at a stated hour. At five o'clock of the following afternoon, according to promise, he met the citizens and the various prominent merchants of the colony then in Williamsburg, and engaged not to execute the Stamp Act without the consent of the Virginia Assembly. He was then carried from the capitol to the coffee-house

[8]J. M. Toner. *George Washington as an Inventor*, etc.

with great rejoicing and an elegant supper was given him. Music, drums, and horns, and then ringing of the bells demonstrated the popular satisfaction, while at night the town was illuminated."

From there he went to Maryland, as he was bound to go, but the reaction he met there was such that he found himself "under a necessity of returning immediately to England."[4]

Washington was not in Williamsburg when these events took place. Had Mercer remained in Virginia he would no doubt have stood side by side with his brother James and with Washington in opposition to the act. He would in all likelihood have risen to high command in the Revolutionary army, as Washington was his friend and knew his military ability. As it was, his life was ruined. There was no future for him in Virginia. His credit in England did not suffer from this episode. In 1769 he was appointed lieutenant governor of North Carolina, but never served. He had returned for a visit to Virginia in 1767, bringing with him his English bride. She died in Richmond and Mercer returned to England where he spent the rest of his life.

He had no land in England and apparently no means of gaining a livelihood. He was obliged to sell and mortgage his Virginia lands. He had conveyed lands to Washington and others in trust to sell, and in that way Washington became acquainted with his business affairs, which were very involved. Washington assisted him in getting the bounty lands in western Virginia to which he was entitled for his service in the campaign of Fort Necessity.

Writing in 1775 Washington said:

"That Colo. Mercer has been a considerable loser in the management of his Estate here, nobody will deny; but has not every gentleman in this country, whose other avocations, or whose inclinations would not permit them, to devote a large portion of their time and attention to the management of their own Estates, shared the same fate? Our Gazettes afford but too many melancholy proofs of it in the sales which are daily advertised; the nature of a Virginia

---

[4]Kate Mason Rowland. *Life of George Mason,* Vol. I, pp. 125-126.

Estate being such, that without close application, it never fails bringing the proprietors in debt annually, as Negroes must be clothed, and fed, taxes paid, &c,&c., whether anything is made or not. . ."[5]

When the differences between England and her American Colonies issued in war, Mercer remained in England and took no part in the contest. Doubts were expressed as to his loyalty. Writing in 1779 to Joseph Wharton, Washington acknowledged the receipt of the "letters you were so obliging as to bring from my old acquaintance and friend Colo. Mercer. A Gentln. for whom I always had a sincere regard. What walk of life he has been in the last four or five years, and what line of conduct he has observed in this great contest I am totally uninformed of, but from the opinion I entertain of his honor, his justice, and his love of this Country, I would feign hope that it has been altogether unexceptionable."[6]

But George Mason, who was Mercer's cousin, felt sure enough of his sympathy to send him a copy of the Bill of Rights he had drafted and which had been approved by the Legislature of Virginia.

Mercer died in England in 1784 in embarrassed circumstances. He left no issue.

James Mercer, the younger brother of George, was graduated from the College of William and Mary in 1767; settled in Fredericksburg, became a lawyer; was a member of the House of Burgesses, of the Virginia Convention, of the Committee of Safety, a delegate to the Continental Congress, and a judge of the First Court of Appeals of Virginia. He was Washington's legal adviser in many matters and is frequently mentioned in his Diaries. He died in 1793.

---

[5] *Writings,* Vol 3, p. 285.
[6] *Ibid.,* Vol. 16, p. 292.

Chapter 4

An English Traveller in Virginia

Archdeacon Burnaby was an Anglican clergyman who received his Master of Arts degree from Cambridge University in 1757. In 1759 and 1760 he travelled through the American Colonies and his *Travels* were first issued in 1775 in the hope that the publication "might in some degree, conduce to" the reconciliation between Great Britain and her Colonies. He died in 1812.

He was a friendly and discriminating observer, and he was the only pre-revolutionary English traveller who described Virginia at any length. The latest reprint of his work was published in 1904 and is now out of print. As he visited the lower Shenandoah Valley shortly after the French and Indian War, and visited Mount Vernon, some of his observations have sufficient interest to reproduce here. He described his visit to Williamsburg:

July 5 (1759)

"The next morning, having hired a chaise at York, a small inconsiderable town, I went to Williamsburg, about twelve miles distant. The road is exceedingly pleasant, through some of the finest tobacco plantations in North America, with a beautiful view of the river and woods of great extent.

"Williamsburg is the capital of Virginia: it is situated between two creeks, one falling into James, the other into York river; and is built nearly due east and west. The distance of each landing-place is something more than a mile from the town; which, with the disadvantage of not being able to bring up large vessels, is the reason of its not having increased so fast as might have been expected. It consists of about two hundred houses, does not contain more than one thousand souls, whites and negroes; and is far from being a place of any consequence. It is regularly laid out in parallel streets, intersected by others at right angles; has a handsome square in the center, through which runs the principal street, one of the most spacious in North America, three quarters of a mile in length, and above a hundred feet wide. At the opposite ends of this street are two public buildings, the college and the capitol: and although the houses are of wood, covered with shingles,[1] and but indifferently built, the whole makes a handsome appearance. There are few public edifices that deserve to be taken notice of; those, which I have mentioned, are the principal; and they are far from being magnificent. The governor's palace is tolerably good, one of the best upon the continent; but the church, the prison, and the other buildings, are all of them extremely indifferent. The streets are not paved, and are consequently very dusty, the soil hereabout consisting chiefly of sand: however, the situation of Williamsburg has one advantage which few or no places in these lower parts have, that of being free from mosquitoes. Upon the whole, it is an agreeable residence; there are ten or twelve gentlemen's families constantly residing in it, besides merchants and tradesmen: and at the times of the assemblies, and general courts, it is crowded with the gentry of the country: on those occasions there are balls and other amusements; but as soon as the business is finished, they return to their plantations; and the town is in a manner deserted."[2]

Burnaby saw Virginia through eighteenth century eyes. It was natural that he should compare Bruton Church with the age-old churches of England to its disadvantage. It was then less than fifty years old and had not the charm that age has given it.

"I departed from Williamsburg, Oct. 1, 1759, in company with another gentleman; and we travelled that day about forty miles, to a plantation in King William county, beautifully situated upon a high hill, on the north side of Pamunky river. A little below this

[1]"These are formed in the shape of tiles, and are generally made of white cedar or of cypress." (Burnaby, p. 34.)

[2]Burnaby, pp. 32-35.

place stands the Pamunky Indian town, where at present are the few remaining of that large tribe, the rest having dwindled away through intemperance and disease. They live in little wigwams or cabins upon the river; and have a very fine tract of land of about 2,000 acres, which they are restrained from alienating by act of assembly. Their employment is chiefly hunting or fishing for the neighboring gentry. They commonly dress like the Virginians, and I have sometimes mistaken them for the lower sort of that people." (p. 62)

The reservation still exists and the customs and manner of life that Burnaby described have not changed greatly in two centuries. A semblance of tribal customs has been preserved. Their reservation is exempted from taxation, and the tribe is governed by a chief and council chosen by themselves. "They live in small frame houses along roads, mostly dirt or gravel. They worship in a church affiliated with the Baptist General Association, send their children to a school provided by the State, and gain their livelihood through farming, hunting and fishing. The women make and sell pottery, shape beads, and fashion pocket books, watch fobs, and like articles. Following custom, the chief and his men make a pilgrimage to Richmond each Thanksgiving and on the steps of the Capitol present freshly killed game, quail, rabbits, turkeys, and occasionally a deer—to the Governor of Virginia, whom they address as Great White Father."[3]

He then travelled to Fredericksburg.

"Fredericksburg is situated about a mile below the Falls of Rappahannock: it is regularly laid out, as most of the towns in Virginia are, in parallel streets.[4] Part of it is built upon the edge of the water for the convenience of warehouses. The town was begun about thirty-two years ago (1727), for the sake of carrying on a trade with the back-settlers; and is at present by far the most flourishing one in these parts." (p. 63)

[3]Virginia *Guide*, p. 601.

[4]The reference to the parallel streets of Williamsburg and Fredericksburg was evidently suggested by the winding streets of the towns and villages of England.

We ferried "over the Rappahannock into the Northern Neck. . . and proceeded through Dumfries, and over Occoquan River to Colchester, about twenty-one miles. These are two small towns lately built for the sake of the back trade; the former on the Quantico, the other upon Occoquan River, both of which fall into the Potomac." . . . (pp. 65-66)

From Colchester Burnaby went about twelve miles farther to Mount Vernon. "This place is the property of Colonel Washington, and truly deserving of its owner. The house is most beautifully situated upon a high hill on the banks of the Potomac; and commands a noble prospect of water, of cliffs, of woods, and plantations. The river is nearly two miles broad, though two hundred from the mouth and divides the dominions of Virginia from Maryland. We rested here one day, and proceeded up the river about twenty six miles to take a view of the Great Falls of the Potomac." (pp. 67-68)

These are described at considerable length. In a new country little altered by civilization, such natural phenomena as falls, caverns, and cascades attract the attention of the traveller. When at Fredericksburg he had visited and described the falls of the Rappahannock above Falmouth. Most motorists crossing the bridge at Falmouth give no more than a passing glance to the rapids.

"In the evening we returned down the river about sixteen miles to Alexandria, or Belhaven, a small trading place in one of the finest situations imaginable. The Potomac above and below the town, is not more than a mile broad, but it here opens into a large circular bay, of at least twice that diameter.

"The town is built upon an arc of this bay; at one extremity of which is a wharf; at the other a dock for building ships; with water sufficiently deep to launch a vessel of any rate or magnitude." (p. 69)

From Alexandria, Burnaby turned south and returned to Williamsburg, after stopping again at Mount Vernon. As he did not see Lord Fairfax when he visited Greenway Court in the Shenandoah Valley, it was at Williamsburg that he met him upon "a visit of ceremony to Lieutenant Governor Fauquier who had lately arrived from England." As Lord Fairfax had the reputation of being reserved and under constraint in the presence of women, Burnaby was agreeably surprised when his Lordship was presented to Lady Fauquier. "He remained in the palace three or four days, and during that time his behaviour was courteous, polite, and becoming a man of fashion." As the only peer resident in Virginia, he aroused curiosity and possibly received unwanted attention.

The Journal continues: "I left Fredericksburg and having ferried over the Rappahannock at the falls, travelled that night to Neville's ordinary about thirty four miles."

The route that Burnaby followed was the one usually taken by travellers from Williamsburg and Fredericksburg to the lower Shenandoah Valley. Neville's Ordinary was kept by George Neville (or Neavill). It was situated at or near the village of Auburn in the present Fauquier County, about five miles east of Warrenton. Like most ordinaries it was at the junction of two roads, one running northerly from Falmouth to Ashby's Gap and the other the Carolina Road, running South through the present Leesburg and Haymarket and crossing the Rappahannock River a short distance above Remington. George William Fairfax and Washington had followed the same road previously on their way to the Shenandoah Valley to survey Lord Fairfax's lands. Neville's Inn had an excellent reputation both for food and accommodations. It stood until 1927.[5]

"I passed over the Pignut and Blue Ridges; and crossing over the Shenandoah, arrived, after a long day's journey of about fifty miles at Winchester. The Blue Ridge is much higher than the Pignut: Though even these mountains are not to be compared with the Alleghany. To the southward, I was told, they are more lofty; and but little, if at all, inferior to them. The pass, at Ashby's Gap, from the foot of the mountain on the eastern side to the Shenandoah, which runs at the foot of the western, is about four miles. The ascent is no where very steep; though the mountains are, upon the whole, I think higher than any I have ever seen in England.

---

[5]Freeman, Vol. 1, p. 209.

When I got to the top, I was inexpressibly delighted with the scene which opened before me. Immediately under the mountain, which was covered with Chamoedaphnes in full bloom, was a most beautiful river; beyond this an extensive plain, diversified with every pleasing object that nature can exhibit; and, at a distance of fifty miles, another ridge of still more lofty mountains, called the Great, or North Ridge[6] which inclosed and terminated the whole.

"The river Shenandoah rises a great way to the southward from under this Great North Ridge. It runs through Augusta county, and falls into the Potomac somewhere in Frederick. At the place where I ferried over, it is only about a hundred yards wide; and indeed it is no where, I believe, very broad. It is exceedingly romantic and beautiful, forming great variety of falls, and is so transparent, that you may see the smallest pebble at the depth of eight or ten feet. There is plenty of trout and other fish in it, but it is not navigable, except for rafts. In sudden freshes it rises above forty or fifty feet. The low grounds upon the banks of this river are very rich and fertile; they are chiefly settled by Germans, who gain a comfortable livelihood by raising stock for the troops, and sending butter down into the lower parts of the country. I could not but reflect with pleasure on the situation of these people; and think if there is such a thing as happiness in this life, that they enjoy it. Far from the bustle of the world, they live in the most delightful climate, and richest soil imaginable; they are everywhere surrounded with beautiful prospects and sylvan scenes; lofty mountains, transparent streams, falls of water, rich valleys, and majestic woods; the whole interspersed with an infinite variety of flowering shrubs, constitute the landscape surrounding them: they are subject to few diseases; are generally robust; and live in perfect liberty: they are ignorant of want, and acquainted with but few vices. Their inexperience of the elegancies of life precludes any regret that they possess not the means of enjoying them: but they possess what

[6] "All these ridges consist of single mountains joined together and run parallel to each other." (Burnaby, p. 73.)

many princes would give half their dominions for, health, content, and tranquillity of mind." (pp. 71-74)

A few miles south of Burnaby's route was the home of Lord Fairfax. Although Burnaby did not see him then, as he was absent from his seat at Greenway Court and, as he says, "was prevented from paying my respects to him," it was evident that his lordship dominated the County of Frederick. He was the County Lieutenant. He owned all the land in the Northern Neck which he had not sold, and was actively engaged in promoting the colonization of the new territory west of Frederick County. He was born in Leeds Castle, Yorkshire, in 1693, and settled in Virginia permanently in 1747 to manage the vast estate he had inherited. He had triumphed in the lawsuit in which a large part of his estate had been questioned by the Virginia government. How had he attained this privileged position?

A brief explanation will show how this happened. While Charles II was a fugitive on the continent and Oliver Cromwell was ruling England, Charles granted to a number of his impoverished favorites all the land between the Potomac and Rappahannock Rivers, not in the possession of persons claiming under prior grants from the Crown. This vast territory was called the Northern Neck. One of the grantees, Lord Culpeper, acquired the shares of the other proprietors.

When the news reached Virginia, it caused great indignation, for the ownership of the soil carried with it the right to convey to tenants who would pay to the proprietor the quit rents which would otherwise be collected for the benefit of the Colony. They were called quit rents because by their payment the tenant was *quit*, or free from all other services.[7] The quit rents were the equivalent of a land tax and were the main source of the revenues of the Colony. Virginia had already been deprived of Maryland by the charter granted to Sir George Calvert. Now she was threatened with the loss of a considerable part of her revenue, for the Northern Neck

[7]H. C. Groome. *Fauquier during the Proprietorship; A Chronicle of the Colonization and Organization of a Northern Neck County.* Richmond, Old Dominion Press, 1927.

Greenway Court, Frederick (Now Clarke) County, Virginia
(Pages 36 to 38)

(From an old print)

Belvoir on the Potomac—Proposed Reconstruction (Pages 50 to 58)

(From a pamphlet on the U. S. Army Engineer Center, Fort Belvoir, Virginia.)

was being rapidly settled. The threat became real when Lord Culpeper became governor of the Colony and set up an office for issuing patents to land in the Northern Neck. After he returned to England he and his successors named agents in the colony who issued patents in the proprietor's name, but signed by themselves under powers of attorney. Lord Culpeper died in 1689, leaving as his only heir a daughter, Catherine, who married Thomas, fifth Lord Fairfax, Baron of Cameron. On her death the proprietorship of the Northern Neck passed by her will to her son, Thomas, Sixth Lord Fairfax in tail male. Since Lord Culpeper's return to England about 1682, none of the proprietors had been in Virginia. Lord Fairfax determined to see his domain. He arrived in Virginia in 1735 and found that a bitter controversy was raging between the Governor and Council of Virginia and his agents as to the correct boundary of the Fairfax patent. Virginia claimed the southern boundary was the Rappahannock. The Fairfax agents claimed the Rapidan was really the "head spring" of the Rappahannock. Both parties were anxious to have the controversy settled, and the matter was appealed to the Privy Council in England. This was the suit of Virginia *vs.* Fairfax, which kept Lord Fairfax in England for several years. After years of litigation the case was settled in favor of Lord Fairfax and a line was directed to be run from the head spring of the Rapidan to the head spring of the Potomac. Thousands of acres east and west of the Blue Ridge were added to Lord Fairfax's domain. When the line was fixed, stones, known as the Fairfax Stones, were erected to mark the headsprings of the two rivers.

In 1747 he returned to Virginia to spend the rest of his long life there. For more than a year he was the guest of his cousin, William Fairfax, at Belvoir, but that was too far away from the Shenandoah Valley where most of the patents were now being issued. So he established quarters at the site of the future Greenway Court. It was there that Washington visited "his Lordship's Quarter" in his first surveying expedition in 1748.

During the French and Indian War, Lord Fairfax stayed courageously at his seat in the Valley "although importuned by his friends and the principal gentry of the colony to retire to the inner settlements for security." Burnaby represents him as saying:

" 'I myself am an old man, and it is of little importance whether I fall by the tomahawk of an Indian or by disease and old age. . . . If we determine to remain, it is possible, notwithstanding our utmost care and vigilance, that we may both fall victims; if we retire, the whole district will immediately break up; and all the trouble and solicitude which I have undergone to settle this fine country will be frustrated; and the occasion perhaps irrecoverably lost.' "[8]

His life at Greenway Court must have been a simple one, far removed as it was from the social and political life of the Colony. The tedium of life among the rough settlers was relieved by occasional visits to Williamsburg, Belvoir, Mount Vernon and at the Bath Warm Springs where Washington met him several times. The Diaries show him dining at Mount Vernon and going fox hunting there; and record Washington going to pay his respects to his Lordship at Belvoir.

Burnaby describes his life at Greenway Court:

"He there lived . . . in the style of a gentleman farmer; or I should rather have said, of an English country gentleman. He kept many servants, white and black; several hunters; a plentiful but plain table, entirely in the English fashion; and his mansion was the mansion of hospitality. His dress corresponded with his mode of life, and, notwithstanding he had every year new suits of clothes, of the most fashionable and expensive kind, sent out to him from England, which he never put on, was plain in the extreme. His manners were humble, modest, and unaffected; not tinctured in the smallest degree with arrogance, pride, or self-conceit. He was free from selfish passions, and liberal almost to excess. The produce of his farms, after the deduction of what was necessary for the consumption of his own family, was distributed and given away to the poor planters and settlers in his neighborhood. To these he frequently advanced money, to enable them to go on with their im-

[8]Burnaby, p. 204.

provements; to clear away the woods, and cultivate the ground; and where the lands proved unfavourable, and not likely to answer the labour and expectation of the planter or husbandman, he usually indemnified him for the expense he had been at in the attempt, and gratuitously granted him fresh lands of a more favourable and promising nature. He was a friend and a father to all who held and lived under him; and as the great object of his ambition was the peopling and cultivating of that fine and beautiful country, of which he was proprietor, he sacrificed every other pursuit, and made every other consideration subordinate, to this great point."[9]

When hostilities against Great Britain began in 1775, he was an old man. Though naturally apprehensive of the effect on his proprietary, it turned out there was no danger. The Commonwealth of Virginia dealt very gently with him. It is a record that every Virginian may be proud of. As he was a citizen of Virginia, the Act of 1777 forfeiting the property of British subjects did not apply to him. Feudal land tenures were abolished by that Act and the quit rents theretofore collected in the name of the King were done away with, but the Northern Neck was specifically excepted from operation of the Act, and Lord Fairfax was suffered to continue in undisturbed possession of his proprietorship during the remainder of his life.[10]

Archdeacon Burnaby in referring to Lord Fairfax's life during the Revolution, says: "So unexceptionable and disinterested was his behavior both public and private, and so generally was he beloved and respected, that during the late contest between Great Britain and America, he never met with the least insult or molestation from either party, but was suffered to go on in his improvement and cultivation of the Northern Neck, a pursuit equally calculated for the comfort and happiness of individuals, and for the general good of mankind."[11]

In 1751 he was joined by his nephew Thomas Bryan Martin, of

[9] *Ibid.*, p. 201.

[10] Groome, H. C. *Fauquier during the Proprietorship*, p. 219.

[11] Burnaby, p. 202.

whom he became very fond, and in 1752 he conveyed to him the Manor of Greenway Court. Martin was "a county lieutenant of Hampshire and a Burgess from that county in 1756-58 and in 1758-61 as a colleague of George Washington (from Frederick County). He died unmarried (in 1798) and left Greenway Court to his housekeeper, Betsy Powers, together with one thousand acres of land surrounding it. . . ."[12] Martinsburg, West Virginia, is named after him.

Greenway Court was nearly two miles south of the village of Whitepost. It is long since gone; replaced by a brick house a century old. Only the little two story Land Office built in 1748 remains, where Lord Fairfax collected his quit rents and kept the folio books of his grants. These last are now in the Capitol in Richmond. About Whitepost the Virginia Guide (p. 442) states that the outstanding feature of the hamlet is "a tall white post surmounted by an old-fashioned lantern that duplicates the one erected by Lord Fairfax to mark the route to his estate."

He never married, having suffered an early disappointment in love, his fiancée having married another man. As Burnaby puts it, "she preferred the higher honour of being a duchess to the inferior station of a baroness."

He died on the ninth of December, 1781, in his eighty-ninth year. Feeling ill, he rode to Winchester to consult his physician, Dr. Cornelius Baldwin, and died in his house. His body was buried in the original parish church of Frederick in Winchester, a large stone building erected by him at his own expense. When the location of that church proved unsuitable and the present Christ Church was built his remains were re-interred there. A tablet to him has been placed on the wall. He devised all his estate to his nephew, the Reverend Denny Martin, a brother of Thomas Bryan Martin. He could not devise his proprietary interest for that was held by him in tail male, and on his death without issue it descended to his brother Robert. He owned, however, a one-sixth interest in the

[12] *Diaries,* Vol. 1, p. 130 (note).

proprietary title in fee simple, and that passed by his will.[13] £47,000 Virginia currency was found in his house after his death.

As Robert was an alien he could not inherit property in Virginia and title passed to the State.

We return now to Burnaby's narrative.

"Winchester is a small town of about two hundred houses. It is the place of general rendevous of the Virginian troops, which is the reason of its late rapid increase, and present flourishing condition. The country about it, before the reduction of Fort du Quesne, was greatly exposed to the ravages of the Indians, who daily committed most horrid cruelties; even the town would have been in danger, had not Colonel Washington,[14] in order to cover and protect it, erected a fort upon an eminence at one end of it, which proved of the utmost utility; for although the Indians were frequently in sight of the town, they never dared approach within reach of the fort. . . ." (pp. 71-75)

"During my stay at this place (Winchester), I was almost induced to make a tour for a fortnight to the southward, in Augusta County, for the sake of seeing some natural curiosities, which, the officers assured me, were extremely well worth visiting: but as the Cherokees had been scalping in those parts only a few days before; and as I feared, at the same time, that it would detain me too long, and that I should lose my passage to England, I judged it prudent to decline it.

"On the 4th of June, therefore, I was enabled to leave Winchester, and I travelled that night about eighteen miles, to Sniker's ferry upon the Shenandoah.

"The next morning I repassed the Blue Ridge at William's Gap, and proceeded on my journey about forty miles."

He spent the night at a vermin-infested house of a poor planter.

"I rose early in the morning, therefore, and proceeded upon my

---

[13]Harrison, Fairfax. "Proprietors of the Northern Neck," *Virginia Magazine of History and Biography,* January 1926, p. 41.

[14]At the time of Burnaby's visit, Washington had retired from the army and married. The garrison at Winchester was commanded by Colonel William Byrd the third, who showed his visitor many courtesies.

journey, being distant from Colonel Washington's not more than thirty miles. It was late, however, before I arrived there, for it rained extremely hard, and a man who undertook to shew me the nearest way, led me among precipices and rocks, and we were lost for about two hours. It was not, indeed, without some compensation; for he brought me through as beautiful and picturesque a scene, as eye ever beheld. It was a delightful valley, about two miles in length, and a quarter of one in breadth, between high and craggy mountains,[15] covered with chamoedaphnes[16] or wild ivy, in full flower. Through the middle of the valley glided a rivulet about eight yards wide, extremely lucid, and breaking into innumerable cascades; and in different parts of it stood small clumps of evergreens, such as myrtles, cedars, pines, and various other sorts. Upon the whole, not Tempe itself could have displayed greater beauty or a more delightful scene."[17]

"At Colonel Washington's I disposed of my horses, and, having borrowed his curricle and servant, I took leave of Mount Vernon the 11th of June.

I crossed over the Potomac into Maryland at Clifton's ferry, where the river is something more than a mile broad; and proceeded on my journey to Marlborough, eighteen miles." (pp. 78-80)

It appears that Burnaby and Washington exchanged letters after the former's return to England, though no copies of Washington's letters appear in Fitzpatrick's *Writings of Washington*. In a letter to a correspondent in London, written in 1774, Washington said: "It gives me sensible pleasure to hear that my old acquaintance and

---

[15]The English habit of calling hills mountains.

[16]"The chamoedaphne is the most beautiful of all flowering shrubs: Catesby in his *Natural History* of Carolina speaks of it in the following manner: 'The flowers grow in bunches on the tops of the branches, to footstalks of three inches long; they are white, stained with purplish red; consisting of one leaf in form of a cup, divided at the verge into five sections. In the middle is a stilus, and ten stamina, which, when the flower first opens, appear lying close to the sides of the cup, at equal distances; their apices being lodged in ten little hollow cells, which being prominent on the outside, appear as so many little tubercles.—As all plants have their peculiar beauties, it is difficult to assign to any one an elegance excelling all others; yet considering the curious structure of the flower, and beautiful apppearance of this whole plant, I know of no shrub that has a better claim to it.' Catesby, Vol. II, p. 98." (Burnaby, p. 80) It is believed to be the mountain laurel.

[17]The valley in which Burnaby got lost was that of the Occoquan.

friend, Mr. Burnaby (for whom I entertained a very sincere esteem) is well; we corresponded for several years after he left this country. . . ."

Burnaby missed seeing the greatest "curiosity" of the Valley, the Natural Bridge, and so did not describe it. Jefferson's description of it as "the most sublime of Nature's works" in his *Notes on the State of Virginia* (pages 33-35) is well known. Washington does not mention being there in either his *Diaries* or his *Writings*, but his initials are pointed out to the modern tourist on a rock about thirty feet above the stream.

The Natural Bridge also fascinated the Marquis François Jean de Chastellux, a general in Rochambeau's Army, who wrote of his travels in America in the years 1780, 1781, and 1782.[18] This charming and intellectual French general gives a vivid account of his visit with Jefferson at Monticello, and his delight in a long conversation with him. He was most enthusiastic over Virginia and its people. He went to Natural Bridge, but Jefferson was unable to accompany him.

---

[18]Chastellux, François Jean, Marquis de. *Travels in North America.*

Chapter 5

Washington as a Burgess

Washington began his career as a member of the House of Burgesses as a representative from Frederick County, elected in July 1758. That was natural. The people of Winchester and the surrounding country regarded him as their savior. He had built a fort for their protection from the Indians and during most of the French and Indian War he had his headquarters in the town in a stone building which is still preserved. He took his seat soon after his marriage in 1759. He was re-elected and continued to represent the county until 1765, when he was chosen along with Colonel John West to represent his home county of Fairfax. He was continuously re-elected until 1775, when he became Commander-in-chief of the American Armies. Although he was appointed a member of the important Committee on Propositions and Grievances, he did not take a prominent part in the deliberations of the House. He was not an orator, and it is believed made no set speeches. He was respected by his fellow burgesses and the public. Except for the clashes with Parliament over the Stamp Act and the subsequent duties on paper, tea and glass, the business which came before the colonial assembly was chiefly of local importance. His mind was practical, not speculative. The resistance of the colonials and the protests of the British merchants led to the repeal of the Stamp Act, but a proviso in the repeal asserted the right of Parliament to tax the American colonists. Washington was strongly opposed to the Act. His sentiments were expressed in a letter to Francis Dandridge.[1] Governor Fauquier was much relieved by the repeal

[1]*Writings*, Vol. 2, p. 425.

as he had written the Earl of Halifax that "government is set at defiance not having strength enough in her hands to enforce obedience."[2]

Any project that seemed likely to be of public benefit appealed to Washington. Thus, he was active in promoting a canal through the Dismal Swamp which would connect the waters of the Chesapeake with those of Albemarle Sound, and he invested heavily as a partner in the enterprise. It did not prove profitable in his lifetime and for many years after. In 1929 title to the canal was acquired by the Federal Government.[3]

After the repeal of the Stamp Act there was a short period of quiet in Virginia, but in 1767 new duties were laid on glass, paper and tea; but to test public opinion in the colonies, a delay of several months was granted before the act became effective. Meanwhile Lieutenant Governor Fauquier died and was succeeded in the autumn of 1768 by Norborne Berkeley, Lord Botetourt, as Governor. For many years the executives of the colony had been lieutenant governors, the titular governor remaining in England and receiving most of the salary and perquisites of the office. Lord Botetourt's appointment as governor was probably due to a desire to conciliate Virginia, though it was suspected that its ulterior purpose was to detach Virginia from the northern colonies. The sequel proved that this purpose, if ever entertained, failed. The Burgesses would not desert the other colonies. Their determination to resist Parliamentary taxation was as strong as that of the New England colonies. They embodied their stand in 1769 in energetic resolves drawn up while sitting behind closed doors. The governor summoned them to meet him in the Council Chamber, and told them they had made it his duty to dissolve them.[4] That was not the end of the matter; the representatives of the people met at once in the Apollo Room of the Raleigh Tavern and passed resolutions establishing a Non-Importation Association. Washington was one of the com-

[2]*Ibid.,* Vol. 2, p. 426 (note).
[3]Virginia *Guide,* p. 91.
[4]In the new election every burgess in the House that had been dissolved, was reelected.

mittee which framed the resolutions. Having done this, the assembly then drank toasts to "the King," "the Queen and Royal Family," "Lord Botetourt," "a Speedy and Lasting Union between Great Britain and her Colonies," "The Constitutional British Liberty in America."[5] Three days later, Washington and the other Burgesses attended the Queen's Birthday celebration at the Governor's Palace.

The Virginians bore Lord Botetourt no ill will for the dissolution of the House of Burgesses. They knew he had done only what he regarded as his duty; that he had acted unwillingly and had avowed his sympathy with their cause.

The governor died soon afterwards in 1770, and was "mourned as 'best of governors and best of men.' "[6]

A life-size white marble figure of Lord Botetourt was placed in the piazza of the Capitol in 1773. "The statue was cleaned twice a year by order of the assembly, even during the Revolution." In 1801 the statue was moved to a prominent place on the William and Mary campus in front of the Wren building. Present-day tourists who are fortunate enough to be in Williamsburg during freshman week, see the freshmen greeting His Lordship in colonial fashion, while upper classmen make sure that the stiff bows of the boys and the cutsies of the girls are performed in the proper manner.

There was another matter, not connected with these political difficulties, in which Washington was deeply interested; that was to get action on the claim of the Virginia volunteers to the western lands promised them.

In 1754 Governor Dinwiddie and the Council had by proclamation authorized a grant of 200,000 acres in the then unsettled back land to those who would volunteer to go to the Ohio and erect and support a fort to be built at the forks of that river. These lands were to be divided amongst them in proportion to their respective ranks. Such a promise could not be carried into effect until after the treaty of 1763, ending the war with France, had been signed.

In 1769, Washington raised the question in the House of Bur-

---

[5]*Diaries,* Vol. 1, p. 125 (note).
[6]Virginia *Guide,* p. 320.

gesses of the veterans' lands, and an address to the governor was voted.[7] As the Governor had recently arrived in Virginia and might not be familiar with the subject, Washington put the matter before him in a long letter.[8]

The Governor and Council confirmed the grant of 200,000 acres to the volunteers but provided that the claimants could make as many as twenty surveys but no more. This limitation may have been prudent, but as the number of claimants greatly exceeded twenty, many of them would have to be included in a single grant. Washington called a meeting at Fredericksburg for the purpose of settling the details of obtaining possession of the lands granted to the officers and men of the First Virginia Regiment. They appointed him their agent and attorney. Washington already had agents on the ground, Captain William Crawford and his brother Valentine. The former acted as his surveyor, choosing desirable tracts for him. Washington determined to see the land himself and chose as his companion, his physician and friend, Dr. James Craik. They took with them servants and pack horses. On the way to Pittsburgh they passed by Great Meadows and the scene of Braddock's defeat, but Washington was too preoccupied with his present business to note this in his Diary. On Oct. 17, 1770 the party arrived at Fort Pitt, where Washington dined at the Officers Club. On the 20th they set out in canoes to paddle down the Ohio to the mouth of the Big Kanawha with Dr. Craik, Capt. Crawford and others. On Oct. 22 they reached "the Mingo Town." A note by the editor states the Mingo Town was on the Ohio about three miles below Steubenville. On Oct. 29, they "went round what is called the Great Bent." On October 31 "the mouth of the Kanhawa was reached making the whole distance from Fort Pitt accordg to my Acct. 266 miles." They ascended the Great Kanawha about 21 miles and then set out on their return. Pittsburgh was reached on Nov. 21 and on the 22nd Washington "invited the Officers of the Fort and other Gentlemen to dine with

[7]Freeman, Vol. 3, p. 238.
[8]*Writings*, Vol. 2, p. 528.

me at Sample's." The editor states that Washington noted an expense with Sample of £26. 1. 10. On December 1 the Diary noted "Reached home. . . . after an absence of 9 Weeks and one Day."[9] There was no time for surveying on this trip. Crawford had already selected fertile tracts which Washington approved, and in the future would survey them and mark corners and line trees. Presumably the whole 200,000 acres were pre-empted, of which Washington was entitled to a large share in his own right and as purchaser from his fellow officers. He seems to have made a large additional purchase from Col. George Croghan of land near Pittsburgh on his own account. He knew he was overextending himself, but he believed passionately in the future of frontier lands.[10] Had not King Carter amassed the greatest fortune in Virginia by his speculations in the then frontier lands in the Northern Neck?

Years afterward toward the close of his life, in a letter to Edward Graham, he explained some of his troubles and how he dealt with them:

"It was with great difficulty after Peace was established in the year 1763 that I could obtain a recognition of the above proclamation; and then instead of assigning a district and permitting every Claimant to locate his own quantum therein, we were compelled to take the whole quantity in twenty Surveys; or rather not allowed to exceed that number. This it was that occasioned so many names to be jumbled together in the same Patent, and has caused the difficulties that have since occured to the Patentees, to obtain their respective quantities. The same happened to myself, but rather than be at the trouble and expense of dealing with others, I bought and exchanged until I got entire tracts to myself."[11]

Back at Mount Vernon, Washington had no occasion to attend the House of Burgesses for the rest of the year. Apparently there was no session that year after his return. He was busy circulating in Fairfax and elsewhere printed copies of the Non-Importation

---

[9]*Diaries,* Vol. 1, pp. 404-452.
[10]Freeman, Vol. 3, p. 265 (note).
[11]*Writings,* Vol. 36, pp. 251-252.

Agreement adopted at Williamsburg. He was also a member of one of the committees for correspondence, whose business it was to unify the colony by resolves of the separate counties and to correspond with like bodies in the other colonies. Fairfax had its own committee—Committee of Safety, it was called. It met in Alexandria in the summer of 1774. Washington was its chairman. George Mason drafted its resolutions. He was eminently fitted for the work. Few men of the day had speculated more deeply upon political theory and the constitutional relations between England and her American Colonies. The resolutions adopted are too lengthy for quotation. They called for a "covenant and association" by the inhabitants of all the colonies not to export their produce to Great Britain nor to import any merchandise (with certain exceptions) shipped from there, nor to buy or purchase any slaves until "free exportation and importation be again resolved on by a majority of the representatives or deputies of the colonies . . . that the legislative power can of right be exercised only by our Provincial Assemblies or Parliaments."

Washington attended the First Continental Congress, held in Philadelphia in September, 1774. Two other delegates, Patrick Henry and Edmund Pendleton, stopped at Mount Vernon to accompany him. Peyton Randolph of Virginia was elected President.

There is no doubt Washington enjoyed being a burgess. It gave him the social life he could find nowhere else in Virginia. He met members of the Council and other political leaders of the Colony; he dined with the Governor, members of the Council, the Speaker of the House, and others. He went to the theater frequently. He purchased things he could not get in Alexandria; heard the latest news from England; transacted the business of the plantations of Mrs. Washington and her children; and arranged for the shipment of their tobacco crop.

Often he took Mrs. Washington and the Custis children with him to Williamsburg, and had dental and other medical work done for all the family. In 1768 he took with him Mrs. Washington, Jacky and Patsy Custis, and Billy Bassett, travelling in the chariot through Caroline, King and Queen and King William counties to Eltham in New Kent County,[12] the seat of Burwell Bassett, who had married Mrs. Washington's sister, Anna Maria Dandridge. Eltham was so important in Washington's social life that a short account of it will be given later.

[12] J. C. Fitzpatrick. *George Washington, Colonial Traveller*, p. 209.

Chapter 6

Friends at Belvoir

No friends of Washington's early life were nearer to him than the Fairfaxes of Belvoir. He owed much of his advancement to the head of the family, the Honorable William Fairfax. He was born in Yorkshire in 1691, and was a cousin of Lord Fairfax of Greenway Court. He was educated in England, gaining a knowledge both of the classics and modern languages. He entered the colonial service, going first to India and then to the Bahama Islands, where he became Secretary of State and acting Governor. There he married Sarah, daughter of Major Thomas Walker. By her he had issue, George William, Thomas, Ann, and Sarah. Thomas was killed in action in 1746 with a French man of war in the East Indies. Ann married Lawrence Washington, and Sarah married John Carlyle. From the Bahamas he went to Salem, Massachusetts, where he obtained the more lucrative position of Collector of Customs. His wife, Sarah, died in Salem. Burnaby relates that on her deathbed she requested her husband after her decease to marry her friend Miss Deborah Clark, from the conviction that she would prove a kind stepmother to her orphan children. This he did and by her had three children, Bryan, William and Hannah. Of Bryan more will be said later. William entered the army and was killed on the Plains of Abraham before Quebec. Hannah married Warner Washington of Gloucester County, a cousin of George Washington.

In 1733 William Fairfax was transferred again, this time to Virginia, where he was appointed Collector of Customs for the South Potomac. "The purpose of this last transfer was to enable him to act as agent for the Northern Neck proprietary in succession to

Robert Carter."[1] He settled first in Westmoreland County, next near Falmouth in King George County and finally in the part of Prince William County, later Fairfax, where in 1741 he had completed the building of Belvoir. He was a burgess from 1741 to 1743, and was advanced to the Council in succession to Commissary Blair. By seniority he became President of the Council. He was a member of the Truro Vestry, and County Lieutenant of Fairfax. He was one of the trustees of Alexandria, and purchased lots 56 and 57 on Prince Street. Washington was under many obligations to him. After the war with the French commenced he was engaged in forwarding militia to Winchester. When the irascible Governor Dinwiddie, ignorant of the capture of Fort Necessity, gave Washington an order to advance to the Ohio and build a fort there to check the French, Washington wrote at great length to William Fairfax. As was his custom he addressed him as "Honbl. Sir." He explained the impossibility of the proposed march, without additional provisions, additional money, and additional men. Nothing more was heard of the plan. Writing from Winchester to his brother John Augustine on May 28, 1755, he said: "I shou'd be glad to hear you live Harmony and good fellowship with the family at Belvoir, as it is in their power to be very serviceable upon many occasions to us, as young beginners. I wou'd advise your visiting often as one step toward it; the rest, if any more is necessary, your own good sense will sufficiently dictate; for to that Family I am under many obligations, particularly to the old Gentleman."[2]

In his trouble with the militia it is not likely that he was much comforted to hear from Colonel Fairfax a reference to like difficulties in the Roman Army: "I am sensible, such a medley of undisciplined militia must create you various troubles, but having Caesar's Commentaries, and perhaps Quintus Curtius, you have therein read of greater fatigues, murmurings, mutinies, and defections, than will probably come to your share, though, if any

[1] Harrison, *Landmarks*, p. 341.
[2] *Writings*, Vol. 1, p. 128.

Courtesy Virginia State Chamber of Commerce

Ossian Hall (Pages 82, 229, and 230)

Courtesy Virginia State Chamber of Commerce

Home of Mary Washington, Fredericksburg, Virginia (Pages 84 and 85)

of those casualties should interrupt your quiet, I doubt not that you would bear them with a magnanimity those heroes remarkably did." It must have been pleasant to have read in the same letter: "The Council and Burgesses are mostly your friends; so that if you have not always the particular instructions from the Governor, you may think necessary and desire, the omission or neglect, may proceed from the confidence entertained of your ability and discretion to act what is fit or praiseworthy."[3]

William Fairfax died on September 3rd, 1757. The tide of war had not then turned in favor of the colonials, and he was spared the news of the death of his son William, in the assault on Quebec. Washington was in Winchester when the news of Colonel Fairfax's death reached him, but he hastened to Belvoir to attend his funeral. William Fairfax's will, recorded in Liber B of the *Fairfax Will Books* devised to his son, George William "My Plantation. . . with all the houses and Edifices thereon called and known by the name of Belvoir"— Belvoir is gone, but its wonderful situation, perched on a steep bluff with a beautiful view of the river and the Maryland hills beyond, remains to testify to the good judgment of its builder in locating it where he did.

Washington's lifelong friend, George William Fairfax, the eldest son of William Fairfax, was born at Providence in the Bahama Islands on January 2d 1724/25. He was educated in England, but apparently never attended a university. He visited Lord Fairfax at Leeds Castle in Kent, and made a favorable impression. His visit probably contributed to remove the strained relation between Lord Fairfax and his Virginia agents. He came back to his father's seat of Belvoir in 1746. He had a prior experience of wilderness life before the surveys he made in company with young Washington in 1748. Soon after his return to Virginia he accompanied John Warner as one of Lord Fairfax's surveyors to the head spring of the Potomac, the westernmost boundary of the Northern Neck, and carved his initials on a tree near the Fairfax Stone. Soon after his

[3]*Ibid.*, p. 385 (note).

return he became a member of Fairfax County Court. In 1748-1749 he was a burgess for Frederick County and it was while in Williamsburg that he met, and won the hand of Sarah Cary, the eldest daughter of Col. Wilson Cary of Ceelys, near Hampton. The Carys belonged to the James River aristocracy, which then dominated the colony. The Colonel was an accomplished classical scholar and had given much time to the education of his daughter. They were married in December, 1748, and took up their residence under the paternal roof at Belvoir. Though they had no children their marriage was a happy one. Sally, as she was called, was intelligent, vivacious and a charming hostess. After the death of her father-in-law, she became mistress of the mansion. Her husband's younger brother, Bryan, and his sister, Hannah (soon to marry Warner Washington), lived there. The great house was filled with guests. There were her own relatives from Hampton and Ceelys, the Blackburns of Rippon Lodge, the McCartys from Cedar Grove, the Waggeners from Colchester, John Carlyle and his wife, Sarah, and many others from Alexandria. Riches, grace and all the amenities of social life were there. To young George Washington, Belvoir was a second home. Like his father, George William Fairfax was one of the original trustees of Alexandria and purchased lots 62 and 63 on the south side of Prince Street. Either he or his father built a house, No. 207 Prince St., which still stands. It is built on lot 57 which he owned as heir of his father.

The Fairfax family owned land in Yorkshire, which would normally pass to George William on the death of the owner. He believed there was an intrigue to deprive him of the inheritance, and that was probably the reason he sailed for England in 1757 shortly after the death of his father. There he came in contact with Lord Fairfax's younger brother, Robert, and urged him to go with him to Virginia, writing "it would be much to your interest to see once what must shortly be your property." He meant that on Lord Fairfax's death without issue, Robert would inherit the Proprietary of the Northern Neck.

On Dec. 12, 1757 he wrote to his wife from London:

Dear Sally:

"I am sorry to say I have not yet succeeded and that it is uncertain whether I shall. But be it as it may, I find it was necessary to be here, and I should not have excused myself if I had not. Mr. Fairfax (Robert) went down to Leeds Castle yesterday and left me to push my own way, and then to follow to spend my Christmas and to prepare for his imbarking with me in March. Therefore I beseech you'll employ old Tom, or get some person to put the garden in good order, and call upon Mr. Carlyle for his assistance in getting other necessary things done about the house in order to receive so fine a gentleman. And I must further recommend, and desire that you'll endeavour to provide the best provisions for his nice stomach, altho: I suppose he will spend chief of his time with his brother.

"However to make his and other company more agreeable I shall endeavour to engage a butler to go over with me at least for one year.

"My Dear, I have often wished for your company to enjoy the amusements of this Metropolis, for I can with truth say, they are not much so to me in my present situation and that I now and then go to a play only to kill time. But I please myself with my country visits imagining the time there will pass more agreeable. Permit me Sally to advise a steady and constant application to those things directed for your welfare, which may afford me the greatest satisfaction upon my arrival.

"Your affect. and loving husband."[4]

Robert Fairfax did not come to Virginia for several years.

After Washington's marriage the families of Mount Vernon and Belvoir lived in close intimacy. By water Belvoir was two miles distant; by land six or seven. Shortly after his marriage Washington noted in his *Diary*: "Colo. Fairfax and Lady and Doctr Laurie dind here. The Dr. went away afterward, but the others stayed." As "Colo. Fairfax and Mrs. Fairfax dind here" the next day, they

[4]Neill, E. D. *Fairfaxes of England and America*, pp. 95-97.

must have made a typical eighteenth century two-day visit. Some time thereafter: "Went with Mrs. Washington and din'd at Belvoir." They played cards, drank Madeira together, and exchanged seeds. Washington and Fairfax went fox hunting together. They were both members of the Truro Vestry, and both purchased pews in the new church, though, as it turned out, George William and his wife made little use of their pews. Both families must have met often at Williamsburg when one was a Councillor and the other a burgess. But this pleasant intimacy lasting nearly fifteen years was now to end. The *Diary* entry of July 8, 1773, reads: "Colo. Fairfax and Mrs. Fairfax came in the aftern. to take leave of us." Fairfax had been "called to England to look after the affairs of Towlston Manor, in Yorkshire, to which he had succeeded under a family entail."[5] The entry in the *Diary* for the next day is, "Mrs. Washington and self went to Belvoir to see them take shipping."

Fairfax expected to return to Virginia, but he knew he would be in England for several years; he therefore resigned his seat in the Council and authorized Washington to advertise Belvoir for rent. This Washington did, inserting notices in the Williamsburg, Maryland and Pennsylvania *Gazettes*.

"June 2, 1774—To be Rented—

"From year to year or for a term of years Belvoir—the beautiful seat of the Hon. George Wm. Fairfax Esq. lying on the Potawmack River in Fairfax County about fourteen miles below Alexandria. The mansion house is all brick, two stories high, with four convenient rooms and a large passage on the lower floor; five rooms and a passage on the 2d; and a servants hall and cellar below; convenient offices, stables, and coach house adjoining, as also a large and well furnished garden stored with a great variety of valuable fruits, All in good condition."

Some time later the furniture was sold by Francis Willis, Fairfax's agent. Washington bought a mahogany sideboard and many other articles, aggregating several hundred pounds. The house was

[5] *Diaries*, Vol. 1, p. 3 (note).

leased to the Reverend Andrew Morton for seven years.[6] After a short stay in London, Fairfax went to Yorkshire to take possession of his ancestral property there.

The Revolutionary War did not stop the correspondence between the two men. Washington knew that Fairfax's sympathies were with the Americans, and while attending the second Continental Congress at Philadephia, he wrote his friend exultingly of Lexington, Concord and Bunker Hill. In another letter he told of his appointment to command the Continental Army, and of his inability to act further as attorney for Fairfax. In a later letter, entrusted to General Burgoyne for safe delivery, Washington gave the Fairfaxes all the news of their family he could gather. He felt sure that letters to him must have miscarried as he had heard nothing from Mr. Fairfax for four years.

Fairfax had appointed Robert Carter Nicholas, the well known James River planter and lawyer, his agent, when Washington was no longer able to act for him. News reached Washington in 1780 that it was proposed in the State Legislature to confiscate Fairfax's land. He wrote to Nicholas:

"I hope, I trust, that no act of Legislation in the State of Virginia has affected, or can affect, the property of this Gentnr. otherwise than in common with every good, and well disposed Citizen of America. It is a well known fact that his departure for England was not only anticedent to the present rupture with Great Britain, but before there was the most distant prospect of a serious dispute with that Country, and if it is necessary to adduce proof of his attachment to the interests of America since his residence there and of the aid he has given to many of our distressed Countrymen in that Kingdom, abundant instances may be adduced, not only by the Gentnr alluded to in his letter of Decr 5, 1779, but by others that are known to me, and on whom justice to Colo. Fairfax will make it necessary to call if occasion should require the facts to be

[6]Dr. Toner thinks he was minister of Drysdale Parish, King and Queen County. *Diaries*, Vol. 2, p. 173.

ascertd."[7] This letter seems to have stopped the proposed legislation. Washington's letter is confirmed by Burnaby's account of his conduct:

"During the ten year contest . . . he received no remittances from his extensive property in that quarter of the world" (Virginia). "This induced him to remove out of Yorkshire, from a house which he had recently furnished, to lay down his carriages, and to retire to Bath, where he lived in a private but genteel manner, and confined his expenses so much within the income of his English estates, that he was able occasionally to send large sums to the government agent, for the use and benefit of the American prisoners."[8]

With the cessation of hostilities, it became possible for the two friends to correspond more freely and Fairfax wrote: "Permit me, tho' an humble individual, and unfortunately out of the way of contributing any mite to the great, the glorious cause of Liberty, to offer my best thanks for all your Exertions, disinterested perseverance to the End of the great work. . . I glory in being called an American. . . During the war I frequently did myself the honor of Addressing a line to you, some of which I hope kis'd your hand, others were I know intercepted, and sent to the Minister, one of which had like to have cost me dear, but happily for me, I was related to a Lady, whose interest at Court saved me from persecution. I every moment expected a Messenger to take me into Custody. . . Indeed my dear Sir, I have been in a very disagreeable Situation, was obliged to leave Yorkshire to get out of the way of being informed against by some Relations, who I apprehended, would have hung me to get my little Estate joining to theirs, but I thank Heaven, you and our brave countrymen, times are greatly altered, and I am now as much Courted as I was before despised as an American. . . It is not possible for you to conceive how I am pestered, by applications, for Letters of Introduction to your Excellency: and other Persons of consequence in Virginia, by men,

---

[7]*Writings,* Vol. 20, p. 318.
[8]Burnaby, pp. 209-210.

that would, twelve months ago, have thought it a reflection upon them to be even seen in my Company."[9]

Washington replied in a friendly letter, expressing his hope "of seeing you and Mrs. Fairfax once more the Inhabitants of Belvoir, and greeting you both there, the intimate companions of our old Age as you have been of our younger years."[10]

Hope that the Fairfaxes might return ended with the burning of Belvoir. Washington described a visit to the ruins in a letter dated February 27, 1785.

". . .I cannot at this moment recur to the contents of those letters of mine to you which I suspect have miscarried; further than that they were all expressive of an earnest wish to see you and Mrs. Fairfax once more fixed in this country; and to beg that you would consider Mt. Vernon as your home until you could build with convenience, in which request Mrs. Washington joins very sincerely. I never look towards Belvoir, without having this uppermost in my mind. But alas! Belvoir is no more! I took a ride there the other day to visit the ruins, and ruins indeed they are. The dwelling house and the two brick buildings in front, underwent the ravages of fire; the walls of which are very much injured: the other Houses are sinking under the depredation of time and inattention, and I believe are now scarely worth repairing. In a word, the whole are, or very soon will be a heap of ruin. When I viewed them, when I considered that the happiest moments of my life had been spent there, when I could not trace a room in the house (now all rubbish) that did not bring to my mind the recollection of pleasing scenes, I was obliged to fly from them; and came home with painful sensations, and sorrowing for the contrast. Mrs. Morton [Wife of Rev. Andrew Morton] still lives at your Barn quarter."[11]

Mr. Fairfax died in 1787. He devised Belvoir to Fernando Fairfax, eldest son of his brother Bryan. He named Washington one of his executors, but he declined to act because of pressure of other

[9]*Writings,* Vol. 27, p. 58 (note).
[10]*Ibid.,* p. 57.
[11]*Ibid.,* Vol. 28, pp. 82-83.

business. He wrote to Fairfax's London agent: "Notwithstanding the long and uninterrupted friendship which subsisted between Colo. Fairfax and myself, and however desirous I may be to give every proof of my affection for him and his amiable relict, yet I must decline acting as executor for his Estate here. . ."[12]

The Belvoir estate is now owned by the United States, which acquired the larger portion in 1912, and is now used as an Engineer Replacement and Training Center. In 1932 overgrowth was cleared and the outline of the mansion and the garden walls disclosed. In the nearby area "is an obelisk erected by Mr. Fairfax Harrison bearing these inscriptions:

" 'Here lies William Fairfax, Esq., 1691-1757 of Belvoir. Born at Towlston in Yorkshire. Died President of the Virginia Council.

" 'Here lies Deborah Clark 1708-1746. Born at Salem in Massachussetts. Died wife of William Fairfax, Esq.

" 'In memory of the second son of William Fairfax, Esq., Thomas Fairfax, 1726-1746, Midshipman, Killed in action against a French squadron on the Coromandel coast.

" 'In memory of the youngest son of William Fairfax, Esq., William Henry Fairfax, 1739-1759, Subaltern in Bragg's (28th) Regiment. Died of wounds received with Wolf before Quebec.'

"This monument is of granite and the shaft is about 12 feet high."[13]

Robert Fairfax finally did make the voyage to Virginia in 1768. Washington records in his Diary on September 6, 1768: "paid a visit to Majr Fairfax (Brother of Lord Fairfax) at Belvoir."[14] Washington met him again over two years later in Williamsburg. He openly showed his disgust at the plain living at Greenway Court, and borrowed all the money he could from Lord Fairfax and later

---

[12]*Ibid.,* Vol. 29, p. 361.

[13]Duhamel, James F. "Belvoir." In Columbia Hist. Soc. of Washington, D. C. *Records,* Vol. 35-36. p. 149. 1935.

[14]*Diaries,* Vol. 1, p. 290.

in England from George William Fairfax. He was a spendthrift, and seems to have expected to recoup his fallen fortunes from the handsome revenue accruing to the Proprietor of the Northern Neck. He outlived his brother and became the seventh Lord Fairfax, but his expectation of revenue from the quit rents of the Northern Neck was doomed to disappointment. Virginia was no longer a British province. He was an alien, and aliens could not inherit from citizens of Virginia. He died in 1793, an old and penniless man.

Washington's relations with George William Fairfax's wife Sarah have been much discussed. He had been often at Belvoir after his brother Lawrence's marriage to Ann Fairfax but the conversation had probably turned mostly on politics, land grants and the affairs of the Ohio Company. When George William brought his bride to Belvoir early in 1749, the mansion acquired a new interest for him. The great house was thronged with visitors, old friends of the neighborhood, and in the winters between sessions of the House of Burgesses, there came relatives and friends from the James River Country. George had never before met such women. His life on the farm on the Rappahannock and on the frontier had not brought him in contact with the elegant social life of Williamsburg and the older settled parts of the colony. At the center of the life at the great mansion presiding over it was young Sarah Fairfax (Sally she was usually called), charming, intelligent, good natured, and something of a coquette. The friendship of young Washington for her lasted the rest of his life. In the last letter he wrote her, after he had retired to Mount Vernon to end his days, he recalled "those happy moments; the happiest in my life which I have enjoyed in your company."

Her attraction is shown by his earliest letters. Setting out with Braddock's army he hopes she will favor him with her correspondence and playfully reminds her that when the General was in Alexandria a Mrs. Wardrope became a greater favorite than Mrs. Fairfax by presenting him with a delicious cake and potted woodcocks.[15] A little later he writes her that a letter from her will "make me happier than the Day is long."[16] After Braddock's defeat, worn out and sick at heart, he returned to Mount Vernon and wrote to Colonel Fairfax inviting him and "the ladies" to visit him. The Colonel replied with a friendly letter welcoming him home, to which Sally Fairfax added in her name and that of two other ladies:

"Dear Sir—After thanking Heaven for your safe return I must accuse you of great unkindness in refusing us the pleasure of seeing you this night. I do assure you nothing but our being satisfied that our Comp would be disagreeable should prevent us from trying if our legs would not carry us to Mount Vernon this night but if you will not come to us tomorrow morning very early we shall be at Mount Vernon.

S. Fairfax
Ann Spearing
Eliz[th] Dent."[17]

This is the only letter of hers to Washington that has survived. In 1756 Washington was on duty at Winchester but in September he found it possible to spend a few days at Mount Vernon to meet the executors of his brother Lawrence. His favorite brother, John Augustine, was there in charge of the estate. John and he were bachelors. He found he needed new shirts and some of his old ones repaired. He might have sent to Alexandria for new ones. Instead he learned through his trusted servant, John Alton, that Sally Fairfax was expecting a seamstress at her house and would willingly take care of his shirts. So he sent her the following letter:

"Mount Vernon, September 23, 1756.

"Dear Madam: John informs me that you told him Miss. Nancy West was to be at your House in a day or two; and that you wou'd, if I sent my Linnen over, give it to Miss. Nancy to make: I shall

---

[15] *Writings*, Vol. 1, pp. 122-123.
[16] *Ibid.*, p. 138.
[17] S. M. Hamilton. *Letters to Washington*, Vol. 1, p. 74.

readily embrace the oppertunity of doing this, tho' I am at the same time, sorry to give you the trouble of directing about the making.

"I have sent a piece of Irish Linnen, a piece of Cambrick, and a shirt to measure by. The Shirt Fits tolerably well, yet, I wou'd have the others made with somewhat narrower Wrist bands: Ruffles deeper by half an Inch: and the Collars by three quarters of an Inch, which is in other respects of proper bigness. If Miss. Nancy will do me the favour to get thread and button's suitable it will oblige me much I have really forget to procure them myself. Please to make my Compts. to Miss. Fairfax and Miss. West when you see her. I am Dr. Madam, etc."[18]

The letter which follows can be best understood by advancing Dr. Fitzpatrick's explanation: "The only authority for this letter that has so far appeared is the text printed in the *New York Herald* (Mar. 30, 1877), and in Welles's *Pedigree and History of the Washington Family* (New York: 1879). The letter was sold by Bangs and Co., auctioneers in New York, and the *Herald*, after printing this letter the day before, merely reported the sale as disposing of two Washington letters, one at $13 and one at $11.50, leaving it a matter of guess as to which one of these prices belonged to this much discussed epistle. The letter drops from sight after this sale, and its present whereabouts is unknown. Constance Cary Harrison, in *Scribner's Monthly* (July, 1876), wrote: 'Mrs. George William Fairfax, the object of George Washington's early and passionate love, lived to an advanced age, in Bath, England, widowed, childless, and utterly infirm. Upon her death, at the age of eighty-one, letters (still in possession of the Fairfax family) were found among her effects, showing that Washington had never forgotten the influence of his youthful disappointment.' But these conclusions are by no means unquestionable. The editor debated for some time the inclusion of this letter and finally concluded to use it after noting its unsettled status."[19]

---

[18]*Writings,* Vol. 1, p. 473.
[19]*Ibid.,* p. 473.

Worthington C. Ford, whose edition of Washington's *Writings* was the standard one before the appearance of Dr. Fitzpatrick's, had printed the letter with reservations.

"To Mrs. George William Fairfax

"Camp at Fort Cumberland, September 12, 1758.

"Dear Madam: Yesterday I was honored with your short but very agreeable favor of the first inst. How joyfully I catch at the happy occasion of renewing a correspondence which I feared was disrelished on your part, I leave to time, that never failing expositor of all things, and to a monitor equally faithful in my own breast, to testify. In silence I now express my joy; silence, which in some cases, I wish the present, speaks more intelligently than the sweetest eloquence.

"If you allow that any honor can be derived from my opposition to our present system of management, you destroy the merit of it entirely in me by attributing my anxiety to the animating prospect of possessing Mrs. Custis, when—I need not tell you, guess yourself. Should not my own Honor and country's welfare be the excitement? 'Tis true, I profess myself a votary of love. I acknowledge that a lady is in the case, and further I confess that this lady is known to you. Yes, Madame, as well as she is to one who is too sensible of her charms to deny the Power whose influence he feels and must ever submit to. I feel the force of her amiable beauties in the recollection of a thousand tender passages that I could wish to obliterate, till I am bid to revive them. But experience, alas! sadly reminds me how impossible this is, and evinces an opinion which I long entertained, that there is a Destiny which has the control of our actions, not to be resisted by the strongest efforts of Human Nature.

"You have drawn me, dear Madame, or rather I have drawn myself, into an honest confession of a simple Fact. Misconstrue not my meaning; doubt it not, nor expose it. The world has no business to know the object of my Love, declared in this manner to you, when I want to conceal it. One thing above all things in this world I wish to know, and only one person of your acquaintance can solve me that, or guess my meaning. But adieu to this till happier times, if I ever shall see them. The hours at present are melancholy dull. Neither the rugged toils of war, nor the gentler conflict of A______ B______s,[20] is in my choice. I dare believe you are as happy as you say, I wish I was happy also. Mirth, good humor, ease of mind, and—what else?—cannot fail to render you so and consummate your wishes.

"If one agreeable lady could almost wish herself a fine gentleman for the sake of another, I apprehend that many fine gentlemen will wish themselves finer e'er Mrs. Spotswood is possest. She has already become a reigning toast in this camp, and many there are in it who intend (fortune favoring) to make honorable scars speak the fullness of their merit, and be a messenger of their Love to Her.

"I cannot easily forgive the unseasonable haste of my last express, if he deprived me thereby of a single word you intended to add. The time of the present messenger is, as the last might have been, entirely at your disposal. I can't expect to hear from my friends more than this once before the fate of the expedition will some how or other be determined. I therefore beg to know when you set out for Hampton, and when you expect to return to Belvoir again. And I should be glad also to hear of your speedy departure, as I shall thereby hope for your return before I get down. The disappointment of seeing your family would give me much concern. From any thing I can yet see 'tis hardly possible to say when we shall finish. I don't think there is a probability of it till the middle of November. Your letter to Captain Gist I forwarded by a safe hand the moment it came to me. His answer shall be carefully transmitted.

"Colo. Mercer, to whom I delivered your message and compliments, joins me very heartily in wishing you and the Ladies of Belvoir the perfect enjoyment of every happiness this world affords. Be assured that I am, dear Madame, with the most unfeigned regard, your most obedient and most obliged humble servant.

"N. B. Many accidents happening (to use a vulgar saying)

---

[20] "Assembly Balls" are probably the words intended.—Ford.

between the cup and the lip, I choose to make the exchange of carpets myself, since I find you will not do me the honor to accept mine."[21]

This letter was sent while Washington was awaiting orders to join General Forbes in the expedition to capture Fort Duquesne. The campaign might prove as bloody as Braddock's. He might never come back. Both he and she knew he was soon to marry Martha Custis, but he seems to have been irresistibly impelled to speak out and draw from her a comment on his declaration of love. If that was his hope he was doomed to disappointment, but from the opening sentence of his next letter, "Do we still misunderstand the true meaning of each other's Letters?"—it is evident she evaded the declaration he had hoped for. She gave him details of her sisters and Nancy Gist and perhaps told him of private theatricals. He replied in a like strain, telling her in detail of Major Grant's defeat before Fort Duquesne and of his apprehension that nothing would come of the campaign for that year and that we shall "retire to the Inhabitants condemned by the World, and derided by our Friends." Washington was mistaken. Forbes captured Fort Duquesne. Some parts of this second letter follow:

"Camp at Rays Town, September 25, 1758

"Dear Madam: Do we still misunderstand the true meaning of each other's Letters? I think it must appear so, tho' I would feign hope the contrary as I cannot speak plainer without. But I'll say no more, and leave you to guess the rest. . . .

"I should think my time more agreable spent believe me, in playing a part in Cato, with the Company you mention, and myself doubly happy in being the Juba to such a Marcia, as you must make.

"Your agreable Letter contained these words. 'My Sisters and Nancy Gist who neither of them expect to be here soon after our return from Town, desire you to accept their best Complimts.&c.'

"Pray are these Ladies upon a Matrimonial Scheme? Is Miss

[21] *Writings,* Vol. 2, pp. 287-289.

Fairfax to be transformd into that charming Domestick—a Martin, and Miss Cary to a Fare? What does Miss Gist turn to—A Cocke? That can't be, we have him here—

"One thing more and then have done. You ask if I am tired at the length of your Letter? No Madam I am not, nor never can be while the Lines are an Inch asunder to bring you in haste to the end of the Paper, You may be tird of mine by (sic) this.

"Adieu dear Madam, you possibly will hear something of me, or from me before we shall meet. I must beg the favour of you to make my Compliments to Colo. Cary and the Ladies with you, and believe me that I am most unalterably. Yr. Most Obedt. & Oblig'd."[22]

With Washington's marriage the romance ended. The friendship remained. He never knew it but Sally Fairfax treasured his first letter and kept it secretly until her death. He was already Virginia's most distinguished soldier, and in her lifetime he was to become the most famous American. The episode is not discreditable to either of the parties. This was not the first time that a man in love with one woman married another. It happened to Sir Thomas More. Nor is it the first time an unmarried man of high character has fallen in love with a married woman. It happened to John Stuart Mill, whom Gladstone called the saint of Rationalism. Mill fell in love with Harriet Handy Taylor. She was a confirmed invalid and lived in the country, where Mill visited her for twenty years, with the full consent of her husband, a man of limited mental powers, but of high character and unselfishness. After Mr. Taylor's death Mill married her.[23]

---

[22] *Ibid.*, pp. 292, 293, 294.

[23] *Encyclopaedia Brittanica,* Eleventh Ed. Article, "John Stuart Mill."

Chapter 7

Marriage and Domestic Life

Washington married Martha Dandridge Custis on January 6, 1759. He was then nearly twenty seven years old and she was nearly a year older. She was the widow of Daniel Parke Custis, a wealthy planter, owning a large tract of land on the Pamunkey and York Rivers known as the White House plantation, and lots in Williamsburg. He died intestate in 1757 at the age of 45 years, leaving besides his land a personal estate appraised at £23,642.[1]

Martha Dandridge was the daughter of John Dandridge of New Kent County. Daniel Parke Custis left two infant children, John Parke Custis (Jackey) and Martha Parke Custis (Patsy). Washington met her on March 16, 1758. George Washington Parke Custis in his *Recollections* states that their first meeting took place in 1758 when Washington ferried the Pamunkey on his way to report to the acting Governor at Williamsburg. There he encountered a Mr. Chamberlayne who insisted that he be his guest at dinner. It was there that he met his future wife. It was love at first sight. Instead of leaving after dinner, Washington stayed for the night, all the next day, and only started for Williamsburg on the day after. As Washington's *Diaries* for 1758 and 1759 are missing or not kept, Custis' account cannot be verified, but there is nothing intrinsically improbable in the story he tells. As the event occurred long before he was born and as he was given to dramatizing (he wrote several plays), it is not certain that the meeting at the Chamberlayne home was the first acquaintance of the parties and it is

[1]Freeman, Vol. 2, p. 300.

Courtesy Virginia State Chamber of Commerce

Kenmore (Page 85)

Eltham (Pages 90 and 94)

(From a drawing published in the William and Mary College Quarterly Historical Magazine, 2d ser., Vol. 23, No. 4, Oct. 1943.)

equally uncertain whether other considerations than pure love did not play a part in the motives of both. Washington was the foremost soldier of Virginia and Mrs. Custis was one of the wealthiest widows in the colony. The marriage took place at the bride's residence, the White House.

There is a persistent local tradition, however, that the ceremony was performed at St. Peter's Church in New Kent County by the Rev. David Mossom. That Parson Mossom was the clergyman is likely, as the White House was in his parish, but the wedding did not take place in the church, which was several miles away, and without heat, as the colonial law forbade the building of chimneys in churches. The Reverend S. B. Chilton, formerly rector of the church, said he found it best not to question the tradition; that any doubt would have given offense to his parishioners.

John Adams is reported to have said that Washington would never have been appointed Commander of the Continental Army or President of the United States if he had not married the rich widow Custis, and David Burns (the "obstinate Mr. Burns," as Washington called him, the original proprietor of the land which is now the south lawn of the Executive Mansion) is credited with a like remark. Both were splenetic, and untrue. Undoubtedly the marriage was a good one for Washington, but his services to his wife and her children outweighed the wealth she brought him. He undertook the management of their lands in Williamsburg and on the York and Pamunkey Rivers, relieving her of a heavy burden, and he became guardian of her children. She had been her own superintendent but Mr. Custis' lawyer had advised before her remarriage that she should employ a trusty steward although he should require high wages.

The marriage also involved Washington in an interminable chancery suit, known as the Dunbar-Parke case, against the estate of Martha's former husband's father. It was begun in the Leeward West India Islands: renewed in the General Court of Virginia, appealed to the English Chancery Court, where the decree of the

General Court was reversed, and the case remanded to Virginia for further proceedings. That was its status when Washington married.[2]

Daniel Parke Custis owned stock in the Bank of England, and Washington received regular dividends, as his wife's personal estate belonged to him, and he also received dividends as guardian of the children. The value of this stock, according to Washington's calculation, was £1650. That was a new experience. There were money lenders in the colonies, but no banks. Many years later when a bank was organized in Alexandria, he became a large stockholder.

After a three months' honeymoon at Martha's house in Williamsburg, in which Washington attended the sessions of the House of Burgesses, the couple and the children left for Mount Vernon, where Washington had started repairing the house. He had occupied Mount Vernon only intermittently during the war. His brother John Augustine had moved away. He had to rely on George William Fairfax to oversee the builder who was doing the repair work. Fairfax had recently returned from England. Washington himself was sick in the early part of 1758 and was at Fort Cumberland and with General Forbes on the march to Fort Duquesne for most of the rest of the year, so he could do little to supervise the job of preparing and beautifying the house for Martha's arrival. The house was painted, new floors were laid, and a new roof put on, but it does not seem to have been enlarged until 1774.

While on the way to Mount Vernon he wrote to his servant John Alton: "I have sent Miles on today to let you know I expect to be up to Morrow, and to get the key from Colo. Fairfax's which I desire you will take care of. You must have the house very well clean'd, and were you to make Fires in the Rooms below it w'd air them. You must get two of the best Bedsteads put up one in the Hall Room, and the other in the little Dining Room that use to be, and have beds made on them against we come. You must also get out the Chairs and Tables and have them very well rubd and

[2] *Ibid.*, pp. 298-301.

cleand; the Stair case ought also to be polished in order to make it look well.

"Enquire about in the Neighborhood, and get some eggs and Chickens, and prepare in the best manner you can for our coming; you need not however take out any more of the Furniture than the Beds and Tables and Chairs in Order that they may be well rubd and cleand."[3]

Back at last in Mount Vernon, he wrote to Richard Washington, then in England: "I am now, I believe, fixed in this Seat with an agreeable consort for life and I hope to find more happiness in retirement than I ever experienced amidst a wide and bustling world."[4] The accumulated deficiencies of years had to be made up. A single invoice of Sundries to be sent by Robert Cary and Company for the use of George Washington in September 1759 includes about two hundred items. Along with this was an Invoice of Sundries for the use of Master John and Miss Patty Custis to be charged to their accounts.

A few of the articles in the first invoice are:

"A Light Summer Suit made of Duroy or &ca. by the measure.
2 best plu Beaver Hats at 21s.
4 psbinding tape.
1 Sword Belt red Morocco or Buff; no buckles or Rings.
2 best two bladed Knives.
2 pr Good Horse Scissars.
6 M Miniken Pins.
2 dozen packs playg. Cards.
1 Hogshead best Porter."

Many of the articles ordered were for Mrs. Washington:

"A Salmon-coloured Tabby of the Inclosed Pattern, with Sattin Flowers to be made in a Sack and Coat.[5]

A Cap, hand'f, Tucker, and Ruffles, to be made of Brussels Lace,

---

[3]*Writings,* Vol. 2, p. 318.
[4]*Ibid.,* p. 337.
[5]The editor's note states "Tabby was a watered silk material or an imitation thereof." *Writings,* Vol. 2, pp. 331-335.

or Point, proper to wear with the above negliglee to cost £20.
2 fine flowered Lawn Aprons.
1 pr. Woman's white Silk Hose.
6 pr Do. fine cotton Do.
1 pr. bla; and 1 pr white Sattan Shoes, of the Smallest fives.
1 fashil Hatt, or Bonnett.
6 pr Women's best kid Gloves.

Also ordered were tools, medicines, soap, and
Directions for the Busts.

4. one of Alexr. the Great, another of Julius Caesar; anr. of Chs.
12.Sweden; and a 4th of the King of Prussia.

Among the things ordered for "Master Custis, six years old," were

6 pr. Gloves, 2 Lac'd Hatts.
4 pr strong Shoes; 4 pr Pumps.
6 pr. fine thrd Stockings.
1 Sumr Suit of Cloathes, to be made of something light and Thin.
10/. worth of Toys.
6 little books for Childn begg. to Read.

For Miss Custis, 4 yrs. old

8 yds of fine printed Linnen at 3/6.
8 pr kid Mitts; 4 pr Gloves.
2 Caps, 2 pr Ruffles, 2 Tuckers, Bibs and Aprons, if fashionable.
6 yds Ribbon; 2 Necklaces.
1 Fash-drest Baby, 10/.; and other Toys 10/.
ginger bread toys"

Other orders included prayer books and Bibles with the Custis' children's names in gilt letters on them. Nor were Washington's orders confined to Cary and Co. Other orders went to Capel and Osgood Hanbury, and to James Gildart.

In her new home Martha's duties were similar to those at the White House, except that she no longer had the care of the plantation. She supervised the dairy, the spinning and the weaving, the house slaves and the management of the household. The tasks proving too onerous, a housekeeper was employed to relieve her.

Martha had never seen Mount Vernon before her marriage. She had spent her life in the lowland country where the hills are mostly rolling undulations and bold bluffs are rare. Now she came to a house in a beautiful setting of green lawns sloping sharply down to the river, with the bluff of Warburton (now Fort Washington) in plain sight. And below her new home lay Belvoir, set high on the precipitous banks of the river. A dozen miles to the south was the wild gorge of the Occoquan. If the country was new to her, so were the people. She knew hardly anyone in Fairfax. She had to make the acquaintance of Washington's friends and neighbors, the Fairfaxes, the Wests, the Alexanders, the Chapmans, the Peakes, the Dulanys, the Manlys, the McCartys, the Cockburns, the Masons, the Bronaughs, the Frenches, the Rev. Charles Green, rector and physician, and the Alexandria people, Carlyles, Ramsays, Gilpins, Fitzgeralds, and many others. The house even then was thronged with visitors. She was no novice in entertaining. Her prior married life had been spent at and near Williamsburg. She had poise and native dignity. Years after, she was described as "a sociable, pretty kind of woman," and her commonplaceness was what Washington needed as a hostess, and he found her the helpmate he wanted.

She had not been a year at Mount Vernon when Washington noted in his diary "January 1, 1760. found Mrs. Washington broke out with the meazles." On the 4th "Mrs. Washington seemed to be very ill wrote to Mr. Green this afternoon desiring his Company to visit her in the Morng." This was the Reverend Charles Green, Rector of Truro Parish. He had practiced medicine prior to his ordination.

"Saturday 5th Mrs. Washington appeared to be something better. Mr. Green however came to see her at 11 o'clock and in an hour Mrs. Fairfax arrived." This was Sally, wife of George William Fairfax. Her sprightly talk must have cheered the sick woman. "The evening being very cold, and the wind high, Mrs. Fairfax went home in the Chariot."

"Sunday 6th. The Chariot not returg time enough from Colo. Fairfax's we were prevented from Church. Mrs. Washington was a good deal better today; but the Oyster Man still continuing his Disorderly behavior at my Landing I was obliged in the most pre-emptory manner to order him and his compy away, which he did not incline to obey till next morning."

The aftermath of the measles hung on for in April he called in Dr. Laurie from Alexandria who "came here I may add Drunk." The doctor stayed all night and was evidently sober in the morning. "Mrs. Washington was blooded by Doctr. Laurie." Dr. Laurie had a contract to attend all Washington's people in Fairfax county for fifteen pounds a year.

Mrs. Washington was a fond mother to her two little children, constantly worrying about them. She wrote to her sister, Mrs. Bassett, about a visit in which, "I carried my little patt with me and left Jacky at home for a trial to see how well I could stay without him tho we were gon but wone fortnight I was quite impatient to get home. If I at any time heard the doggs barke or a noise out, I thought thair was a person sent for me. I often fancied he was sick or some accident had happened to him, so that I think it is impossible for me to leave him as long as Mr. Washington must stay when he comes down."[6]

Little "patt" early showed signs of epilepsy. In 1768 Dr. Rumney was sent for to attend her. At the end of July 1769, "set out with Mrs. Washington and Patsy Custis for the Frederick Springs." Travelling leisurely, stopping at his brother's and at Winchester, he arrived at the Springs on August 6th. He occupied the house of his friend, Colonel George Mercer. He found it needed repairing and ordered the erection of an arbor for further comfort and made arrangements for procuring meats, vegetables, butter and eggs, as he proposed to stay for some time. Actually he stayed two months. and dined with Lord Fairfax, George William Fairfax, Lord Fairfax's brother, Robert, Mr. Warner Washington, Colonel Stephen,

[6]Ford, *True George Washington,* p. 96.

and many others. He "rid with Mrs. Washington and others to the Cacapehon (Capon) to see the prospect from thence." He had taken his chariot for the convenience of Mrs. Washington and Patsy. Presumably the chariot was used to see the "prospect." It broke down, much to his disgust, on the way home. Patsy derived no benefit from the waters. Mount Vernon was reached on the 12th of September.[7]

This was not Washington's first visit to the Springs. He had been there in 1761 and had written the Reverend Charles Green that while food was abundant, lodging was almost impossible to secure as there were about 200 people at the place, "full of all manner of diseases and complaints . . . Had we not succeeded in getting a tent and marquee from Winchester we should have been in a most miserable condition here." He stayed a fortnight and in the end found "my fevers are a good deal abated."[8]

The Warm Springs in Berkeley County, Virginia (now in Morgan County, West Virginia) were known to the Indians, but until the capture of Fort Duquesne the danger from the Indians prevented their development as a health resort. Lord Fairfax gave the springs to Virginia in 1756, "that those healing waters might be forever free to the publick for the welfare of suffering humanity."[9]

The most lively account of the Warm Springs in the eighteenth century was given by Philip Vickers Fithian, an itinerant Presbyterian clergyman who visited there in 1775. The year before he had been a tutor in the family of Councillor Carter of Nomini Hall. On this occasion he apparently went out of his way for a "change from the primitive society among which he had been travelling for ten weeks." He found that a "Huge Stone tumbled from the mountain directly to the Drinking Spring." He continues, "Drank early and freely of the Waters—about four hundred now present. Near one half of these are visibly indisposed." He names various

[7] *Diaries*, Vol. 1, p. 336 *et seq.*
[8] *Writings*, Vol. 2, p. 365.
[9] Carl Bridenbaugh. "Baths and Watering Places of Colonial America," *William and Mary Quarterly*, April 1946.

people he met, Col. (Fielding) Lewis of Fredericksburg, Dr. Holmes, Mr. Finley and Mr. Williamson of Alexandria, Mr. Blain of Maryland, Mr. Washington, Major Willis and others.

"Parson Allen of Frederick in Maryland left Bath this morning. It is said he has been mobbed by the ladies. Tickets going about for a Ball this Evening. Parson Wilmore is said to be the verriest Buck in Town." Such gayeties were permissible to Episcopal clergymen. They shocked but interested this sober Presbyterian.

"In one part of this little bush Village a splendid Ball—At some distance and within hearing, a Methodist Preacher was haranguing the People. . . In our dining Room Companies at Cards, five and forty, whist, Alfours Callico Betty etc."[10]

"Mr. Biddle, one of the Delegates for the Province of Pennsylvania, at the Con. Congress is here and much disordered with the Rheumatism."

The next day "from twelve to four this Morning soft & continual Serenades at Different houses where the Ladies lodge. Several of the Company, among many the Parson, were hearty."[11]

"In October 1776 an act was passed establishing the town of 'Bath' at Warm Springs in Berkeley County. Fifty acres were set aside to be divided into lots and streets on which 'to build convenient houses to accommodate numbers of infirm persons who frequent these springs yearly.' One large spring was designated as 'suitable for a bath.' Management of the bath and buildings was placed under the superintendence of a board of trustees, among whom were Bryan Fairfax, Samuel and Warner Washington and Thomas Hite."[12]

Little Martha Custis continued to decline; her fits recurred more frequently. One curious remedy was tried. "Joshua Evans, who came here last Night put an Iron Ring upon Patsy for Fitts." The

[10]Note by the editors: "five and forty was a game somewhat resembling euchre . . . All-Fours was a high, low, jack, game type, the forerunner of auction pitch and very popular for gambling."

[11]Fithian *Journal,* Vol. 2, pp. 125-126. (Princeton University Press).

[12]Carl Bridenbaugh. "Baths and Watering Places of Colonial America," *William and Mary Quarterly,* April 1946.

editor of the *Diaries* explains in a note this was "one of the old superstitions of the curative properties of iron mingled with the symbolism of the ring."[13] The end came on the nineteenth of June 1773. "At home all day. About five o'clock poor Patsy Custis Died Suddenly."[14]

The next day Washington wrote Burwell Bassett: "It is an easier matter to conceive than to describe the distress of this Family; especially that of the unhappy Parent of our dear Patsy Custis when I inform you that yesterday removed (sic) the Sweet Innocent Girl Entered into a more happy and peaceful abode than any she has met with in the afflicted Path she hitherto has trod.

"She rose from Dinner about four o'clock in better health and spirits than she appeared to have been in for sometime, soon after which she was seized with one of her usual Fits. and expired in it, in less than two minutes without uttering a word, a groan or scarce a sigh. This sudden, and unexpected blow, I scarce need add has almost reduced my poor Wife to the lowest ebb of Misery; which increased by the absence of her son."[15]

John Parke Custis was not at Mount Vernon when his sister died. Washington was determined he should have the best education in the colonies. He placed him under the care of the Reverend Jonathan Boucher at Annapolis. The boy was then (1768) fourteen years old and had received some instruction from Mr. Magowan, who lived in Maryland across the river from Mount Vernon. Boucher suggested a European trip with him, the Custis estate paying the expense of both. Washington thought well of the project, but on making inquiries of the expense, concluded he could not, as guardian, sanction it without an order of court, and the matter was dropped. He wrote to Boucher in 1770: "According to appointment, Jacky Custis now returns to Annapolis. His mind is a good deal released from Study, and more than ever turned to Dogs, Horses and Guns; indeed upon Dress and equipage, which till of

[13] *Diaries*, Vol. 1, p. 313.
[14] *Ibid.*, Vol. 2, p. 115.
[15] *Writings*, Vol. 3, p. 138.

late, he has discovered little Inclination of giving into."[16] In a later letter: "In respect to the kinds and matter of his Studying, I leave it wholly to your better Judgment; had he begun, or rather, pursued his Study of the Greek Language, I should have thought it no bad acquisition, but whether to acquire this now, he may not forego some more useful branches of learning, is a matter worthy of consideration. To be acquainted with the French Tongue, is becoming a part of polite Education." And he went on to name Arithmetic, Mathematics, Philosophy, Moral and Natural, as desirable studies for "a Gentleman."[17] While with Boucher, Jacky was inoculated for smallpox in Baltimore, but Washington took care that the boy's mother knew nothing about it until his recovery. Eventually Washington took young Custis to Kings College (now Columbia University), New York City, apparently on Boucher's recommendation. While there, at the age of eighteen he became engaged to Eleanor Calvert, daughter of Benedict Calvert of Mt. Airy, Prince Georges County, Maryland, without the knowledge of his mother or Washington. The match was one to which no exception could be taken on the score of the young woman's character or family; the objection was that a marriage at this time would prevent the completion of his education. Washington wrote to Calvert that "Miss Nellie's amiable qualifications stand confessed at all hands; and that an alliance with your Family, will be pleasing to his.

"This acknowledgment being made you must permit me to add Sir, that at this, or in any short time, his youth, inexperience, and unripened Education, is, and will be insuperable obstacles in my eye, to the completion of the Marriage."[18]

Writing to Burwell Bassett he stated his apprehension as to Jack's marriage more plainly: "not that I have any objection to the match, as she is a girl of exceeding good character; but because I fear, as he has discovered much fickleness already, that he may either change, and therefore injure the young lady, or that it may

[16] *Ibid.*, p. 35.
[17] *Ibid.*, p. 36.
[18] *Ibid.*, p. 130.

precipitate him into a marriage before I am certain, he has ever bestowed a serious thought of the consequences; by which means his education is interrupted and he perhaps wishing to be at liberty again before he is fairly embarked on those important duties."[19]

Washington had his way, temporarily, but in the end he was obliged to yield and he wrote the Rev. Myles Cooper, President of Kings College, that he had hoped by Custis's "continuance at that place under a Gentleman so capable of instructing him in every branch of useful knowledge, as you are" to have completed his education, "but these hopes are at an end; and at length, I have yielded, contrary to my judgment, and much against my wishes, to his quitting college, in order that he may enter soon into a new scene of Life, which I think he would be much fitter for some years hence, than now; but having his own inclination, the desires of his mother and the acquiessence of almost all his relatives, to encounter, I did not care, as he is the last of the family, to push my opposition so far; and therefore, have submitted to a kind of necessity."[20]

The marriage took place at Mount Airy on the 3d of February 1774. Mrs. Washington, apparently, did not attend, probably she did not care to join in the festivity so soon after Patsy's death. The couple stayed at Mount Airy for several months and then moved to Custis's White House estate on the Pamunkey River. There they lived until 1778. Both husband and wife were anxious to get back to the neighborhood of Mount Vernon and Mount Airy: so anxious that Custis entered into contracts with Robert and Gerard Alexander to buy their plantations on the Potomac above Four Mile Run. They moved into Robert Alexander's house on the river just north of the Run, and gave it the name of Abingdon. The bargain with Robert Alexander was a preposterous one. In telling Washington about it, Custis wrote; "I have agreed to give him twelve pounds per acre, and at the expiration of 24 years to pay him the principal with compound interest."[21] Washington was dum-

[19] *Ibid.*, p. 134.
[20] *Ibid.*, pp. 167-168.
[21] Custis manuscript, Library of Congress.

founded. He replied: "As a friend and one who has your interest at heart, let me entreat you to consider the consequences of paying compound interest. . . . I presume you are not unacquainted with the fact of 12,000 pounds at compound interest amounting to upwards of 48,000 pounds in twenty-four years."[22]

At the siege of Yorktown Custis served as a volunteer aide-de-camp on Washington's staff, contracted camp fever and was taken to Eltham where he died. In a letter from Mount Vernon to Lafayette, Washington wrote:

"On that day I arrived at Eltham (the Seat of Colo. Bassett) time enough to see poor Mr. Custis breathe his last; this unexpected and affecting event threw Mrs. Washington and Mrs. Custis (who were both present) into such deep distress, that the circumstances of it and a duty I owed to the deceased in assisting at his funeral rights prevented my reaching this place till the 13th."[23]

There were four children of the marriage, Elizabeth, born in 1776, married Thomas Law, the English speculator, who played a considerable part in the development of the "Federal City." The well known Rodgers family of Baltimore, donors of Druid Hill Park, descend from this marriage. Martha, born in 1777, married Thomas Peter of Georgetown, builder of Tudor Place, which her descendants still occupy. Eleanor, born 1779, married Washington's nephew, Lawrence Lewis. They built Woodlawn, on a part of the Mount Vernon estate overlooking the Washington and Richmond Highway. Lastly, George Washington Parke Custis, born 1781, built Arlington Mansion. Washington adopted the two younger children, and they were reared at Mount Vernon. The widow and the two older children returned to Abingdon. In 1783 she married Dr. David Stuart, by whom it is said she had twelve children. Before remarrying she must have tried to get Lund Washington to sound out George Washington on the subject, but he declined to commit himself. He wrote Lund: "For my own part, I never did, nor do I believe I ever shall give advice to a woman who

[22]*Writings*, Vol. 12, p. 266.
[23]*Ibid.*, Vol. 23, p. 340.

is setting out on a matrimonial voyage, first, because I never could advise one to marry without her own consent, and secondly, because I know it is to no purpose to advise her to refrain when she has obtained it."[24] He went on, however, to tell Lund the sensible advice he would give her if she asked his opinion.

Dr. David Stuart

From the time of his marriage Dr. Stuart became one of Washington's most intimate friends. He studied medicine, but seems not to have practiced, at least, after his marriage. Both his father and grandfather had been Rectors of the still standing St. Paul's Church in King George County, Virginia. His grandfather, David, seems to have been involved in the abortive Jacobite rising of 1715 and fled to Virginia. He claimed descent from the royal house of Stuart, and shortly after his arrival he was given charge of St. Paul's Parish. He died in 1749 and was succeeded by his son, the Rev. William Stuart, who resigned because of ill health some years before his death in 1796. The two Stuarts, father and son, ministered to this church nearly eighty years. Dr. Stuart was a son of this William. He was a member of the Fairfax County Court. In 1786 he was elected to the House of Delegates, "Colo. Mason receiving 109 votes; Dr. Stuart 105 and Capt. West 84." This was an important election, for at the ensuing session the Assembly elected delegates to the Constitutional Convention in Philadelphia, which framed the Constitution of the United States. After his marriage he resided at Abingdon until 1792 when as administrator of John Parke Custis he deeded the Abingdon tract back to Robert Alexander under a compromise agreement, ratified by an act of the Virginia Legislature. He then moved to Hope Park, an estate of 2000 acres belonging to him, situated about five miles northwest of Fairfax Court House. He continued to reside there until after Washington's death. His residence there was the probable reason of his being named by the State Legislature trustee for the

[24] *Ibid.*, Vol. 27, p. 157.

town of Centerville in 1792 and of Providence (now Fairfax Court House) in 1805.

Her mother's remarriage and the removal of the family to Hope Park did not meet the approval of her daughter Elizabeth (Eliza), who subsequently made an unfortunate marriage to Thomas Law. At Abingdon she was near Mount Vernon, Alexandria and Georgetown, with balls, dances and visits. Hope Park she considered in the wilderness. A letter of hers written in 1808, after her separation from her husband, was printed in the *Virginia Magazine of History and Biography* for April 1945. An extract from it is given here:

"Two years after my father's departure my mother gave her hand to Dr. Stuart—she chose the man she believed would make the best Guardian for her children—Dr. S. was not then the gloomy Mortal he has been since—he had just returned from Europe—where he received every advantage of Education and was one of the most learned men of his day—he was a Man of respectable family & a Character free from reproach, he had studied the profession of Medicine & I believe was qualified to make a conspicuous figure in it—he had little fortune & my mothers friends disapproved of the choice she made but she was independent of them & finding herself incapable of managing her own, or her childrens property determined to marry Dr. S. he became her husband & the guardian of her children's fortune—. . . the place she was to remove to was one Dr. S.—had purchased with the wish to acquire property—The place had nothing to recommend it was twenty miles from Alexandria."

Dr. Stuart's important appointment was his choice by President Washington as one of the three Commissioners for the laying off of the Federal City. His colleagues were Thomas Johnson, afterward Governor of Maryland, and Daniel Carroll of Forest Glen, Maryland. The Commissioners had a gigantic real estate problem on their hands. Without other assistance than modest appropriations by Maryland and Virginia, they were to lay off the new city, grade its streets, pay for surveying, and other help, raise funds for building the Capitol, White House and other public buildings from the proceeds of the sale of the public's half of the newly formed lots.

As Dr. Stuart was one of the family, Washington frequently consulted him on domestic problems after he came back to Mount Vernon in 1797.

George Washington Parke Custis (called Washingon) was the chief problem. Washington would have liked to enter him in the College of Massachusetts, as he called Harvard, "but if he should go contrary to his inclination, and without a disposition to apply his time properly, an expense without any benefit would result from the measure," so he sent young Washington to Hope Park, hoping that Mrs. Stuart (his mother) and the Doctor could find out his wishes. He was finally sent to St. John's College at Annapolis, but he would not study and soon quit. Washington wrote of him: "I believe Washington means well, but has not resolution to act well." When war with France appeared imminent, Washington designed to procure young Custis a Cornetcy in a troop of Light Dragoons to be commanded by Lawrence Lewis. This pleased Custis, but the danger of war soon disappeared. Washington wrote to him repeatedly admonishing him to study and showing pleasure when his letters indicated progress, but he knew Custis' indolence and closed one letter with these words: "And let me exhort you, in solemn terms, to keep steadily in mind the purposes and the ends for which you were sent to the seminary that you are now placed at, and not disappoint the hopes which have been entertained from your going thither, by doing which you will ensure the friendship, & of. . ."[25]

Washington visited Hope Park several times. His *Diary* of May 19, 1798 records: "About 8 o'clock in the forenoon Mrs. Washington and myself set out on a visit to Hope Park and the Federal City. Got to the former to Dinner and remained there until morning when we proceeded to the City. Dined at Mr. Thomas Peter's and remained there until Wednesday, and then went to Mr. Law's and remained there until friday."[26] Washington's will contained

[25] *Ibid.*, Vol. 36, p. 258.
[26] *Diaries*, Vol. 4, p. 277.

this bequest: "To Doctor David Stuart I give my large shaving and dressing Table and my Telescope." Dr. Stuart was living at Hope Park when Washington died. His last home was at Ossian, a mile south of Annandale. It is one of the show places of Fairfax County, and is described in the Virginia *Guide*: "This white frame house, flanked by boxwood and oak trees, was built on the Ravensworth estate before the Revolution . . . After 1804 it was the home of Dr. David Stuart." The name was probably given by Dr. Stuart, after the legendary Irish hero, Ossian, about whom James Macpherson wrote the widely known poem in the late eighteenth century.

Dr. Stuart survived his wife and died in 1814. He devised Ossian to his son William Shalto Stuart. (Fairfax Will Book K 1, p. 238.)

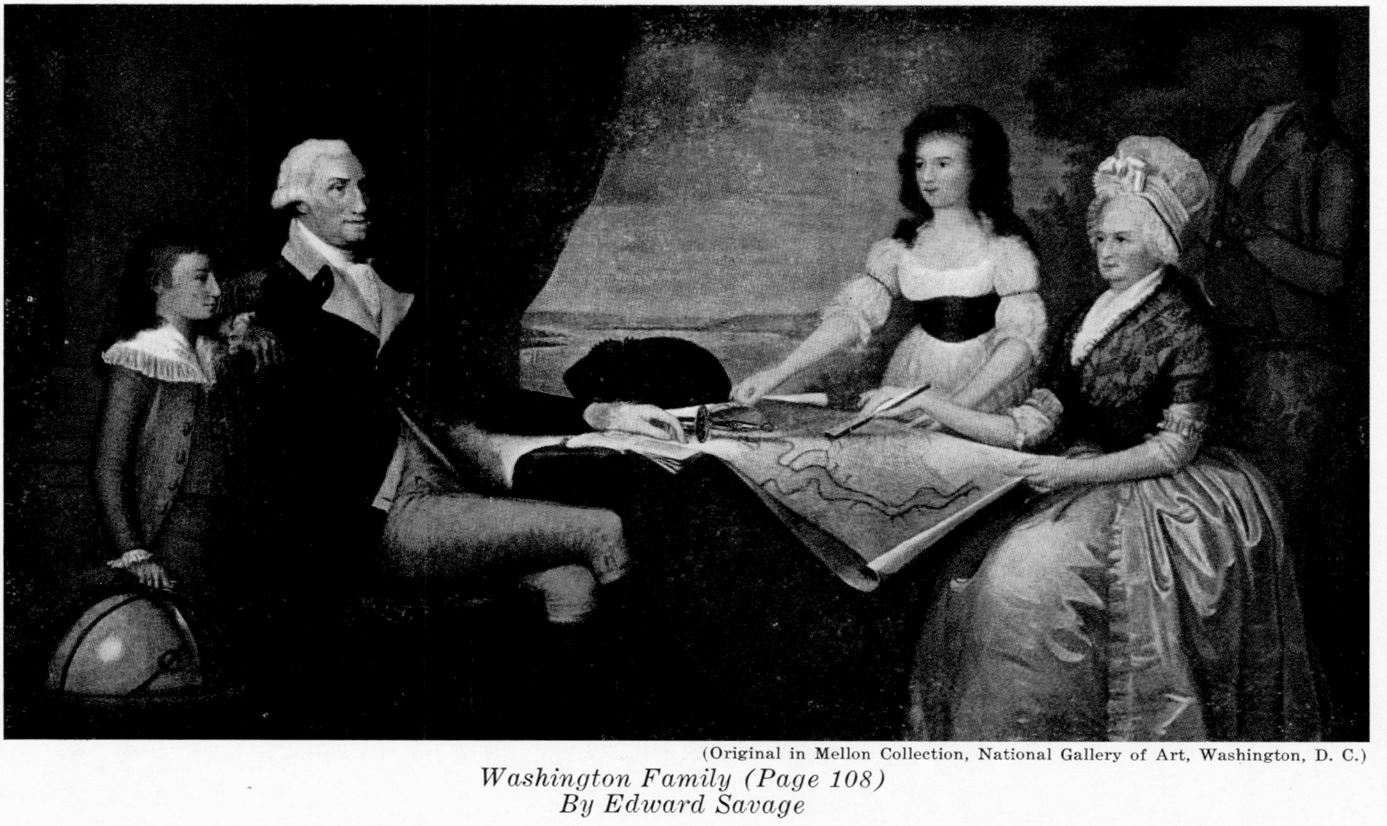

(Original in Mellon Collection, National Gallery of Art, Washington, D. C.)

Washington Family (Page 108)
By Edward Savage

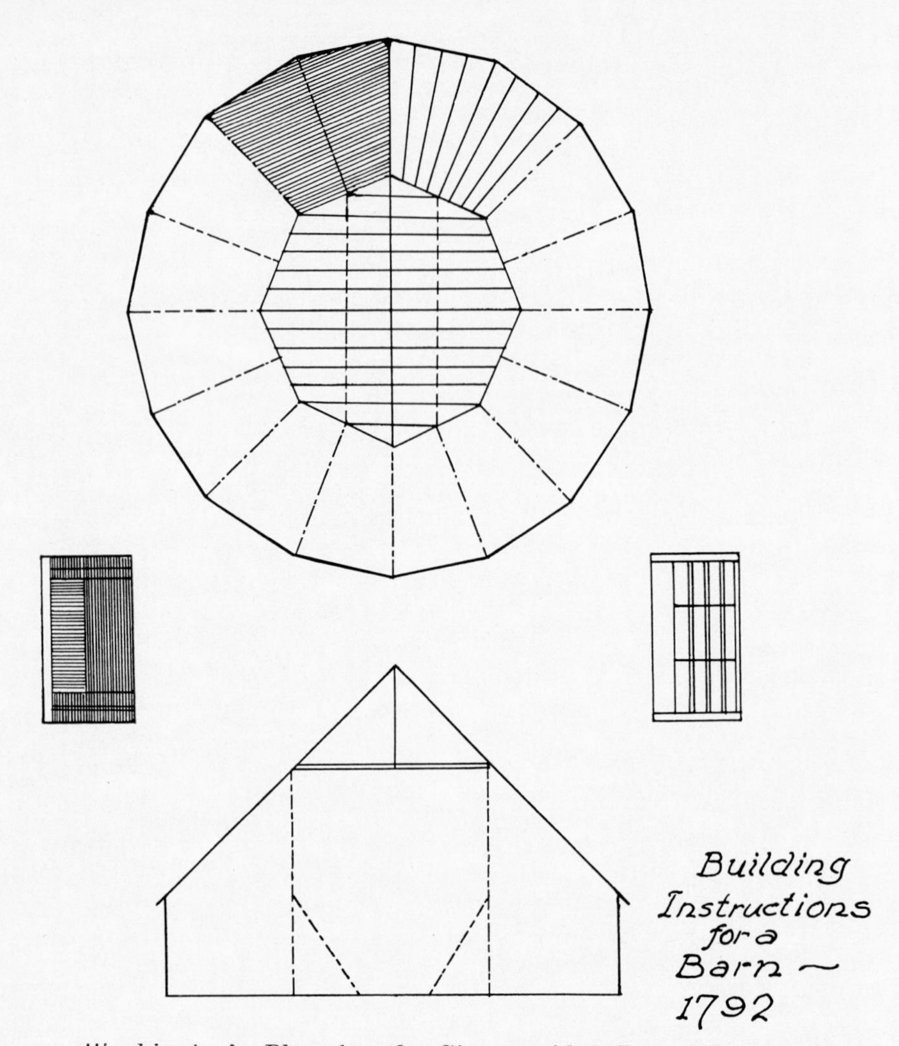

Washington's Plan for the Sixteen-sided Barn (Page 119)

(Drawn by Mrs. Elizabeth S. Adams from the copy in Fitzpatrick's edition of the Writings of Washington, v. 32, p. 285)

Chapter 8

Washington's Relatives

Washington's mother was born Mary Ball. She was the daughter of Colonel Joseph Ball of Epping Forest, Lancaster County. The house in which she was born has long since disappeared and has been replaced by a frame house bearing the same name. Her father and mother both died when she was a girl and she was left to the guardianship of George Eskridge, whose home was at Sandy Point on the Potomac River. It is probable that Washington derived his Christian name from this George Eskridge and that her marriage to Augustine Washington took place at Sandy Point. She owned a plantation, conveyed to her by her father, situated near the falls of the Rappahannock River, adjoining the Ferry Farm of her husband, Augustine. She owned it when she died.[1] After his death she continued to live on the Ferry Farm and was guardian of her son George, to whom this farm was devised by his father, and with his consent, appropriated the profits to her own use after he became of age.[2]

During the French and Indian War he wrote to her inviting her to "spend the chief part of your time at Mount Vernon, as you say, where I am certain everything will be order'd as much for your satisfaction as possible in the Situation we are in." The letter was written from Fort Cumberland, and Mrs. Washington's son, John Augustine, was then living at Mount Vernon.[3] Neither Washington's surviving *Diaries*, nor his published correspondence show that

[1]See Washington's letter to his sister Elizabeth. *Writings,* Vol. 30, p. 402.
[2]See Washington's letter to her. *Writings,* Vol. 29, p. 159.
[3]*Writings,* Vol. 1, p. 36.

she ever visited him there. They do show him stopping at his mother's many times, often giving her sums of money from two to six or seven pounds, spending nights at her farm and taking meals with her. When in Philadelphia in 1774 he purchased a riding chair and a cloak for his mother.[4]

It was therefore with surprise and indignation that in 1781 he received a letter from Benjamin Harrison, Speaker of the Virginia House of Delegates:

"Some Gentn. of the last Assembly proposed to apply to that body for assistance to your mother, who they said was in great want, owing to the heavy taxes she was oblig'd to pay; I took the liberty to put a stop to this supposing you would be displeased at such an application, I make no doubt but the assembly would readily grant the request, and it now only rests with you to say whether it shall be made or not."[5]

In answer he wrote:

"My Dr. Sir; Upon my return to this place last night, I met your private and friendly letter of the 25th of February. I do not delay a moment to thank you for the interesting matter contained in it, and to express my surprise at that part which respects a pension for my mother.

"True it is, I am but little acquainted with her present situation, or distresses, if she is under any. As true it is, a year or two before I left Virginia (to make her latter days confortable, and free from care) I did, at her request but at my own expence, purchase a commodious house, garden and Lotts (of her own choosing) in Fredericksburg, that she might be near my Sister Lewis, her only daughter; and did moreover agree to take her Land and negroes at a certain yearly rent, to be fixed by Colo. Lewis and others (of her own nomination) which has been an annual expence to me ever since, as the Estate never raised one half of the rent I was to pay. Before I left Virginia, I answered all her calls for money; and since that period, have directed my Steward to do the same. . . .

---

[4]*Diaries,* Vol. 2, p. 169 (note).
[5]*Writings,* Vol. 21, p. 341 (note).

But putting these things aside, which I could not avoid mentioning, in exculpation of a presumptive want of duty on my part; confident I am that she has not a child that would not divide the last sixpence to relieve her from real distress. This she has been repeatedly assured of by me: and all of us, I am certain, would feel much hurt, at having our mother a pensioner, while we had the means of supporting her; but in fact she has an ample income of her own."[6]

Mary Washington lived in the house in Fredericksburg from 1772 until her death in 1789. The northern wing was added after she died.

Washington was the oldest of the five children of the marriage of Augustine and Mary Washington. The others were his sister Elizabeth and his brothers, Samuel, John Augustine, and Charles.

Elizabeth (whom Washington often called "Betty") was born in 1733 and died in 1797. She was the second wife of Fielding Lewis, whom she married in 1772. After his marriage he began building the stately house which he called Millbank, but which is now known as Kenmore. He was an earnest patriot in the Revolution, fitting out troops at his own expense. He was chief commissioner for the manufacture of small arms in Fredericksburg, and used his own money when the public funds were exhausted. When he died in 1782, he left a debt of £7000 and a mortgage on Millbank. His widow struggled to maintain the home but in the end was forced to sell it.[7]

In 1795 she bought Millbrook in Spotsylvania County. "Two death notices that appeared in Fredericksburg newspapers, April 11 and April 12, 1797, both saying 'Mrs. Betty Lewis relict of the late Fielding Lewis,' died 'at her seat in this county,' would seem to fix Mrs. Lewis's death at Millbrook and not elsewhere as frequently asserted."[8]

Three of her four sons, Howell, Robert and Lawrence, were suc-

[6] *Ibid.*, pp. 340-342.
[7] Virginia *Guide*, p. 224.
[8] *Ibid.*, p. 506.

cessively employed by Washington in clerical and other capacities. Just before he assumed the presidency, he wrote to his sister about employing Robert:

"My dear Sister: Since you were speaking to me concerning your Son Bob, I have thought it probable that I may have occasion for a young person in my family of good disposition, who writes a good hand, and who can confine himself (to) a certain reasonable number of hours in the 24 to the recording of letters in books, which will be provided for their reception from the separate papers on which they now are and will be first draughted.

"If Bob is of opinion that this employment will suit his inclination, and he will take his chance for the allowance that will be made (which cannot be great) as there are hundreds who would be glad to come in. I should be very glad to give him the preference. He will be at no expence (except in the article of clothing) as he will be one of the family and live as we do. . .

"If he comes, it may be with his Aunt, (and at her expence, as she will want some body to accompany her) when I send my horses back after I am fixed in New York.[9]

More will be said later of Lawrence Lewis and his marriage to Eleanor Parke Custis.

Their eldest son, Fielding Lewis, displeased Washington and received a caustic letter from Mount Vernon in 1786:

"Sir—[ominous beginning] Your letter of the 11th of Octor. never came to my hands until yesterday. Altho' your disrespectful conduct toward me, in coming into this country and spending weeks therein without ever coming near me entitles you to very little notice or favor from me; yet I consent that you may get timber from off my land in Fauquier County to build a house on your lot in Recter town. Having granted you this, now let me ask what your views were in purchasing a Lott in a place which, I presume, orginated with and will end in two or three Gin Shops, which probably will exist no longer than they serve to ruin the proprietors,

[9] *Writings,* Vol. 30, pp. 228-229.

and those who make the most frequent applications to them."[10]

But Washington was wrong. Rectortown still exists, a lovely straggling village set among the fertile rolling farms of northern Fauquier.

Samuel Washington was born in 1734 and died in 1781. He moved into the Shenandoah Valley and his home, Harewood, in Berkeley County, now in West Virginia, is still standing. He married five times. He became much embarrasssed by debt and Washington loaned his considerable sums of money.

In a letter Jan. 16, 1783 to his brother John Augustine, Washington asked: "In Gods name how did my Brother Saml. contrive to get himself so enormously in Debt? Was it by purchases? By misfortunes? or shear indolence and inattention to business? From whatever cause it proceeded, the matter is now the same, and curiosity only prompts the enquiry."[11]

And in his will Washington forgave the "Estate of my deceased brother, Samuel Washington, from the payment of the money which is due me. . ."[12] This amounted to about £1000. He also acquitted the sons of Samuel, namely George Steptoe and Lawrence Augustine Washington, from the payments for sums advanced for their education.

It appears that the young men were at one time being educated at the academy of the Reverend Stephen Bloomer Balch, the Presbyterian clergyman of Georgetown, whom Washington esteemed highly.

For Thornton, another son of Samuel, Washington obtained a commission of ensign during the Revolutionary War. He assumed the care of Harriet, Samuel's daughter, who lived in his household for several years. She was a constant care and vexation to him, for he wrote to his sister Betty: she has "no disposition to be careful of her clothes," which are "dabbed about in every hole and corner."[13] He was finally rid of her when she married Andrew Parks

[10]*Ibid.*, Vol. 29, p. 101.
[11]*Ibid.*, Vol. 26, pp. 41-42.
[12]*Ibid.*, Vol. 37, p. 281.
[13]*Ibid.*, Vol. 32, p. 176.

in 1796 and moved to Kanawha Salines, now Malden, West Virginia, where she died in 1822.[14] Washington's ledger contains an entry—"By Miss Harriot Washington—gave her to buy wedding clothes $100."

John Augustine Washington (1736-1787) was Washington's favorite brother. His letters to him were usually addressed, "Dear Jack" and he called him "the intimate companion of my youth and the friend of my ripened years."

After residing at Mount Vernon during Washington's service in the war against the French, he settled in Westmoreland County at Bushfield. He married Hannah Bushrod. Philip Vickers Fithian, who, with others, dined there, said: "His House has the most agreeable situation, of any I have yet seen in Maryland or Virginia; the broad Potowmack, which they account between 7 and 8 Miles over washes his Garden on the North, the River Nomini is within a stone throw on the West, a levil Country on the East."[15]

On January 10, 1787 Washington noted in his *Diary*: "I rec'd by express the acct. of the sudden death (by a fit of the Gout in the head) of my beloved brother, Colo. John Auge. Washington."

By his will Washington devised Mount Vernon and the Mansion House Farm to John Augustine Washington's son Bushrod, "partly in consideration of an intimation to his deceased father, while we were bachelors, and he had kindly undertaken to supervise my Estate during my Military Services in the former war between Great Britain and France, that if I should fall therein, Mount Vernon . . . should become his property."

Bushrod Washington married Ann, the daughter of Colonel Thomas Blackburn of Rippon Lodge, Prince William County.[16] Washington was proud of his success as a lawyer and as a judge, and in his later years, consulted him about legal matters, and employed him when suing or being sued. A sketch of him is contained in Lanman's *Biographical Annals*:

"He was born in Westmoreland County, Virginia, June 5, 1762;

---

[14] *Ibid.*, Vol. 35, p. 16 (note).
[15] *Journal*, 1773-1774, p. 89 (Williamsburg Restoration Historical Studies, No. 30).
[16] *Ibid.*, Vol. 2, p. 64n.

graduated at William and Mary College in 1778; studied law, and was successful in the profession; served as a soldier in the Revolution; as a member of the Virginia House of Delegates; was a member of the Convention to ratify the Federal Constitution; and he resided both in Alexandria and Richmond. He was the first President of the Colonization Society; and in 1798 he was appointed by President Adams a Justice of the Supreme Court of the United States; he published two volumes of Reports of the Court of Appeals of Virginia, and four volumes of Reports of the Third Circuit of the United States Court. He was a favorite with his uncle, the first President; and he died in Philadelphia, November 26, 1829; he was a devisee of Mount Vernon and a man of ability and high character."[17]

His brother Corbin married Hannah Lee, daughter of Richard Henry Lee. His sister Mildred married Hannah's brother, Thomas Lee. The oldest sister, Jane, married her cousin, William Washington.

Charles Washington was the youngest brother of George Washington. He was born in 1738 and died in 1799. He married, before he was twenty-one years old, Mildred, daughter of Colonel Francis Thornton of Fall Hill, Spotsylvania County. He must have lived in Fredericksburg for some time as there is a small brick house there known as the Charles Washington house. At a later date, he followed the example of his brother, Samuel, and moved to the lower Shenandoah Valley, where he established himself at Happy Retreat, now called Mordington.[18] He laid off the town of Charlestown in Berkeley County, now in West Virginia. He died so shortly before his brother, that the latter left unchanged the bequest; "To my brother, Charles Washington the gold headed cane left me by Doctr. Franklin in his will."

In the genealogy Washington prepared in 1792, he stated: "Charles Washington has four children, George Augustine,

[17]Lanman, Charles. *Biographical Annals of the Civil Government of the United States.* 1876. p. 451.

[18]West Virginia *Guide,* p. 205.

Frances, Mildred and Samuel. George Augustine married Frances Basset, daughter of Colo. Burwell Basset of New Kent; Frances married Colo. Burgess Ball . . . Mildred and Samuel are unmarried."[19]

Eltham

Eltham was the seat of Colonel Burwell Bassett, in New Kent County on the south side of the Pamunkey River, several miles from the present village of West Point and eighteen miles northeast of Williamsburg. In 1757 he married Anna Maria, a daughter of John Dandridge. In 1759 George Washington married her sister, Martha Dandridge Custis. The Bassetts had been in Virginia since 1644, and soon became prominent. The grandfather of Burwell Bassett was a member of the Council; his father, William, was a Burgess and built Eltham about 1730. The families of Mount Vernon and Eltham became intimate after Washington's marriage. The house lay slightly off Washington's route to and from Williamsburg, but he usually found time to visit there, sometimes riding out to spend the night and returning to Williamsburg the next morning. When Mrs. Washington accompanied him, she usually stayed with her sister. In May 1771 the Washingtons spent about ten days at Eltham, going to St. Peter's Church, to the "White House," where they had been married, and attending the theater at Williamsburg. In April 1772 "with Colo. Bassett and Lady, and their three daughters; set off for Mount Vernon." The visit lasted more than two weeks, during which the whole party dined at Belvoir. Washington took the Bassetts to Pohick Church and took the "Colo" to Court at Alexandria with him, and fox hunting.[20]

When Washington was about to set out for the Warm Springs in the hope of benefiting Patsy Custis, he invited the Bassetts to accompany him. "You will have occasion to provide nothing, if I can be advised of your intentions before the wagon comes down for my necessaries, so that I may provide accordingly."[21]

[19]*Writings,* Vol. 32, p. 30.
[20]*Diaries,* Vol. 2, pp. 16-19, 60-62.
[21]*Writings,* Vol. 2, p. 511.

During the Revolutionary War, Bassett looked after the business of Mrs. Washington and the Custis children in New Kent County, and Washington's western lands. He wrote to Bassett from his camp at Cambridge: "I thank you heartily for the attention you have paid to my landed affairs on the Ohio, my interest in which I shall be more careful of, as in the worst event they will Serve for an asylum."[22]

Writing again on April 22, 1779 about the depreciation of the Continental currency: "ten thousand pounds will not compensate the losses I might have avoided by being at home, and attending a little to my own concerns. I am now receiving a Shilling in the pound in discharge of Bonds which ought to have been paid me, and would have been realized before I left Virginia, but for my indulgence to the debtors."[23]

In 1785 the families were drawn closer together by the marriage of Washington's nephew, George Augustine Washington, to Bassett's daughter Fanny (Frances). Washington wrote Bassett: "It has ever been a maxim with me thro' life, neither to promote nor to prevent a matrimonial connection, unless there should be something indispensably requiring interference in the latter: I have always considered marriage as the most interesting event of one's life, the foundation of happiness or misery; to be instrumental therefore in bringing two people together who are indifferent to each other, and may soon become the objects of hatred; or to prevent a union which is prompted by mutual esteem and affection, is what I never could reconcile to my feelings; and therefore, neither directly or indirectly, have I ever said a syllable to Fanny or George upon the subject of their intended connexion; but as their attachment to each other seems to have been early formed, warm and lasting, it bids fair to be happy; if therefore you have no objection, I think the sooner it is consummated the better.

"I have just now informed them (the former thro' Mrs. Washington) that it is my wish they should live here."[24]

[22] *Ibid.*, Vol. 4, p. 359.
[23] *Ibid.*, Vol. 14, p. 432.
[24] *Ibid.*, Vol. 28, p. 152.

George Augustine was the son of Washington's youngest brother, Charles. The marriage was made possible by Washington offering them a temporary home at Mount Vernon and later making it more permanent by appointing George Augustine as his manager. But Washington in his sympathetic affection for the young couple sought to make their "situation more stable and pleasing." So on October 25, 1786 he wrote to George as follows: ". . . It is my present intention, to give you, at my death, my landed property in the neck; containing by estimation, between two and three thousand acres (by purchases from William Clifton and George Brent) and that the reasons why I mention the matter to you at this time are, that you may, if you choose it, seat the negroes which Colo. Bassett has promised you, upon that part of the tract, on which Samuel Johnson formerly lived. And under this expectation and prospect, that you may, moreover, when it perfectly suits your inclination and convenience, be preparing for, and building thereon by degrees.

"You may say, or think perhaps, that as there is a contingency tacked to this intimation, the offer is too precarious to hazard the expence of building; but if Mrs. Washington should survive me there is a moral certainty of my dying without issue, and should I be the longest liver, the matter in my opinion is almost as certain; for whilst I retain the reasoning faculties I shall never marry a girl; and it is not probable that I should have children by a woman of an age suitable to my own, should I be disposed to enter into a second marriage." He further states that to prevent any possible loss to his nephew, if he should "be deprived of the fee simple in the land . . . I will pay the cost of any buildings which you may erect on the premises. . ."[25]

George Augustine was in ill health and went south for some time, but received little benefit from the change. Washington had advised him on the site of his house, and building had begun before his death, in February 1793. On learning of his death Washington wrote to his widow:

---

[25]*Ibid.*, Vol. 29, pp. 28-29.

"My dear Fanny: To you, who so well know the affectionate regard I had for our departed friend, it is unnecessary to describe the sorrow with which I was afflicted at the news of his death, although it was an event I had expected many weeks before it happened. To express this sorrow with the force I feel it, would answer no other purpose than to revive, in your breast, that poignancy of anguish, which, by this time, I hope is abated. Reason and resignation to the divine will, which is just, and wise in all its dispensations, cannot, in such a mind as yours, fail to produce this effect."[26]

He insisted that she and the children return to Mount Vernon to live. Fanny married Tobias Lear and died in the spring of 1796. Washington bequeathed to the two sons, George Fayette and Charles Augustine Washington, his River Farm subject to the life estate of Tobias Lear to a portion of it.

The reason for the bequest is stated in Washington's will:

"In consideration of the consanguinity between them and my wife, being as nearly related to her as to myself, as on account of the affection I had for, and the obligation I was under to their father when living, who from his youth had attached himself to my person, and followed my fortunes through the viscissitudes of the late Revolution; afterwards devoting his time to the Superintendence of my private concerns for many years, whilst my public employments rendered it impracticable for me to do it myself, thereby affording me essential Services, and always performing them in a manner the most felial and respectful. . ."[27]

Burwell Bassett died during Washington's first term as President and he wrote a letter of condolence to his son Burwell on the loss of "your father and my friend for whom when alive, I had the sincerest regard."

This son (1764-1841) built Bassett Hall in Williamsburg. He served for twenty years in Congress.[28] It is not known why he abandoned Eltham. Burwell Bassett had other sons, John and William (Washington's Billy Bassett). One of them may have lived

[26]*Ibid.*, Vol. 32, p. 354.
[27]*Ibid.*, Vol. 37, p. 289.
[28]Kibler, J. Luther. *Historic Virginia Landmarks*, p. 51.

there. Eltham was burned in 1876. In his *Mansions of Virginia*, Thomas T. Waterman states "one of the dependencies survived until recently when the brick walls were taken down for use in the Williamsburg Restoration."

The Rev. Arthur Gray concludes his article on the "White House" as follows. "The Management of these estates (Custis), his long stays at Eltham, his hunting and fishing excursions along the Pamunkey, his many visits to friends and relatives through this valley, all these give this section the right, more than any part of America, to the title the people like to use: 'Washington's Playground'."[29]

[29]Gray, Arthur. "The White House—Washington's Marriage Place," *Virginia Mag. of Hist. and Biog.*, Vol. 42, 1934, p. 240.

Chapter 9

Agricultural Pursuits

The land Washington inherited from his brother did not satisfy him; he wished to farm on a larger scale. By constantly purchasing adjoining lands, the estate grew to such a size that it was found necessary to subdivide it into several tracts (eventually five). Each was operated as a separate farm, with its own overseer and its own gang of negro slaves. A house was provided for the overseer and his family and cabins for the slaves, who had their own little gardens and the use of animals to till them. Each farm drew on the whole for needed supplies, and as occasion demanded, the workmen on one plantation were temporarily transferred to another. Separate books were kept for each farm, showing what crops had been planted or harvested each week, how each laborer's time had been spent, and all details of the operation.

Washington gave names to his five farms. The River Farm included all the land east of Little Hunting Creek and contained over 2000 acres. Dogue Run Farm contained 649 acres. The mill was on this parcel. Muddy Hole Farm containing 476 acres lay along the westerly side of Little Hunting Creek. Union Farm containing 928 acres lay along the estuary of Dogue Run. The balance of the estate, which was by far the largest, was the Mansion House Farm.

In 1786 Washington wrote to Arthur Young, the English agricultural correspondent of his later years: "Agriculture has ever been amongst the most favorite amusements of my life, though I never possessed much skill in the art, and nine years total inattention to it, has added nothing to a knowledge which is best understood from practice. . ."

When he began farming he did what all the other planters in Fairfax did, he made tobacco his main crop. There was a ready market for it in England. It gave him a balance in his factor's hands on which he could draw to pay for needed imports. He soon found that the soil of his Mount Vernon land was not suited to the culture of the best tobacco. It could not compete with the tobacco grown on his dower lands or on the lands of his wards on the York and Pamunkey Rivers, nor could he get as good a price for it. The freight charges were higher, as few tobacco ships came to the upper Potomac. At times he had to send his tobacco to Westmoreland County to get cargo space. His letters to Cary and Co. are full of complaints on this score. He knew tobacco was exhausting his soil, and in 1768 he wrote to Capel and Osgood Hanbury: "Having discontinued the growth of Tobo. myself, except at a plantation or two upon York River, I make no more of that Article than barely to furnish me with Goods."[1]

Next to tobacco, corn was the major crop in the early years at Mount Vernon. There were plenty of uses for it. It was food for stock, and when ground into corn meal, it supplied food for the slaves of the plantation. Later when he had a distillery he had need of more corn. He aimed to sell corn but more often was obliged to buy. Thus in 1760: "Called at Mr. Possey's (Posey) . . . and desir'd him to engage me 100 Bar'ls of Corn upon the best terms he could in Maryland."[2]

Alexandria and Colchester were turning to the flour trade and Washington gladly substituted wheat for tobacco and in 1765 was sending a large consignment to Carlyle and Adam of Alexandria at fifty-eight pounds to the bushel, to be ground at their mill on Four Mile Run. Later he ground it at his own mill on Dogue Run. He was proud of his wheat and wrote: "No wheat that has ever fallen under my observation exceeds the wheat which some years ago I

[1]*Writings*, Vol. 2, p. 485.
[2]*Ibid.*, p. 341.

cultivated extensively." After threshing, he had it barrelled by his own coopers. He exported much of it to the West Indies. It has been said that the barrels were passed without inspection, but this, like many other stories told about him, cannot be true. The Virginia law provided for inspection and any official in the West Indies who passed it without inspection would have been in danger of losing his job.

Writing to Arthur Young in 1792 Washington described the condition of the average Virginia estate in his younger days: "A piece of land is cut down and kept under constant cultivation, first in Tobacco and then in Indian Corn (two very exhausting plants) until it will yield scarcely anything; a second piece is cleared and treated in the same manner; then a third, and so on, until probably, there is but little more to clear. When this happens, the owner finds himself reduced to the choice of one of three things; either to recover the land which he has ruined, to accomplish which he has perhaps neither the skill, the industry nor the means; or to retire beyond the Mountains; or to substitute quantity for quality in order to raise something. The latter has been generally adopted; and with the assistance of horses, he *scratches* over much ground, and Seeds it, to very little purpose. . ."[8]

In contrast to this method we have Washington's proceedings as described in his *Writings* and *Diaries*. Whenever he was at Mount Vernon, he was a careful observer of the crops and of the way "his people" handled them. He seemed particularly interested in his wheat crop, seeking to employ practices that would minimize damage from the Hessian fly, rust and other diseases and pests. From his *Diaries*, 1769, these items are selected:

"June 27, Began in the afternoon to cut my Wheat at Doeg Run Quarter with Jonathan Palmer and 6 other Cradlers.

"June 28, Elijah Houghton joind the above at the same place. The whole made but a bad day's work. They complain of the Straw cutting very hard.

"Note. The Wheat this year appeard different from what it did

[8]*Ibid.*, Vol. 32, p. 68.

last year, the straw being quite changd (even the Knobs and joints, nearly so) when the Grain was not hard. On the Contrary last year the grain was tolerably hard, whilst part of the Straw retained a good deal of green.

"29. Eliab Roberts, William Acres, Joseph Wilson and Azel Martin set into work to day and I think worked but indifferently. . . .

"30. The Rest of the Cradlers and hands went into the Neck and began there abt. 10 Oclock, Making a poor days work. . .

"July 1st. Went into the Neck to my Harvest People and returned to Dinner."

Thus from farm to farm he observed his "harvest people," recording his visits almost daily, sometimes with other members of his family, or with visitors, until on July 15 he sums up his findings in a note:

"From the remarks and observations made this year in Harvesting my Wheat, it appeared evident that 10, and sometimes 9, Cradlers (according as the Wheat was thick or thin) were full suff. to keep the rest of my hands employ'd; and it likewise appeard, that it was evidently to my advantage to employ my own hands to Cradle the Wheat rather than to hire any at all, as these may be got for 2 shilgs. or half a Crown a day, whereas the Wages of the White Cradlers are exorbitantly high. But if Wheat of different kinds are sowed so as to prevent the Harvest coming on at once, it is my opinion that hirelings of all kinds may be dispensed with. The Rakers in the generality of the Wheat is sufficient to Rake and bind after a Cradle, and the rest of the hands can manage (after the water Carriers and Cooks are taken out) to get the Wheat into convenient places and attend the Stackers. Two, and sometimes three, Stackers will Stack as fast as it is cut and I am of opinion that two brisk hands is sufft. for this purpose.

"From experience it has been found advantageous to put the Cradlers and their attendants into at least 3 Gangs. The Stops and delays by this means are not so frequent, and the Work much better attended to, as every Mans work is distinguishable, and the

Mount Eagle (Pages 130 and 290)

Photographed by Alexandria Studio

Old Entrance to Mount Vernon (Page 132)

Photographed by Mrs. Margaret B. Stetson

whole Cradles not always stopping for every little disorder that happens to each respective one, as is the case when they cut altogether."[4]

It was the customary practice at that time to thresh grain either by beating it with a hickory flail, or by treading it out with horses. Washington used the latter method, though he considered it dirty and wasteful.

When he read that a threshing machine had been invented he wrote to Arthur Young, who told him of Winlaw's and a Scotch machine. Washington was interested but decided to delay ordering one, fearing that any machine might be "too complicated for common and unskilled labourers." In January 1790 he went on horseback to see the Winlaw machine on the farm of Baron Poellnitz near Murray Hill, and described it in his *Diaries*.

"Called on my ride on the Baron de Polnitz, to see the operation of his (Winlaw's) threshing machine. The effect was, the heads of the wheat being separated from the straw, as much of the first was run through the mill in 15 minutes as made half a bushel of clean wheat—allowing 8 working hours in the 24, this would yield 16 bushels pr. day. Two boys are sufficient to turn the wheel, feed the mill, and remove the threshed grain after it has passed through it. Two men were unable, by winnowing, to clean the wheat as it passed through the mill, but a common Dutch fan, with the usual attendance, would be *more* than sufficient to do it. The grain passes through without bruising and is well separated from the chaff. Women, or boys of 12 or 14 years of age, are fully adequate to the management of the mill or threshing machine. Upon the whole, it appears to be easier, more expeditious, and much cleaner way of getting out grain than by the usual mode of threshing; and vastly to be preferred to treading, which is hurtful to horses, filthy to the wheat, and not more expeditious, considering the numbers that are employed in the process from the time the head is begun to be formed until the grain has passed finally through the fan."[5]

---

[4]*Diaries,* Vol. 1, pp. 338-339.
[5]*Ibid.*, Vol. 4, pp. 72-73.

The subject continued to occupy his mind, and in October 1793, he wrote a private letter to Governor Henry Lee of Virginia:

"I have always (from the accts. given of it) entertained a high opinion of Colo. Taliaferros threshing machine but knew at the same time I had no stream that could supply water for one on any of my Farms. This was confirmed when Mr. Payne came hither and exam'd them. The model brought over by the English Farmers may also be a good one, but the utility of it among careless Negros and ignorant Overseers will depend *absolutely* upon the simplicity of the Constructn; for if there is any thing complex in the machinery it will be no longer in use than a mushroom is in existance. I have seen so much of the beginning and ending of these new inventions, that I have almost resolved to go on in the old way of treading until I get settled again at home, and can attend myself to the management of one. As a proof in point of the almost impossibility of putting the Overseers in this Country out of the track they have been accustomed to walk in, I have one of the most convenient Barns in this, or perhaps any other Country, where 30 hands may with great ease be employed in threshing; half of the Wheat of the Farm was actually stowed in this Barn in the straw by my order for threshing; notwithstanding, when I came home about the Middle of September, I found a treading yard not 30 feet from the Barn door, the Wheat again brought out of the Barn and horses treading it out in an open exposure liable to the vicissitudes of weather. I am now erecting a building for the express purpose of treading. I have sanguine expectations of its utility; and if I am not deceived in them it may afford you some satisfaction when you come into this part of the Country to call and look at it. . ."[6]

The barn referred to must have been his sixteen sided barn described later.

Nearly three years later in a letter to Thomas Jefferson after discussing malicious attempts to embitter him towards Mr. Jeffer-

---

[6]*Writings*, Vol. 33, pp. 132-133.

son, he turns to a friendly discussion of farm practices and ends thus:

"If you can bring a moveable threshing Machine, constructed upon simple principles to perfection, it will be among the most valuable institutions in this Country; for nothing is more wanting, and to be wished for on our farms. Mrs. Washington begs you to accept her best wishes, and with very great esteem etc."[7]

Letters to his manager, James Anderson, in the following year show the plans being made for erecting a threshing machine. And in June, 1797 he wrote to William Booker:

"Sir: From the good report I have had of your improved threshing machine, I am desirous of getting one or two of them erected; and as expeditiously as possible.

"The Scantling for two, upon the Plan of Mr. Jefferson and others, of the Scotch machine, had been got before I received the account of yours; and may, I presume, be appropriated to the latter. The purpose therefore of this letter, is to know if you would undertake to erect mine; Or, if your other engagements should prevent your personal attendance, whether a person in whose knowledge and skill in the matter, you cd. place *entire* confidence, could be sent; or, lastly, whether you could spare time to make me a visit for the purpose of directing my own Carpenters (six or 7 in number, and some of them competant to follow any direction) to proceed to the execution, and for which due conpensation would be made you."[8]

Booker's machine was finally erected on Union Farm, but it broke down and Booker was urged to come and repair it. Washington apparently decided the machine was worth further trial, for a note in the *Diaries*, August 14, 1798, states that William Booker of Richmond built a threshing machine for the River Farm at the cost of fifty dollars.[9]

During the last quarter of the eighteenth century, many in-

---

[7]*Ibid.*, Vol. 35, p. 122.
[8]*Ibid.*, pp. 477-478.
[9]*Diaries*, Vol. 4, p. 282 (note).

ventors were experimenting with threshing machines. But it was not until about 1830 that they began to be produced and used to any great extent.

The crops raised on the farms were many and varied. Besides wheat, which became the staple crop, oats, barley, buckwheat and rye were grown. Hemp and flax were raised, hemp for ropes and twine; flax for homespun clothing. Washington practiced rotation of crops and kept a record of the succession of crops planted in the different fields. When possible the fields were fenced. The master of Mount Vernon had a low opinion of hedges. He once said that "no hedge could keep out four-footed, or two-footed hogs." He was always in search of manure, animal, vegetable or mineral. He experimented with plaster of Paris, but later discontinued its use as he could not discover that his "Wheat had derived any benefit from the Plaister of Paris which has been sprinkled thereon."[10]

He admired the English system of husbandry and asked George William Fairfax (then in England) if he thought "a sober, industrious and knowing Farmer might be had to take care of our plantations . . . to be stocked with a competent number of Plows, Black Cattle, Sheep and hogs? When I speak of a knowing farmer, I mean one who understands the best course of crops; how to plough, to sow, to mow, to hedge, to Ditch, and above all, Midas like, one who can convert everything he touches into manure, as the first transmutation towards gold. . ."[11]

Anyone who has seen the tidy Devonshire fields with small piles of manure closely spaced understands why Washington admired the "course of husbandry as practiced in the best Farming Counties of England."

From the time that he first came into possession of Mount Vernon, he had an active interest in improving his agricultural practices; through reading as shown by the books listed in his orders on Cary & Sons; through his own experiments as recorded in his *Diaries*; and through correspondence with Arthur Young, Sir John

---

[10] *Ibid.*, Vol. 2, p. 374.
[11] *Writings*, Vol. 28, p. 186.

Sinclair and other well known British Agriculturists, and with his planter friends in Virginia, writing, "I shall always feel myself obliged by your communicating any useful discovery in Agriculture."

The following experiments have been selected from his *Diaries*:

On Apr 14-1760, . . . "mixed my Composts in a box with ten Apartments in the following manner, viz: in No. 1 is three pecks of the Earth brought from below the Hill out of the 46 Acre Field without any mixture; in No. 2 is two pecks of the said Earth and one of Marle taken out of the said Field, which Marle seemed a little Inclinable to Sand;

3. Has 2 Pecks of sd. Earth and 1 of Riverside Sand;
4. Has a Peck of Horse Dung;
5. Has mud taken out of the Creek;
6. Has Cow Dung;
7. Marle from the Gullys on the Hill side, wch. seemed to be purer than the other;
8. Sheep Dung;
9. Black Mould taken out of the Pocoson on the Creek side;
10. Clay got just below the Garden.

All mixd with the same quantity and sort of Earth in the most effectual manner. . .

In each of these divisions were planted three grains of Wheat, 3 of Oats and as many of Barley—all at equal distances in Rows, and of equal depth. . ."[12]

On May 1st he found some seeds coming up with "The two grains in No. 8 . . . rather the strongest, but upon the whole No. 9 was the best."

On Sunday, May 11th, 1788—"Counted the number of the following articles which are contained in a pint; viz. of

"The small round pease commonly called Gentlemans's Pease . 3144
"Those brot. from York Rivr. by Majr. G. Washington 2268
"Do. Those brot. from Mrs. Dangerfield's 1375
"Those given by Hezh. Fairfax 1330

[12] *Diaries*, Vol. 1, p. 153.

"Large, and early black eye Pease 1186
"Bunch hominy Beans 1473

"Accordingly, a bushel of the above, allowing 5 to a hill, will plant the number of hills wch. follow: viz.

1st Kind	40243	4th Kind	17024
2. Ditto	29030	5. Ditto	15180
3. Ditto	17200	6. Ditto	........18854."[13]

Washington paid equal attention to his orchards. His *Diaries* contain frequent references to planting, transplanting, and grafting fruits and nuts of various kinds, pears, peaches, apples, cherries, and others.

In 1760 he grafted "plumbs," "New Town Pippins," Burgamy and English "pairs" (he usually spelt pears, "pairs"), "Carnation Cherries," "Grape vines." The grape vines, and no doubt many other plantings, or graftings came from Col. Mason. The Masons had been established in Dogue Neck long before the Washingtons gave Mount Vernon its name, and their plantation was no doubt well stocked with a variety of plants not yet planted at Mount Vernon.

Other friends sent him trees and plants. In a letter from Philadelphia to his manager in the spring of 1795 he enclosed a "List of Plants which were sent by a Gentleman of Jamaica to Norfolk for me. If they should have been forwarded to Mount Vernon desire Elher to pay particular attention to them."

This same letter states that he has sent "a bundle of Pekan, or Illinois nuts . . . which desire the gardener to plant along with those sent some time ago."[14] There were many other plantings and in the autumn when the slaves were not busy they were set to barrelling filberts, walnuts, chestnuts, and hickory nuts. These accounts and his orders for shipments from England of Jordan almonds, French walnuts and other nuts, lend credence to the statement by Prince de Broglie that "at dessert he eats an enormous

[13] *Ibid.*, Vol. 3, p. 346.
[14] *Writings*, Vol. 34, p. 205.

quantity of nuts, and when the conversation is entertaining he keeps eating through a couple of hours. . ."[15]

Agriculture held first place at Mount Vernon, but the fisheries were also important. Washington engaged in fishing primarily for profit, but he loved fishing for itself. On his trip along the Ohio and the Great Kanawha Rivers, he fished repeatedly. Most of the fish caught were eaten; others may have been given to Indian traders. But he fished for sturgeon at Eltham, for sheepshead at Nomini. He certainly was not fishing there for profit.

At Mount Vernon it was different. His great family of slaves had to be fed. Their diet was chiefly corn pone, buckwheat cakes, rye bread, turnips, onions and lentils and the like. Fish formed the larger part of their flesh diet.

Washington had seines at the old Posey fishery, which he continued to operate, and at his own fishery further up the river. His boatmen drew the seines ashore by ropes around windlasses. In a letter to Arthur Young written in 1793, describing his estate, he wrote: "This River which encompasses the land . . . is well supplied with various kinds of fish at all Seasons of the year; in the Spring with the greatest profusion of Shad, Herring, Bass, Carp, Perch, Sturgeon, & ca. Several valuable fisheries appertain to the estate; the whole shore in short is one entire fishery."[16]

Shad seems to have been caught at the Posey fishery in the deep water off the mouth of Dogue Run. The herring came in shoals. So many were caught that the cooper of the estate could not make enough barrels and Washington had to send to Alexandria for more. What could not be eaten fresh was salted in barrels and stored for future use or sold. In 1772 "the latter part of April and the beginning of May, Washington sold over eleven thousand fish, mainly herring."[17]

On April 6, 1785 he noted, "Sent my Shad Sein and Hands to the Ferry to commence Fishing for Messrs. Douglas & Smith (Alexandria merchants) who had engaged to take all the Shad

[15]Ford, p. 194.
[16]*Writings*, Vol. 33, p. 176.
[17]*Diaries*, Vol. 2, p. 62 (note based on Ledger B).

and Herring I can catch in the Season, the first at 15/. a hundred, and the other at 4/. a thousand."[18]

Other contracts were made. In 1770 he made one with Mr. Robert Adam for "the Fish catch'd at the Fishing Landing I bought of Posey."[19]

Washington gave permission to many of his neighbors to fish off his shore and gave away fish to poor people of the neighborhood. Fish that could not be disposed of any other way was used for fertilizer.

Washington usually spoke of his slaves as "my people." That did not imply any disinclination to use the word "slave," but his slaves were his workmen. He knew their names and tested their capacities for the different kinds of plantation labor. When away from Mount Vernon, he wrote to his managers giving detailed directions for the employment of each gang. Among his slaves were blacksmiths, carpenters, bricklayers, mill hands, spinners and other trades.

In winter when the cultivation of crops was impossible Washington set his slaves, men and women, to preparing fences to enclose his fields. Thus he notes: Monday, January 21st, 1788, "Rid to the Ferry, French's, Dogue run, and Muddy hole Plantations.

"The women at the first were at wk. in the New grd. The Men were set to getting Rails.

"At French's two men were cutting Trunnels for Fences and the women were carrying Rails from the swamp side to the division fence between the two Plantations.

"At Dogue run, the Men were cutting and mauling of Rails, the Women at the New ground at the Home House.

"At Muddy hole 2 Men were cuttg and Mauling, 1 Carting, and the Women at the New Ground.

"From the Neck eight Women were also at this place grubbing."[20]

---

[18]*Ibid.*, p. 357.
[19]*Ibid.*, Vol. 1, p. 367.
[20]*Ibid.*, Vol. 3, p. 299.

Washington was reluctant to part with a slave and turn him over to a new master who might not use him humanely. He sold slaves occasionally when he had too many at a particular plantation or too many doing the same kind of work but he never parted families. He watched over their health. The physicians who attended his family, attended the slaves when sick. He sometimes advertised for runaway slaves. He paid the Reverend Charles Green of Truro Parish for catching and returning one. If a slave was incorrigible, he was sent to Jamaica or other West Indies islands to be sold. A Cash Memorandum Book item reads: "Gave my servant Christopher to bear his expenses to a person in Lebanon, Pennsylvania, celebrated for curing persons bitten by mad animals $25." Christopher came back probably benefited. He had his master's pocketbook in mind for he returned $12. "The person celebrated for such cures was Dr. Henry William Stoy."[21]

One slave deserves particular mention because of Washington's affection for him; William Lee (Billy), purchased from the Lee family. When Washington was surveying his land on Four Mile Run, "my servant William (one of the Chain Carriers) fell, and broke the pan of his knee, wch. put a stop to my Surveying; and with difficulty I was able to get him to Abingdon, being obliged to get a sled to carry him on, as he could neither walk, stand, or ride."[22] When Washington was elected President, Billy wanted to accompany his master to New York, but gave out in Philadelphia. Lear (Washington's private secretary) wrote to Clement Biddle on behalf of the President that "He would thank you to propose it to Will to return to Mount Vernon when he can be removed for he cannot be of any service here, and perhaps will require a person to attend upon him constantly, if he should incline to return to Mount Vernon, you will be so kind as to have him sent by the first Vessel that sails for Alexandria after he can be removed with safety, but if he is still anxious to come on here, the President

---

[21]*Ibid.*, Vol. 4, p. 262 (note).
[22]*Ibid.*, Vol. 2, p. 366.

would gratify him, Altho' he will be troublesome. He has been an old and faithful Servant: this is enough for the President to gratify him in every reasonable wish."[23]

Washington continued to bear Lee in mind, for to David Humphreys who was visiting Mount Vernon, he wrote: "you will have no occasion for Horses, for mine will always be at your service; and very little for a servant, as your old acquaintance, Will, who is scarcely fit for anything else, can whiten your head, and many idlers about the house can blacken your shoes."[24]

In the Washington family group painted by Edward Savage about 1795, the General is shown in military uniform, Mrs. Washington, the two Custis children in the background, William Lee in a black suit, white shirt and dark cravat.

In his will Washington provided "And as to my Mulatto man William (calling himself William Lee) I give immediate freedom; or if he should prefer it (on account of the accidents which have befallen him, and which have rendered him incapable of walking or of any active employment) to remain in the situation he now is, it shall be optional in him to do so. In either case however, I allow him an annuity of thirty dollars during his natural life, which shall be independent of the victuals and cloaths he has been accustomed to receive, if he chuses the last alternative; but in full, with his freedom if he prefers the first; and this I give him as a testimony of my sense of his attachment to me, and for his faithful services to me during the Revolutionary War."[25]

And so this "faithful servant" lives in the memory of posterity by Savage's painting and still more by his master's appreciation of his worth.

Washington realized the limitations of the individual in carrying on experiments, especially his own, as he had spent so many years in public life. In March, 1790 he wrote to Baron Poellnitz who had written him "on the subject of establishing a farm under public

[23]*Writings,* Vol. 30, p. 308 (note).
[24]*Ibid.,* Vol. 28, p. 464.
[25]*Ibid.,* Vol. 37, p. 277.

patronage for the purpose of encreasing and extending agricultural knowledge":

"As I have passed a considerable portion of my life very satisfactorily in the business of agriculture, it will be understood, that I am alike fond of it on individual account, and on account of its public emoluments. But, however convinced I am of the great advantages to be derived to the Community from improvements in it, however susceptible of improvements I consider the present state of farming in this Country, and however desirous I am of seeing these improvements take place immediately, yet, in my public capacity, I know not whether I can with propriety do anything more at present, than what I have already done. I have brought the subject in my speech, at the opening of the present Session of Congress, before the national Legislature. It rests with them to decide what measures ought afterwards to be adopted for promoting the success of the great objects, which I have recommended to their attention. . ."[26]

He had no party "whip" to push the scheme through Congress. Moreover, he added, "the subject of Finance has not yet received such a form as may justify any considerable new expenditures."

Baron Poellnitz "had an experimental farm near Murray Hill, and one of his ideas, which he suggested to Washington, was the establishment of such a farm under the Government. Poellnitz can thus be credited with being the father of our Government Experiment stations of to-day."[27]

Washington was also interested in establishing Agricultural Societies. October 17, 1796 he wrote to Landon Carter:

"Nothing has contributed, nor will any thing contribute more to effect these desirable purposes than the establishment of Agricultural Societies in this, as they have been in other countries: that the community may derive advantages from the experiments and discoveries of the more intelligent communicator through such channels. Besides the numerous local Societies which are to be found

---

[26] *Ibid.*, Vol. 31, pp. 23-24.
[27] *Diaries*, Vol. 4. p. 72 (note).

in all parts of Great Britain and Ireland, a national one is now established under the auspices of the government of those countries; which will, I conceive, be found among the most useful and beneficial institutions in them, if it is prosecuted with as much assiduity as it has commenced, under Presidency of Sir Jno Sinclair."[28]

Nearly a year later he wrote to William Strickland, in England, "I have endeavoured, both in a public and private character, to encourage the establishment of Boards of Agriculture in this country, but hitherto in vain. . ."[29]

He had in his final message to Congress, December 7, 1796 urged the "primary importance" of agriculture and recommended "the establishment of Boards, composed of proper characters, charged with collecting and diffusing information, and enabled by premiums, and small pecuniary aids, to encourage and assist a spirit of discovery and improvement."[30]

He was interested in agricultural statistics too. "There is, in the *Washington Papers*, at the end of the year 1789, a 4-page, folio Tabular statement of crops, showing the work done at the Mount Vernon farms—plowing, seeding, planting, etc., together with a calculation of the costs of the plantings. It is labeled 'First statement of the Crops in 1789.' "[31]

It was many years later that the first agricultural statistics were collected in a division of the Patent Office, and it was not until 1862 that a Commissioner of Agriculture was appointed, and the status of Executive Department was not attained until 1889. Two years earlier state agricultural experiment stations were established. Nearly a century had elapsed since Washington made his recommendations to Congress.

[28] *Writings*, Vol. 35, pp. 246-247.
[29] *Ibid.*, p. 501.
[30] *Ibid.*, pp. 315-316.
[31] *Ibid.*, Vol. 30, p. 486 (note).

Chapter 10

Managers

During the French and Indian War Washington's younger brother, John Augustine, lived at Mount Vernon and managed the plantation. Washington wrote him frequently during the war but found little time to deal with business affairs so far as his existing letters show. After his marriage he was his own manager, though he had overseers for his different farms. During the Revolutionary War he employed his distant cousin, Lund Washington. He was fortunate to get him. Lund was born in 1737 and died in 1796. In his youth he had been manager of a large estate in Albemarle and Orange Counties. He was next appointed manager of Ravensworth in Fairfax County by its owner, Major Henry Fitzhugh.[1]

He made regular reports "detailing all the events that occurred on the plantation, his purchases, sales, payments of money, the kinds and quantity of produce, occupation of laborers, and whatever else could tend to explain the precise condition of the business in his hands. The General's answers to these letters are said to have been destroyed, but a number of Lund Washington's letters have been preserved and copies of them are in the Library of Congress."[2] Washington entrusted to him much personal business, affairs of the Custis estate, drafting of contracts and leases of Washington's lands. He did not need to give him minute directions as to farming, for Lund was quite capable of running the plantation. He made extensive repairs to the Mansion. Washington directed that, "the chimney in the new room should be exactly in the middle

[1]Slaughter. *History of Truro Parish*, p. 110.
[2]*Writings*, Vol. 4, p. 114 (note).

of it—the doors and everything else to be exactly answerable and uniform—in short, I would have the whole executed in a masterly Manner." He built the present brick barn in 1782, and he added to the mansion by raising and enclosing the north end.[3]

Early in the Revolution, the last royal governor, Lord Dunmore, had been driven from the mainland and had taken refuge on the frigate *Fowey*. He cruised up and down the Chesapeake Bay, committing depredations. Washington became apprehensive lest he should seize Mrs. Washington. He wrote Lund:

"I can hardly think that Lord Dunmore can act so low, and unmanly a part, as to think of siezing Mrs. Washington by way of revenge upon me; however, as I suppose she is, before this time gone over to Mr. Calvert's, and will soon after returning, go down to New Kent, she will be out of his reach for 2 or 3 months to come, in which time matters may, and probably will, take such a turn as to render her removal either absolutely necessary, or quite useless."[4]

In 1775 he wrote Lund: "Let the Hospitality of the House, with respect to the poor, be kept up. Let no one go hungry away. If any of these kind of People should be in want of Corn, supply their necessities, provided it does not encourage them in idleness; and I have no objection to your giving my Money in Charity, to the amount of forty or fifty Pounds a Year, when you think it well bestowed. What I mean, by having no objections is, that it is my desire that it should be done. You are to consider that neither myself or Wife are now in a way to do these good Offices."[5]

When in 1781 Lord Cornwallis carried the war into Virginia and British frigates were again in the Chesapeake Bay, Washington, fearing damage to Mount Vernon with consequent plunder and loss of slaves, was again aroused. He was shocked and indignant when he received word that about fifteen slaves had been taken. He wrote to Lund "that which gives me most concern, is that you

---

[3]Charles C. Wall. "Notes on the Early History of Mount Vernon," *William and Mary Quarterly*, April 1945, page 180.

[4]*Writings*, Vol. 3, pp. 432-433.

[5]*Ibid.*, Vol. 4, p. 115.

should go aboard the enemys Vessels and furnish them with refreshments. It would have been a less painful circumstance to me, to have heard, that in consequence of your non-compliance with their request, they had burnt my House, and laid the Plantation in ruins. . . I am thoroughly persuaded that you acted from your best judgment; and believe, that your desire to perserve my property and rescue the buildings from impending danger, were your governing motives. But to go on board their Vessels; carry them refreshments; commune with a parcel of plundering Scoundrels, and request a favor by asking the surrender of my Negroes, was exceedingly ill-judged, and 'tis to be feared, will be unhappy in its consequences, as it will be a precedent for others, and may become a subject of animadversion."[6] A note by the editor states that five of these slaves were recovered in Philadelphia and one after the siege of Yorktown.

Actually there was little danger of the destruction of the mansion. The burning of Mount Vernon would have aroused indignation, not only in America, but in England, where the war, now in its sixth year, was unpopular and was prolonged only by the obstinacy of the King and Lord North. It had created a formidable coalition of European powers against Great Britain.

The wanton destruction of private homes was unusual, though Wye House of the Lloyds on the Eastern Shore of Maryland was burned by the British. The seizure of slaves in the southern colonies became more common toward the end of the war.

About 1785 Lund Washington expressed his wish to retire from the management of Mount Vernon. He had been the superintendent of the estate for ten years. While reluctant to let him go, Washington was not the man to urge another to stay against his wishes. He accordingly wrote to Lund: "However unlucky I may have been in Crops &c of late years, I shall retain a grateful sense of your endeavors to serve me, for as I have repeatedly intimated to you in my Letters from Camp, nothing but that entire confidence

[6] *Ibid.*, Vol. 22, pp. 14-15.

which I have, could have made me easy under an absence for almost nine years from my family and Estate, or could have enabled me, consequently, to have given not only my time, but my whole attention to the public concerns of this Country for that space."[7] Earlier in the letter he had said that he could not keep Lund longer in his employ than suited his (Lund's) interest.

In a note to an article on Elizabeth Washington of Hayfield by William Buckner McGroarty, appearing in the *Virginia Magazine of History and Biography*, April 1925, it is stated: "General Washington returned from the War of Independence $15,000 in debt; to liquidate this indebtedness he sold to his manager 360 acres of the western section of Mount Vernon for the above named sum." The authority quoted by Mr. McGroarty is, "The Memorial to Washington"; Callahan, 1923.

Lund Washington built Hayfield on the land so acquired.[8] It was situated on the Back (now Telegraph) Road to Alexandria from Pohick Church. It was burned about thirty years ago. Its location is shown by a marker on the road. Hayfield is still a farm. Washington's will bequeathed mourning rings of the value of one hundred dollars each to five persons, one of them was Elizabeth Washington of Hayfield. She was the widow of Lund Washington. The will adds: "these bequests are not made for the intrinsic value of them, but as mementoes of my esteem and regard."

After Lund Washington, the manager was a Mr. Bloxham, an Englishman, who desired to return to England in 1789. Washington, who was then President, authorized his nephew, George Augustine Washington, to employ Anthony Whiting of Chestertown, Maryland. Whiting was required to make weekly reports and "use his best skill to carry into effect the present rotation system of cropping." Whiting gave satisfaction and continued as manager until his death in 1793. In one of his early letters Washington desires him "to be particularly attentive to my Negros in their

---

[7]*Ibid.*, Vol. 28, p. 319.

[8]A picture of Hayfield is given in the Virginia Magazine of *History and Biography*, April, 1925, facing page 154.

Courtesy Publishers Homes and Gardens in Old Virginia

Wellington *(Page 138)*

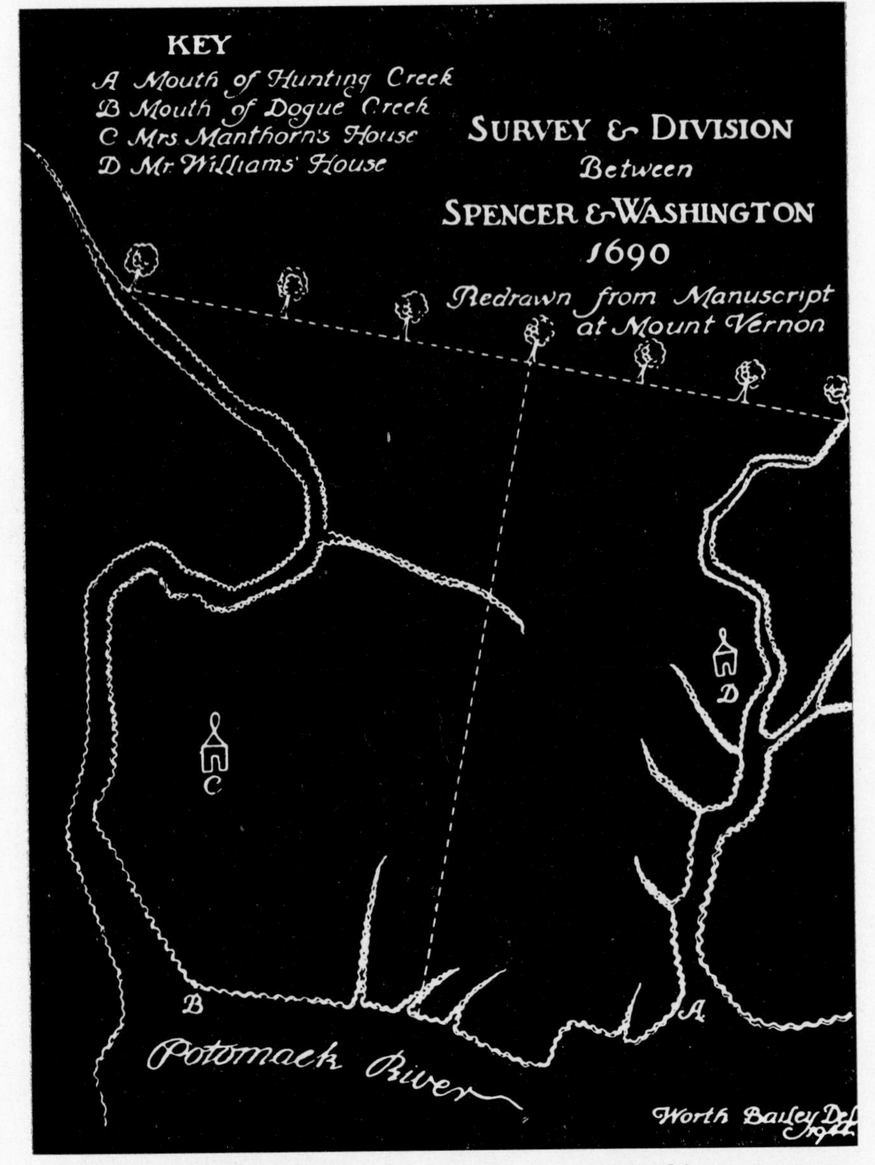

Survey and Division Between Spencer and Washington, 1690
(Page 133)

Courtesy Charles C. Wall, Resident Superintendent, The Mount Vernon Ladies' Association of the Nation

sicknesses; and to order every Overseer *positively* to be so likewise; for I am sorry to observe that the generalty of them, view these poor creatures in scarcely any other light then they do a draught horse or Ox," and "if their disorders are not common and the mode of treating them plain, simple and well understood, send for Doctr. Craik in time."[9]

But for all his anxiety that his negroes should be cared for when sick, he did not propose to be imposed upon, for he wrote: "What is the matter with Old Frank, that he is always (almost) on the Sick list? I am inclined to believe that he finds the House too comfortable to quit, or he would not be so often and so long in it at a time."[9]

He wrote to Whiting almost weekly and in one letter explained his procedure: "Whenever I set down to write you, I read your letter, or letters carefully over, and as soon as I come to a part that requires to be noticed, I make a short note on the cover of the letter, or piece of waste paper; then read on to the next, noting that in like manner; and so on until I have got through the whole letter and reports. Then in writing my letter to you, as soon as I have finished what I have to say on one of these notes, I draw my pen through it and proceed to another, and another, until the whole is done, crossing each as I go on, by which means if I am called off twenty times whilst I am writing, I can never with these notes before me finished or unfinished, omit anything I wanted to say."[10] While Whiting was manager, Washington directed that the name "Union Farm or Plantation" be given to the lands formerly called "Ferry and French's."

After Whiting's death in 1793 Washington wrote to Arthur Young a letter, parts of which are set out here.

". . .All my landed property East of the Apalachian Mountains is under Rent, except the Estate called Mount Vernon. This, hitherto, I have kept in my own hands; but from my present situation; from my advanced time of my life; from a wish to live free from

---

[9]*Writings*, Vol. 32, pp. 184, 319.
[10]*Ibid.*, p. 467.

care, and as much at my ease as possible during the remainder of it; and from other causes which are not necessary to detail, I have, latterly, entertained serious thoughts of letting this estate also, reserving the Mansion house farm for my own residence, occupation, and amusement in agriculture; provided I can obtain what in my own judgment, and in the opinions of others whom I have consulted the low Rent which I shall mention thereafter; and provided I can settle it with *good* farmers.

"The quantity of ploughable land (including meadow); the relative situation of the farms one to another; and the division of these farms into seperate inclosures; with the quantity and situation of the Woodland appertaining to the tract, will be better delineated by the sketch herewith sent (which is made from actual surveys, subject nevertheless to revision and correction) than by a volume of words.

"No estate in United America is more pleasantly situated than this. It lyes in a high, dry and healthy Country 300 miles by water from the Sea, and, as you will see by the plan, on one of the finest Rivers in the world. Its margin is washed by more than ten miles of tide water; from the bed of which, and the enumerable coves, inlets and small marshes with wch. it abounds, an inexhaustible fund of rich mud may be drawn as a manure; either to be used seperately, or in a compost, according to the judgment of the farmer. It is situated in a latitude between the extremes of heat and cold, and is the same distance by land and water, with good roads and the best navigation (to and) from the Federal City, Alexandria, and George town; distant from the first twelve, from the second nine, and from the last sixteen miles. . . .

"There are, as you will perceive by the plan, four farms besides that at the Mansion house: these four contain 3260 acres of cultivable land; to which some hundreds more, adjoining, as may be seen, might be added, if a greater quantity should be required; . . .

"On what is called Union farm (containing 928 acres of arable and Meadow) there is a newly erected Brick Barn equal perhaps to any in America, and for conveniences of all sorts, particularly for sheltering and feeding horses, cattle &c., scarcely to be exceeded anywhere. . . .

"Dogue run farm (650 acres) has a small but new building for the Overlooker; one room only below, and the same above, 16 by 20 each; decent and comfortable for its size. It has also covering for forty odd negroes, similar to what is mentioned on Union farm. It has a new circular barn now finishing on a new construction; well calculated, it is conceived, for getting grain out of the straw more expeditiously than in the usual mode of threshing. There are good sheds also erecting, sufficient to cover 30 work horses and Oxen.

"Muddy hole farm (476 acres) has a house for the Overlooker, in size and appearance nearly like that at Dogue run, but older. The same kind of covering for about thirty negroes, and a tolerably good barn, with stables for the work horses.

"River farm which is the largest of the four, and seperated from the others by little hunting Creek, (contains 1207 acres of ploughable land), has an Overlookers Ho. of one large and two small rooms below, and one or two above; sufficient covering for 50 or 60 Negroes like those before mentioned. A large barn and stables (gone much to decay, but these will be replaced next year with new ones). . . .

"I would let these four farms to four substantial farmers, of wealth and strength sufficient to cultivate them; and who would insure to me the regular payment of the Rents; and I would give them leases for seven or ten years, at the rate of a Spanish milled dollar, or other money current at the time, in this country, equivalent thereto, for every acre of ploughable and mowable ground within the Inclosures of the respective farms, . . ."[11]

A copy of the plan or map enclosed in the letter is in the George Washington Atlas in the Library of Congress.

Nothing tangible came of this letter, except that Washington received an inquiry from an Englishmen, Richard Parkinson, to

---

[11] *Ibid.*, Vol. 33, pp. 175-179.

whom he replied by two letters printed in Fitzpatrick's *Writings of Washington*. Parkinson paid a visit to Mount Vernon and was dissatisfied with what he saw. He considered the land and the crops poor, and had had no experience with slave labor. It was just as well, for Washington would never have been satisfied to have been a stranger to his mill, his sixteen-sided barn, or his distillery.

Washington's next manager was William Pearce of Kent County, on the Eastern Shore of Maryland. Although Washington had never been further south on the Eastern Shore of Maryland than the ferry from Annapolis to Chester River, he thought favorably of its agriculture, and was predisposed to employ Pearce, as he, like Whiting, came from that section. His contract with him called for an annual salary of one hundred Guineas, a dwelling house, meats and provisions, fodder for his horses, allowance of a negro woman to cook for his family, a negro boy and girl for help. Besides managing and cultivating the farm, Pearce was to have control over the Overseers of the different farms with authority to engage and dismiss them.[12] The names of these overseers appear in subsequent letters, Stuart, Crow, McKay, Butler, Davy, Thomas Green (overseer of the carpenters). Washington warned that Green will "require your closest attention . . . to keep him from flying from one thing to another without system." As to his negro carpenters, "there is not to be found so idle a set of Rascalls."

While Bloxham was manager a new barn was built on Union Farm. The general plan of the barn was suggested by Arthur Young for Washington wrote to him in 1788: "The building of a Brick Barn has occupied much of my attention this Summer. It is constructed somewhat according to the plan you had the goodness to send me: but with some additions. It is now, I believe, the largest and most convenient in this Country."[13] This was the barn of which Washington wrote the French "Minister and Madame de Brehan expressing a desire to walk to the New Barn we accordingly did so, and from thence through French's Plantation to my Mill

---

[12] *Ibid.*, pp. 97-100.
[13] *Ibid.*, Vol. 30, p. 152.

and from thence home, compleating a tour of at least seven Miles."[14]

This was not the well known sixteen-sided or circular barn. That was on the Dogue Run Farm, built while Pearce was manager by Thomas Green the head carpenter. It is described in an advertisement of lease in 1796: "a new brick barn with an open circular floor to thresh, or tread on, through which the grain passes to the floor below."[15] This barn was two stories high.

The threshing was to be done on the second floor, with "interstices between the treading floor," wide enough to let the grain filter through to the lower floor, but not too often, "lest the straw should work into them and choke the passage of the grain . . . to make the difficulty of cleaning the grain much greater." The plan Washington drew for this barn is in the Washington Papers in the Library of Congress. The treading floor was in the center with solid flooring on all sides, except a runway on one side by which the animals could reach the treading floor.

The same advertisement states that on the River Farm there is "an old barn (now in use) and a brick one building 60 by 30 feet, besides ends and wings sufficient for stabling 20 working horses and as many oxen."

In 1796 Pearce's rheumatism obliged him to retire. Washington wrote of him: "Mr. Pearce who at present looks after my business is a person with whose management I am very well pleased. He is a man of property, of great integrity, very great industry, and much experience in the superintendence of a large concern, having been the manager for a Gentn on the Es (Eastern Shore) for fifteen or eighteen years before he came to me."

His next and last manager was James Anderson. He had a trying experience. Several months after he began his management, Washington's second term as President expired, and Anderson was under daily surveillance, as Washington rode over his farms every day. This irked Anderson so much that he threatened to resign. Wash-

---

[14]*Diaries*, Vol. 3, p. 441.
[15]*Writings*, Vol. 34, p. 435.

ington answered his complaints in a long letter: "If I cannot remark upon my own business, passing every day under my eyes, without hurting your feelings, I must discontinue my rides, or become a Cypher on my own Estate." Their differences must have been patched up as the last letter Washingon wrote was addressed to him.

Chapter 11

Amusements

From early manhood Washington patronized the theater. The first dramatic performance he witnessed was the *Tragedy of George Barnwell*, when he was in the Barbadoes with his brother Lawrence. "The character of Barnwell and several others was said to be well performed." While in Dumfries on other business in 1771 he attended a play called *The Recruiting Officer*. There is no record of a theater there, so the play was probably performed in a tavern or store. In Williamsburg in Washington's burgess days, there was a theater known as the Hallam Playhouse, named after Mrs. Hallam, whose company toured the American Colonies in the early eighteenth century. Washington seems to have attended plays whenever his duties as burgess required his presence in the Capital. During ten days in October and November, 1771, he went "to the play" four times. His ledger entry for this period shows, "By Sundry Play Tickets £4. 10. 0," indicating he took others with him. There was no regular theater building in Alexandria until 1797,[1] but plays were performed as early as 1768, for that year Washington, Mrs. Washington, Patsy Custis, and Milly Posey saw two plays there. When in Annapolis attending the races, he went to the play repeatedly. While President he gained a much needed relaxation by going to see plays, where he occupied a box. He combined pleasure with entertaining distinguished guests: . . ."sent tickets to the following ladies and gentlemen, and invited them to seats in my box, viz:—Mrs. Adams (lady of the Vice Presi-

[1]Gay Montague Moore. *Seaport in Virginia*, p. 28.

dent), Genl. Schuyler and lady, Mr. King and lady, Majr. Butler and lady, Colo. Hamilton and lady, Mrs. Green—all of whom accepted and came, except Mrs. Butler, who was indisposed."[2] A note to the diaries states the play was *The Toy or a Trip to Hampton Court*. At Philadelphia he saw performed *The Child of Nature*, the *Lock and Key*, and the *Way to get Married*. These were ephemeral productions, but he saw more noteworthy drama, *The School for Scandal*, *Julius Caesar*, and *Hamlet*. Few Presidents have attended the theater more frequently than he. Once while attending the theater in Philadelphia, *Hail Columbia* was sung for the first time. On May 27, 1798 he wrote the author, Joseph Hopkinson, thanking him for a copy of the song.[3]

Like most Virginia gentlemen of his day, he kept race horses and patronized the sport. Some of his favorite horses were named "Leonidas," "Sampson," "Steady," "Traveller," "Magnolia," "Blueskin," and "Nelson." The last two were horses he rode in the Revolution.[4] A nearby race track was Bogges at the head of Pohick Bay. A letter from George Mason to him is headed, "Race Course at Bogges." There were other tracks at Cameron and Alexandria. He was Secretary of the Alexandria Jockey Club. Nearest of all to his home was Accotink, four miles from Mount Vernon, where he went to a purse race and entered one of his horses and paid Robert Sandford twelve shillings to ride him. The most famous course within riding distance from Mount Vernon was at Annapolis. Thither he set out in company with John Wormeley, younger brother of Ralph Wormeley of Rosegill, who had traveled 140 miles to join him.[5] They seem to have had an extraordinarily good time. They lodged with the Rev. Jonathan Boucher, dined with Governor Eden, and "went to the Play and Ball afterwards." Next

---

[2]*Diaries*, Vol. 4, p. 54.

[3]*Writings*, Vol. 36, p. 274.

[4]Paul L. Haworth. *George Washington, Country Gentleman*, p. 131.

[5]John Wormeley was a Tory in the Revolutionary War and became a captain in the British Army. After the conclusion of hostilities he consulted Washington about return to Virginia. In a letter he wrote to Governor Harrison from Norfolk, he states that General Washington saw no impropriety in his return. A note by the editor of the *Diaries* states that Wormeley was restored to his Virginia citizenship in 1783. (Hening, XI-316), *Diaries*, Vol. 2, p. 34.

day they "dined at Doct. Steward's (Stuart) and went to the Play and Ball afterwards." The following day, "dined at Mr. Ridout's, and went to the Play after it," the next day: "dined at Mr. Carroll's and went to the Ball." This "Mr. Carroll" may have been "the father of Charles Carroll of Carrollton." Among other notables they dined "with Majr. Jenifer and suppd at Daniel Dulany, Esqrs."[6] Though they went for the races, Washington makes no mention of them but in his ledger he made an entry: "by John Parke Custis at ye Annapolis Races £8."

He indulged in moderate betting, not only at horse races, but at cards, at his own home, at Williamsburg, Fredericksburg, Annapolis and other places, and he kept records of his gains and losses. The editor of the *Diaries* computed his gains and losses for the years 1772, 1773 and 1774. His losses were £78. 5. 9 and his gains £72. 2. 6.

If the diaries reflect Washington's tastes—as they undoubtedly do—he was no devotee of cock fights. The indexes show but a single reference to the sport. On his return from Barbadoes in 1752 he noted in his journal: "A Great Main of . . . cks fought in Yorktown . . . tween Glouster and York for '5 pistoles each battle and 100 ye odd.' I left it with Colo. Lewis before it was decided and had part of his chariot to his house."[7]

The sport most often alluded to is fox hunting. Washington was passionately devoted to it. The index to the *Diaries* shows over one hundred references to it. Was it the pursuit and killing of the fox that attracted him? George Mercer's description of him concludes with: "he is a splendid horseman." He loved to feel a horse under him; to ride at breakneck speed, leaping fences, turning obstacles with the hounds yelping—that must have been the charm. It was a gentleman's sport, brought from the mother country, it was also a social pastime. With him at one time or another were the Alexanders, Capt. Posey, Mr. Chichester, Mr. Triplett, Mr.

---

[6]*Diaries*, Vol. 2, pp. 34-35.

[7]*Diaries*, Vol. 1, p. 36. "Colo. Lewis" was probably Warner Lewis of Warner Hall, Gloucester County, who was born in 1720.

Peake, Lord Fairfax and his brother Robert, Bryan Fairfax, Mr. Manley, Capt. McCarty, Alexander Henderson, Hector Ross, Lund Washington and hundreds of others. One conspicuous name is missing—George Mason of Gunston Hall.

A favorite form of social gathering in the Virginia of the eighteenth century was the barbecue. Washington attended many—at Alexandria, Fredericksburg, where he "dined at the Barbicue with a great deal of Company." His favorite spot was nearer his home, at Accotink,[8] where on one occasion he "went to a Barbicue of my own giving." At another time: "Went with the above company to a Boat Race and Barbicue at Johnson's Ferry." The company consisted of Mr. and Mrs. Custis (John Parke Custis and wife), Miss Calvert and Mr. Tilghman.[9]

Washington took chances in raffles and lotteries. The latter are looked upon with disfavor today and are prohibited by law in many States; not so in the eighteenth century. The original wooden Christ Church in Alexandria was built with money raised by a lottery. Selling lottery tickets was a favorite method of starting a new town. Thus we find him corresponding with Lord Stirling in 1775 about "six tickets wch. I kept on my own account, two of them were fortunate, viz.

"One of £200 No. 58 in the division of Wenhams great Lot, in the Hardenberg's Patent in Ulster County near Rochester" and he speaks of 12 more tickets which he owned. In a letter to Edmund Randolph he speaks of the "list of associates [of whom he was evidently one] who purchased 100 Tickets in the lottery of the deceased Colo. Byrd."

Washington first mentions dancing in a letter to Mrs. George William Fairfax written from Fort Duquesne in 1758 as A——— B———s. The initials stood for Assembly Balls. Shortly after his marriage in 1760, he "went to a Ball in Alexandria where Music and Dancing was the chief entertainment." From then on, there are numerous references to the Assembly Balls in Alexandria; thus

[8]Accotink is a modern village about four miles southwest of Mount Vernon, on the Richmond Road where the creek of that name empties into Accotink Bay.

[9]*Diaries*, Vol. 2, p. 150.

in April, 1768: "We (Mrs. Washington, Patsy Custis, and Miss Betsy Ramsay) went up to Alexa. to a Ball." The next day "We returned from Alexandria thro Snow."[10] "January 12, 1769: In ye afternoon went up to Alex. to ye Monthly Ball."[11]

"Went up in the afternoon with Mrs. Washington, J. P. Custis, Miss Custis and Milly Posey to a Ball in Alexandria. Lodged in my own House in Town." That was in July, 1772. One of these balls was given by Washington himself to celebrate his reelection to the House of Burgesses. "December 4th 1771. Went up to the election and the Ball I had given at Alexa." His account book shows that the expenses of the election and ball amounted to over twenty-five pounds.

Most of the balls must have been held in Gadsby's Tavern, where there was a large assembly room, with a high balcony for musicians.

During the Revolutionary War the Army spent the winter of 1779-1780 at Morristown, New Jersey, where the officers subscribed money for the promotion of a dancing assembly. An agreement was drawn up and signed by Washington and 34 other officers.[12]

Official balls were held in New York and Philadelphia throughout his Presidency. This is the toast proposed at one of them:

"May the members thereof and the *Fair* who honor it with their presence long continue in the enjoyment of an amusement so innocent and agreeable."[13]

After his retirement from public office, Washington felt too old to dance. In 1799 he received an invitation from the Managers of the Alexandria Dancing Academy. He replied: "Mrs. Washington and myself have been honoured with your polite invitation to the assemblies in Alexandria this winter, and thank you for this mark of your attention, but alas! our dancing days are no more."[14]

---

[10] *Ibid.*, Vol. 1, p. 264.
[11] *Ibid.*, p. 308.
[12] *Writings*, Vol. 18, p. 261 (note).
[13] *Ibid.*, Vol. 35, p. 397.
[14] *Ibid.*, Vol. 37, p. 425 (note).

Eleanor Parke Custis, Mrs. Washington's granddaughter, grew into a beautiful young woman as fond of dancing as her "grand-papa" had ever been. Washington twitted her about her professed indifference to young men. The humor is a trifle forced, but the advice was sound:

". . . Let me touch a little now on your Georgetown ball, and happy, thrice happy, for the fair who were assembled on the occasion, that there was a man to spare; for had there been 79 ladies and only 78 gentlemen, there might, in the course of the evening, have been some disorder among the caps; notwithstanding the apathy which *one* of the company entertains for the 'youth' of the present day, and her determination 'never to give herself a moment's uneasiness on account of any of them.' A hint here; men and women feel the same inclinations to each other *now* that they always have done, and which they will continue to do until there is a new order of things, and *you*, as others have done, may find, perhaps, that the passions of your sex are easier raised than allayed. Do not therefore boast too soon or too strongly of your insensibility to, or resistance of, its powers. In the composition of the human frame there is a good deal of inflammable matter, however dormant it may lie for a time, and like an intimate acquaintance of yours, when the torch is put to it, *that* which is *within you* may burst into a blaze; for which reason and especially too, as I have entered upon the chapter of advices, I will read you a lecture drawn from this text.

"Love is said to be an involuntary passion, and it is, therefore, contended that it cannot be resisted. This is true in part only, for like all things else, when nourished and supplied plentifully with aliment, it is rapid in its progress; but let these be withdrawn and it may be stifled in its birth or much stinted in its growth. For example, a woman (the same may be said of the other sex) all beautiful and accomplished, will, while her hand and heart are undisposed of, turn the heads and set the circle in which she moves on fire. Let her marry, and what is the consequence? The madness *ceases* and all is quiet again. Why? not because there is any diminution in the charms of the lady, but because there is an end of hope.

Hence it follows, that love may and therefore ought to be under the guidance of reason, for although we cannot avoid first impressions, we may assuredly place them under guard; and my motives for treating on this subject are to show you, while you remain Eleanor Parke Custis, spinster, and retain the resolution to love with moderation, the propriety of adhering to the latter resolution, at least until you have secured your game, and the way by which it may be accomplished."[15]

Life was pleasant at Mount Vernon in the halcyon days between Washington's marriage and the Revolution. Busy with the farms that he loved, yet not too busy to hunt foxes with his friends. He was surrounded by congenial friends who visited him, and whom he visited. Every few days he was at Alexandria. On gala nights the chariot rumbled up to the balls, where he knew everybody. No wonder that in after years he looked back to those days as the happiest of his life. That old society is dead and gone. Southern Fairfax has a larger population now, and it has comforts and conveniences unknown in Washington's day, but it lacks the homogeneity and charm of its eighteenth century social life.

[15]*Ibid.*, Vol. 34, pp. 91-92.

Chapter 12

Mount Vernon

We are apt to forget how late in the colonial era southern Fairfax became a part of the richer and more prosperous society of the longer-settled tidewater country. William Fairfax completed the building of Belvoir in 1741. Virginia had then a history of over a century and a quarter. Alexander Spottswood, Virginia's most colorful governor, was dead. The capital of the colony had been transferred from Jamestown to Williamsburg nearly half a century. Until 1730 when Prince William County was organized, the part of it later incorporated in Fairfax was frontier country, only a few years removed from Indian occupation. Many of the most famous homes of the tidewater aristocracy had been built before Fairfax became a County in 1742. The Lees had built Stratford; Councillor Carter, Nomini Hall; Landon Carter, Sabine Hall; the Burwells, Fairfield; the Pages, Rosewell; the Byrds, Westover; the Wormeleys, Rosegill; the Nelsons, the Nelson Hall at Yorktown. The pattern of Virginia colonial society was already formed. The Fairfax society was merely an extension of it. It was Washington and Mason who gave it distinction, as Jefferson gave distinction to Albemarle and Madison to Orange.

Until the construction of the George Washington Memorial Boulevard the visitor to Mount Vernon crossed Great Hunting Creek by a bridge from the south end of Henry Street. This bridge was erected before 1810.[1] Its object was not to reach Mount Vernon, but to reduce the distance from Alexandria to the Occoquan, Fred-

[1] *Landmarks of Old Prince William*, p. 571.

ericksburg, and further south. Before then the traffic going south had had to cross Cameron Run at a ford which Moses Ball, who was born in that vicinity in 1717, called "the wading place." The crossing is now made by a bridge and the road is called the Telegraph Road. Before the telegraph poles were put up, it was called the Back Road to Pohick Church. When Washington travelled from Alexandria to Mount Vernon he followed this route. There was never a town at the crossing, though there was an abortive effort made to locate one there instead of at Alexandria. It was known as Cameron and was a place of muster for the Fairfax militia; it had a racecourse, and it was a junction of roads leading southerly and westerly. There was an ordinary there kept by John Minor.

John Minor was a Justice of the Fairfax County Court on its establishment in 1742; a Vestryman of Truro Parish in 1744, where he is styled Capt. John Minor. He married a daughter of Dennis McCarty of Cedar Grove, Fairfax County. In 1745 he purchased land from Moses Ball at Cameron and established his ordinary. He died in 1752 and was succeeded by his son John, who sold the Minor tract in 1767 to Thomas Shaw. (Fairfax D. B., G: 195)

One of his sons, Nicholas, after his father's death purchased land in what soon became Loudoun County and opened an ordinary on the site of the future Leesburg. He laid off streets and lots and was instrumental in establishing the town.

Soon after crossing the run the road to Mount Vernon and the neighboring plantations left the main road, branched to the left, and led up a sharp hill, where the Civil War Fort Lyon was later erected, and reached the plateau above Hunting Creek estuary. This plateau commanded a beautiful view of the estuary and of the river.

After Alexandria became a town, the situation had the added attraction of nearness to a business and social center. Nearby was the home of Colonel John Colvill.

Though forgotten except by the student of local history, Colvill played a considerable part in the early history of Northern Virginia, ranking after William Fairfax, but standing beside Lawrence Washington and John Carlyle. He was a Vestryman of Truro Parish from 1734 to 1748, a Burgess from Fairfax from 1744 to 1748. A note to the *Diaries* (vol. 1, page 214) states: "John Colvill was trading in the Potomac in his own ship about 1730, and soon thereafter seated himself at 'Clish,' on the lower side of Great Hunting Creek. He served as justice and Burgess and accumulated large bodies of land, chiefly in the Catoctin neighborhood. . . Meanwhile his brother, Thomas, had emigrated to Cecil County, Maryland, but on John's death, removed to 'Clish' to administer on John's estate." Bryan Fairfax subsequently purchased four hundred acres of the Clish estate on which he built Mount Eagle. Among John Colvill's numerous patents was one for 5688 acres on Difficult Run, which he subsequently sold to William Fairfax in 1740 (Prince William D. B., Liber E, folio 203), by deeds of lease and release. He died in 1756 leaving a will recorded in the Fairfax Will Book B-97. It contained bequests for a natural daughter Catherine, and her mother. He devised a life estate to his brother Thomas, and the residue to his cousin, the Scotch Earl of Tankerville. Thomas persuaded Washington to become one of his executors. "In the end this duty brought to Washington a heavy burden of responsibility and much annoyance by reason of the claims upon him by Colvill's English kin, who were induced to believe that a fortune was due them, which Washington was wrongfully withholding." (*Diaries*, Vol. 1, p. 214, note) Washington's correspondence shows that it was not until 1797 that the estate was finally closed. Colonel John Colvill called his estate Cleesh, not Clish.

When Washington was halfway from Cameron to Mount Vernon he passed near the home of a man he knew well. This was John West, Junior of West's Grove,[2] located on the northerly branch of Little Hunting Creek. The Wests were a family of political importance in the Fairfax County of Washington's day. The father of this John West was Hugh West, who was elected a member

[2]Prince William D. B., Liber D, folio 36, 195.

Courtesy Virginia State Chamber of Commerce

George Washington's Mill (Pages 147 to 149)

Courtesy Virginia State Chamber of Commerce

Woodlawn (Page 153)

of the Truro Vestry in 1744.[3] He owned a warehouse and adjoining land, which was taken for Alexandria on the founding of that town in 1749, and was named as a trustee for it in the Act of Assembly. He was a Burgess for Fairfax from 1752 to 1754. He died shortly afterward, leaving several sons, one of whom was John West, Junior. The records do not show why he was called junior. It may have been to distinguish him from his uncle, John West, whom Washington referred to as Colonel. He was assistant Surveyor of Fairfax County and as such laid off Alexandria. Young Washington assisted him. He married Catherine, daughter of Colonel John Colvill. He purchased a pew in Christ Church, Alexandria for £33. With Washington he was executor of the will of his wife's uncle, Thomas Colvill. When Washington was put in command of the Continental Army, he was no longer able to take an active part, and said that West did not pay enough attention to the management of the trust estate. He was elected to the Assembly of 1776 in place of his uncle, Colonel West, who had retired. He died in 1777 leaving a will recorded in the Fairfax Will Book D. He was survived by three sons, Thomas, Hugh and John.

Just before Washington reached his own land, he passed close to the house of his nearest neighbors, the Peake family. Like the Washingtons, the Peakes had moved to Fairfax County from further down the Potomac River. In 1668 the first of the family in Virginia obtained a large grant of land on Potomac Creek in Stafford County. The head of the family in Washington's day was William Peake. He was a member of the Vestry of Truro Parish from 1733 to 1744 and again from 1749 to 1762 when he died and Washington was chosen to fill the vacancy.[4] As Washington's *Diaries* never give him any designation other than "Mr. Peake" and from the fact that none of the family held an elective office in the county, it may be assumed that the Peakes belonged to the minor gentry. William Peake was often at Mount Vernon and

[3]Slaughter. *History of Truro Parish in Virginia*, p. 21. Some of the facts stated here have been taken from a sketch of the West family given in Harrison, *Landmarks of Old Prince William*, Vol. 1, p. 138.

[4]*History of Truro Parish in Virginia*, by Philip Slaughter, pp. 7 and 34.

joined Washington in fox hunts. He left sons, William and Humphrey, a daughter, Nancy, and perhaps other issue. Humphrey seems to have been the most prominent member of the family. He dined frequently at Mount Vernon and was Washington's companion in frequent fox and duck hunts. When he was sick Washington and his wife visited him. An entry in the *Diaries*, under date of January 13th 1785, probably refers to Humphrey Peake: "Was invited and went to the Funeral of Mr. Peake, who died on Tuesday night. Returned to Dinner accompanied by the Revd. Doctr. Griffith." Dr. Griffith was Rector of Christ Church, Alexandria.

Washington's will refers to the "land of the late Humphrey Peake."

After travelling this road for seven miles Washington reached Mount Vernon. The last two miles ran through his own land. He approached his mansion through a gate by which stood a porter's lodge. Here he got his first glimpse of his home and the Bowling Green in front of it. He opened this approach in 1769, for his diary records: "At home all day opening the Avenue to the House, and for bringing the road along."[5] The vista remains, but the road is now closed to the public. In the eighteenth century all visitors to Mount Vernon passed through this gate. Those from Alexandria and points north left the main road (now U. S. Highway No. 1) at Gum Spring where it enters the Mount Vernon estate of Washington's day. Those coming from Colchester and points south left the highway near Woodlawn, and reached the gate and lodge by a road passing near Washington's Mill.

The history of the Mount Vernon tract begins with the patent issued to Nicholas Spencer and John Washington in 1674 for five thousand acres in Stafford County, situated on the Potomac River, between Little Hunting Creek and Dogue Creek. It was issued by Lord Culpeper, then Governor of Virginia and also Proprietor of the Northern Neck.

Of the two patentees Nicholas Spencer was the more important.

[5]*Diaries*, Vol. 1, p. 308.

He was a cousin of Lord Culpeper. He was a member of the Council of the colony and held the Secretaryship, the most lucrative office next to that of governor. He lived at Nomini on the Potomac River in Westmoreland County, which was sold in 1710 to the father of Councillor Carter of Nomini Hall. Spencer owned valuable estates in Bedfordshire, Huntondonshire and Essex. This may have been one reason for his return to England, where he died. His memory was long cherished in Virginia. No member of the Council from the Northern Neck exercised a greater influence before Thomas Lee of Stratford, also a member of the Council living in Westmoreland, where Spencer had lived three-quarters of a century before.

The location of the patent was skillfully chosen between two creeks with a straight back line. This eliminated such controversies and suits as vexed the Alexanders and their neighbors on the west over the location of the rear line of the six thousand acre tract patented by Robert Housing (or Howson) in 1669. The patentee was by law required "to seat or plant upon it within 3 Years after the Date of the Patent. . . Seating by their Law, is reckon'd the Building of an House, and keeping a Stock one whole Year . . . otherwise it lapses again to the King."[6] These conditions were complied with, as is shown by a Survey and Division between Spencer and Washington—made in 1690. This plat is now at Mount Vernon, and a photostat of it is reproduced here through the courtesy of Mr. Charles C. Wall. It shows that Lawrence Washington received in this partition, twenty-five hundred acres bordering on Little Hunting Creek and that Madame Spencer (presumably the widow of Nicholas Spencer) received twenty-five hundred acres bordering on Dogue Creek. No building is shown on the site of the Mount Vernon house. A house called Mrs. Manthorn's is located on the Spencer tract, and Mr. Williams' house is located on the Lawrence Washington tract. Both these houses have long since disappeared. Lawrence Washington was the son of Colonel John Washington, the emigrant, and also the grandfather of Lawrence and George Washington. This Lawrence Washington died

[6]Hartwell, Blair and Chilton. *Present State of Virginia*, p. 19.

in 1698. Sometime between 1690 and his death, he may have built a small house or "quarter," which is now incorporated in the center of the present Mount Vernon Mansion. In an article in the *William and Mary Quarterly* for April, 1945, Mr. Charles C. Wall, resident Superintendent of Mount Vernon, sets out his reasons for believing this to be true. One piece of evidence "is the so-called cornerstone of the Mansion, which reposed in a basement wall, until it was removed for better preservation and replaced by a facsimile thirty five years ago. . . It is now displayed in the museum in a special case. This stone bears the initials L. W. and a heart flanked by two halberds, all framed within a geometric border. . . It has often been remarked that certain walls in the Mansion basement might well relate to an earlier structure. . . . These walls are of stone; their surfaces have disintegrated with time and, more significant, several of them bear no functional relation to the present structure. . . . We regret that the cornerstone bears no date, but it is more suggestive of the seventeenth than of the eighteenth century in its design. We know also that Augustine Washington and Lawrence Washington, his son, knew and used the family coat-of-arms. May we not infer that it would have been used on a cornerstone had one been placed by either of these gentlemen?"

Although stated before, it may be well to recapitulate the title to the Mount Vernon estate from Lawrence Washington to Augustine Washington. Lawrence devised to his daughter Mildred, "all my land in Stafford County lying upon hunting Creek." She married Roger Gregory, and in 1726 Mildred and her husband Roger released the plantation to her brother Augustine, father of George Washington.

As to the enlargement of the mansion after it became the property of George Washington, Mr. Wall writes: "General Washington inaugurated a comprehensive plan for the enlargement of his Mansion House, replacement of outbuildings and extension of formal planted areas adjacent thereto in 1774. He himself raised and enclosed the addition to the south end of the Mansion before he was called to a wider field of activity as Commander-in-Chief of the Continental Army. Lund Washington, kinsman and wartime manager, raised and enclosed the addition at the north end and completed other major features of the plan."[7] This last statement needs qualification: The north end of the house includes the banquet hall. The outside walls of this end were no doubt completed as stated. The interior of the banquet hall was unfinished, as shown by Washington's letters of 1785 and 1786. John Rawlings contracted to do the plastering and interior decoration. Apparently he did not do the work himself but employed one Tharpe. Washington noted in his *Diary* that on August 25, 1786, "Mr. Rawlings from Baltimore and Mr. Tharpe came here before dinner to measure the work which had been done for me and to receive payment,"[8]

In his *Mansions of Virginia*, Thomas Tileston Waterman says: "Mount Vernon is the perfection of Virginia Colonial Architecture. It has an incomparable setting on the banks of the Potomac and is an amazingly personal document of Washington, the planter." Waterman's detailed and illuminating description of the interior is too long to quote here. Instead Snowden's briefer, if less professional account is given:

"The interior of the old house remained unchanged; but wings were added and the exterior remodelled. Its appearance to-day is as when completed then (1785-87). It was of the most substantial frame-work (cut in imitation of stone), two stories and attic in height, ninety-six feet in length by thirty in depth, with a piazza fifteen feet in depth extending along the entire eastern or river front, supported by square columns twenty-five feet in height, over this a light balustrade, and in the centre of the roof an observatory and spire. There were seven high dormer windows—three on the eastern side, one on each end, and two on the western or lawn side. The ground floor contained six rooms . . . with the old spacious hall . . . extending through it from east to west, and the stairway. On the south side of the hall was the parlor, library, and breakfast-room, from which last a narrow staircase ascended to the private

[7]Wall, p. 180.
[8]*Diaries*, Vol. 3, p. 108.

study on the second floor; on the north side a music-room, parlor, and dancing-room, in which when there was much company the guests were sometimes entertained at table. The principal feature of this room was the large mantelpiece, wrought in Italy, of statuary and Sienite marbles, exquisitely carved in every part, bearing in relief scenes in agricultural life. The interiors of the new rooms were finished to correspond with the old ones. At the same time were built, near the mansion, on either side, a substantial kitchen and laundry, connected with it by colonnades, These, with other outlying buildings there erected, all remain, with the exception of an extensive conservatory."[9]

Since Snowden wrote in 1894, the balustrade has been removed, as it was discovered that it was not there originally, but was added later by Bushrod Washington.

The first deed enlarging the Mount Vernon tract from its original twenty-five hundred acres was made to Lawrence Washington. On March 2d 1738, William Spencer, reciting himself the grandson of Nicholas Spencer, conveyed two tracts to Lawrence for the consideration of £75. These tracts were in the Parish of Truro, then in Prince William County: the first containing 200 acres and bounded in part by the Potomac River and being the same formerly leased by Frances Spencer to Capt. William Harrison. Metes and bounds are given, but the description cannot be plotted as it depends upon the location of trees and swamps not now to be identified. The second parcel contained 56 acres on Dogue Run.[10] The Washington Mill was subsequently built on this parcel.

The ownership of the mill was claimed by Lawrence's father in his will admitted to probate five years later:

"Imprimis I give unto my son Lawrence Washington and his heirs forever all that Plantation and Tract of Land at Hunting Creek in the County of Prince William Containing by Estimation two thousand five hundred acres with the water mill adjoyning thereto and lying near the same. And all the slaves, Cattle and

---

[9]Snowden, W. H. *Some Old Historic Landmarks* (ed. of 1894), pp. 65-66.
[10]Prince William D. B. D, pp. 112-115.

Stocks of all kinds whatsoever and all the household Furniture possessed by my said son Together with the said Plantation Tract and Mill."[11] The conjectural explanation of this claim is that Augustine Washington paid the £75 consideration, and therefore claimed ownership of the mill. In March 1738 Lawrence had not reached his majority and probably did not have the money to make the purchase.

In 1751 Lawrence Washington acquired from Thomas Marshall twenty-two acres on Dogue Run.[12] Marshall had gotten the land from William Spencer: so when George Washington acquired his title by the will of his brother, the estate comprised 278 acres in addition to the original estimated 2500 acres.

Washington was a persistent purchaser of adjoining lands and when he died his Mount Vernon estate comprised over eight thousand acres. His first considerable purchase was the Clifton tract of 1207 acres, for which he agreed to pay £1150 on Feby 26, 1760. Clifton afterwards tried to get out of his bargain under pretense of his wife not consenting to acknowledge her Right of Dower and "by his shuffling behaviour . . . convinced me of his being the trifling body represented." On March 11 "Visited at Colo. Fairfax's and was informed that Clifton had sold his land to Mr. Thompson Mason which fully unravelled his conduct on the 2d and convinced me that he was nothing less than a thorough pac'd Rascall, disregardful of any engagements of words or oaths not bound by penalties."[13]

It turned out the whole tract was mortgaged to Charles Carroll, and there were other claims against it amounting to nearly £1000. The land was sold by foreclosure in a Chancery suit, and all Clifton's land, amounting to over 1800 acres, was sold to Washington,[14] who made a separate farm of it which he called his River Farm. It was separated from the rest of his estate by Little Hunting Creek. He subsequently added to it by the purchase of 238 acres from

[11] *Wills of George Washington and his Immediate Ancestors,* Ford, W. C., ed., p. 45.
[12] Fairfax D. B. C, p. 159.
[13] *Diaries,* Vol. 1, p. 137.
[14] The details are set out in a note in *Diaries,* Vol. 1, pp. 163-164.

Charles Brent.[15] This appears in a "List of Lands given unto the Clerk of Fairfax County to pay taxes for the year 1763: lot of Mr. Clifton 1806 acres; lot of Mr. Brent 238 acres."

Washington bequeathed the use of 360 acres of River Farm to his Secretary: "To Tobias Lear, I give the use of the Farm which he now holds, in virtue of a Lease from me to him and his deceased wife (for and during their natural lives) free from Rent, during his life." Lear occupied the house on the farm which was probably built by Clifton before 1760. After his death in 1816, the farm, which had become known as Walnut Tree Farm, passed according to the will, to George Fayette Washington and Charles Augustine Washington, who had inherited the whole of River Farm, 2077 acres.

"The farm was occupied by two generations of the Washington family, Charles A., a grandnephew, being the last, until 1859."[16] This house with the addition of wings and other changes is the present Wellington, owned by Mr. and Mrs. Malcolm Matheson.

On the land bought from Clifton there was a spring, and a ferry and fishing landing, both called Johnson's from the tenant Samuel Johnson. The *Diaries* record two outings here:

May 7, 1774, "Went with the above Company (Mr. and Mrs. Custis and Miss Calvert and Mr. Tilghman) to a Boat Race and Barbicue at Johnson's Ferry. . ."[17]

September 10, 1785 "Rid with Fanny Bassett, Mr. Taylor, and Mr. Shaw, to meet a Party from Alexandria at Johnson's Spring (on my Land where Clifton formerly lived) where we dined on a cold dinner brought from Town by Water, and spent the Afternoon agreeably, returning home by Sun down or a little after it."[18]

Possibly the agreeable afternoon was spent at or near the spot where the present public picnic tables stand on the Mount Vernon Boulevard with a fine view across the Potomac to Fort Washington.

Washington eventually got in all the Spencer half of the original

---

[15]Fairfax County D. B.-D, folio 839.
[16]Snowden, 3rd ed., p. 27.
[17]*Diaries*, Vol. 2, p. 150.
[18]*Ibid.*, p. 412.

five thousand acre patent. As before noted 278 acres came to him from his brother Lawrence. In Liber D of the land records of Prince William County there are recorded in the years 1738 and 1739 a series of deeds from William Spencer, grandson of Nicholas Spencer, to Lawrence Washington, Zephaniah Wade, George Harrison, Richard Osborn, and to Zephaniah Wade and Samuel Magruder, trustees, and to William Marshall, conveying about twenty-five hundred acres. The deeds to Marshall—lease and release—were recorded on November 27th 1739 in Liber D, folios 289 to 291 and 291 to 293, and conveyed to said Marshall eight hundred acres "and all the land the aforesaid William Spencer hath any right to of the aforesaid five thousand acres."

It would be interesting to trace the titles of these grantees of William Spencer to George Washington, but the loss of about half of the Fairfax deed books covering the years when these interests were acquired makes it impossible to trace them and the matter is in no event of much consequence.

When Washington became the owner of Mount Vernon after the death of his brother Lawrence and the settlement with his widow, Ann Fairfax Lee, his nearest neighbor was "Capt." John Posey who owned a farm of 200 acres on the estuary of Dogue Creek. He had acquired it from Washington's youngest brother, Charles, by lease and release,[19] who in turn must have derived his title directly or by mesne conveyance from William Spencer. The first entry in the Washington papers relating to Posey was prophetic of their subsequent relations. "April 1750 Winchester £2,—account with John Posey."[20] He was an amiable, shiftless, irresolute man with a Micawber-like belief that his business troubles would soon take a favorable turn. Washington seems to have been genuinely fond of him for he went hunting with him many times; he dined at Mount Vernon with his first wife, and Washington visited him, usually on the way to his mill.

---

[19]Fairfax D. B. D, pp. 669-670. This deed also conveyed another tract of 145 acres in the branches of Muddy Hole.

[20]Ledger A, (Washington Papers, Library of Congress).

Besides his farm Posey had a valuable fishery and operated a public ferry to Thomas Marshall's on the Maryland shore. His optimism led him to run for Burgess in 1769 against two such formidable candidates as Washington and Colonel John West. He did, however, attain the dignity of a vestryman of Truro Parish from 1765 to 1770.[21]

Posey acted as Washington's agent in the purchase of 210 acres on Dogue Run from William and Diana Whiting for £75. It adjoined property that Washington already owned on the Run. As the Whitings lived in Nangemy Parish, Charles County, Maryland,[22] which Posey knew, and Washington did not, his services may have increased Washington's disposition to help him in his financial difficulties. The transaction seems to have been consummated in 1764. The deed was recorded in one of the lost Fairfax deed books.

In 1765 Washington very unwillingly and to stave off other creditors, loaned Posey £700 and took a mortgage on his land and chattels. He was therefore surprised when in 1767 he received a letter asking an additional loan. He wrote Posey "that instead of being able with the money I agreed to lie somewhat longer out of to discharge your debts, that you wanted to borrow a further sum of £500 to answer this purpose. I was in hopes, and you gave me the strongest assurance to believe, that when I lent you . . . the first sum of £700, you could therewith discharge not only all your creditors, but in two years time sink the principal, which was lent to effect that end; how it comes to pass that instead of being prepared in twice two years to discharge my claim, you should require £500 more to satisfie others, is, as I first said, entirely beyond my comprehension, and leaves but too much cause to apprehend, that if you could be supplied with the further sum required, it would afford but temporary relief; and that at the end of another prefixed period you would be as unprepared and as reluctantly then, as now (to) part with your effects to discharge this debt." and he advised

[21] Slaughter. *History of Truro Parish*, p. 122.
[22] *Diaries*, Vol. 1, p. 339 (note).

Posey to sell his land and make a new start in the "New Settlements upon Monongahela. . . . For proof of which only look to Frederick, and see what Fortunes were made by the Hite's and first takers up of those lands; Nay, how the greatest Estates we have in this Colony were made, was it not by taking up and purchasing at very low rates the rich back Lands which were thought nothing of in those days, but are now the most valuable lands we possess?"[23]

But Posey had no mind to take this advice, nor could Washington have expected that he would. Other creditors were pressing him, John West and Colonel Mason. Washington, however, became surety to the extent of three hundred pounds on the debt to Mason. At the end of a second letter, he adds a postscript: "I have this Instant been informed that you have declard you paid me all you owed me except abt. £20; does such disingenuity as this deserve any favour at my hands? I think any body might readily answer for you, No."[24]

Posey took refuge in Maryland, and there hit upon a new scheme to retrieve his fallen fortunes. He wrote Washington this letter:

"I could have been able to (have) Satisfied all my old Arrears, Some months Ago by marrying (an) old widow woman in this County. She has Large sums (of) cash by her and Prittey good Est.—She is as thick as she is high—and she gits drunk at least three or four (times) a week—which is Disagreeable to me—has a Valiant Sperrit when Drunk—its been (a) Great Dispute in my mind what to Doe,—I believe I shu'd Run all Risk's—if my Last wife, had been an Even temper'd woman—but her Sperrit has Given me such (a) Shock—that I am afraid to run the Resk Again, —when I see the object before my Ey(e)s, (it) is Disagreeable."[25]

He must have married, for Washington's next letter of June 11, 1769 begins: "Hearing from your Son Price and by the Maryland Gazette that you are again entered into the estate of Matrimony, I wish you joy." Then he gave in detail the desperate state of Posey's

---

[23]*Writings*, Vol. 2, pp. 445-456, 458-459.
[24]*Writings*, Vol. 2. pp. 476-477.
[25]Hamilton. *Letters to Washington*, Vol. 4, p. 66.

affairs; stating that a Bill in Chancery had been filed by Hector Ross and others against Posey and himself to sell the land. He then offered to buy the two hundred acres himself, and settle with Ross, Mason and West. Posey did not get the money he expected from his marriage,[26] and apparently did not accept Washington's offer. The deed by which Washington acquired title was recorded in one of the lost Fairfax deed books, but Washington recorded in his *Diary*: "October 23d 1769, Went to Posey's sale." A note by the editor states: "Hector Ross and others obtained a judgment in chancery in the Fairfax Court and the sale of Posey's effects was ordered." So it seems Washington acquired title as the highest bidder at the foreclosure sale. Posey had still six acres purchased from Thomas Hanson Marshall and freed from the lien of his debts by the chancery sale. This he sold to Washington in 1769.[27] He called his plantation, "Rover's Delight."[28] Washington changed its name to "Ferry Farm." He was at Mount Vernon again in 1772, for Washington's Cash Memorandum book for October 14th contains an entry: "By cash, paid Capt. Posey for his Right to 3000 acres of land under ye King's Proclamation of October, 1763. 5 half Joes £11.11.3." He disappears from Washington's Writings. The only other entry on the Fairfax records that has been found mentioning him is the will of Thomas Ford which refers to one of his daughters as Ann, wife of John Posey. He probably continued to live in Charles County, Maryland. Washington bore Posey no ill will. Why should he? He had obtained 210 acres which he needed to round out his estate, a valuable deep water fishery and a ferry which he maintained until about 1790 when "George Augustine Washington, on behalf of the President of the United States, petitioned the Virginia Legislature for permission to close the ferry, which had been operated since 1753 from the land of John Posey, now the property of George Washington (known as the Ferry Farm) to the land of Thomas Marshall in

[26]See Washington's letter to Hector Ross. *Writings*, Vol. 2, p. 525.
[27]*Diaries*, Vol. 2, p. 66.
[28]*Writings*, Vol. 28, p. 166,

Maryland."[29] The ferry was unprofitable and required keeping open a road to it that he wished to close.

Posey had sons, John Price, Thomas, Lawrence; a daughter Milly and perhaps others. Price turned out badly. He was manager for the land of John Parke Custis on the Pamunkey when the latter died in 1781. Washington heard that he had mismanaged the estate, sold slaves and pocketed the money. He wrote him a scathing letter threatening him with prosecution, and in a letter to Bartholomew Dandridge termed him "a most consumate villain" and in a later letter: "Pray, what has become of that Superlative Villain, Posey?"

He contributed to the education of both Thomas and Lawrence. There was one member of the Posey family who won the hearts of the whole Mount Vernon family. She was Milly (Amelia). She was a friend of Patsy Custis. Washington paid for her dancing lessons: "Patsy Custis and Milly Posey went to Colo. Mason's to the Dancing School." The editor of the *Diaries* notes: "By Mr. Christian, Entrance for P. Custis and Milly Posey £2."[30] This was in April 1770 after Milly's father had decamped. She must have lived somewhere in the neighborhood. Mr. Christian was the travelling dancing master who appears in Philip Vickers Fithian's *Journal* in 1773 and 1774 as having classes at Nomini Hall, Bushfield, Chantilly and Stratford. In 1772 there is an entry in the *Diaries*: "Went up in the afternoon with Mrs. Washington, J. P. Custis, Miss Custis and Milly Posey to a Ball in Alexandria."[31] And again: "Rid to my Harvest field in the Neck, with Mrs. Washington, Patcy and Mill(y) Posey." Nor did Washington or Mrs. Washington's interest in her stop with Patsy's death. Mrs. Washington regarded her as protégé, and Washington in his wartime letters to Lund Washington mentions her again and again. Thus: "My best wishes to Milly Posey and all our Neighbors and friends."[32] The last mention of her is in a letter to Lund

[29] *Ibid.*, Vol. 31, p. 134 (note).
[30] *Diaries*, Vol. 1, p. 373.
[31] *Ibid.*, Vol. 2, p. 71.
[32] *Writings*, Vol. 5, p. 462.

dated March 18th, 1781. "She (Mrs. Washington) joins me in best wishes for you, Mrs. (Lund) Washington and Milly Posey."[33] She was then a young woman probably over 25, but she was still "Milly" to Washington. Though she never speaks for herself, the record leaves the impression that she was a lovely young woman. One would like to know more about her. Where did she live? Why does she so suddenly disappear from the Mount Vernon circle of friends? Did she marry, and if so, whom?

Washington appears to have been satisfied with the back line of the Spencer-Washington Patent. The map of his estate which he sent to Arthur Young in 1793 shows his westerly line as extending from a branch of Little Hunting Creek to a branch of Dogue Run, which is substantially the back line of the original patent. The additional tracts he acquired were those of Clifton and Brent on the easterly side of Little Hunting Creek; lands embraced in the Spencer 2500 acres, and lands subsequently devised to Lawrence Lewis and his wife Eleanor.

The list of his taxable lands submitted to the Clerk of Fairfax County in 1761[34] includes two parcels of 135 acres each "bot of William and George Ashford." Their deed to Washington dated January 29, 1761 recites that they derive title from a deed of their father Michael Ashford, made in 1729 and from his will proved in 1734. The two tracts embraced land on both sides of Dogue Run.[35] The consideration is £150 for each.

The same tax list also includes 500 acres "bot of Darrel." This was conveyed to Washington by Sampson Darrell by deed dated in July 1761, and was recited to be the same land granted to Sampson Darrell, grandfather of the grantor, by the Proprietor's deed dated November 28th 1694. It could not have been part of the Spencer Tract.[36]

Sampson Darrell was sheriff of Fairfax County in 1767, and with John Posey was appointed by the Truro Vestry processioner

[33]*Ibid.*, Vol. 21, p. 387.
[34]*Ibid.*, Vol. 2, p. 390.
[35]Fairfax D. B. E, pp. 22, 24.
[36]Fairfax D. B. D, pp. 681-683.

of the land between Hunting Creek and Dogue Run. The Fairfax records do not show a will of his nor any adminstration on his estate. He left a son, Augustine, who was at Mount Vernon several times. There was an estate called Darrell's Hill between Alexandria and Mount Vernon, to which Washington refers several times, but whether that was the home of Sampson Darrell or his brother William is not known.

Washington's next purchase was from Thomas Hanson Marshall of Marshall Hall, Maryland. It will be remembered that William Marshall, probably the father of Thomas Hanson, had acquired eight hundred acres from William Spencer by the deed recorded in the Prince William deed book D. From his camp at White Plains he wrote Lund Washington in August, 1778:

"I have premised these things to shew my inability, not my unwillingness, to purchase the Lands in my own Neck at (almost) any price. and this I am yet very desirous of doing if it could be accomplished by any means in my power, in the way of Barter for other Land; for Negroes (of whom I every day long more and more to get clear of) or in short for any thing else (except Breeding Mares and Stock of other kinds) which I have in my possession; but for money I cannot, I want the means. Marshalls Land alone, at the rate he talks of, would amount to (if my memory of the quantity he holds, is right) upwards of £3000, a sum I have little chance, if I had much inclination, to pay; and therefore would not engage for it, as I am resolved not to incumber myself with Debt.

"Marshall is not a necessitous Man, is only induced to offer his Land for Sale in expectation of a high price; and knowing perhaps but too well my wish to become possessed of the Land in that Neck will practice every deception in his power to work me (or you in my behalf) up to his price, or he will not sell."[87]

Washington thought the land he wished to purchase contained about 500 acres. He must have bought it, as the index of Fairfax

[87] *Writings*, Vol. 12, pp. 326-327.

deeds show such a conveyance, but the Liber in which it was recorded is missing.

After his acquisition of the Marshall lands Washington owned all the land in his neck between Little Hunting Creek and Dogue Run, except two contiguous parcels, one, held by Elizabeth Dulany, wife of Benjamin Dulany, daughter and devisee of her father, Daniel French,[38] subject to the life estate of her mother, Penelope French; the other belonging to the estate of Harrison Manley, whose executors were William Triplett and others. The French tract comprised about 500 acres, the Manley parcel 142 acres. They lay, like a Naboth's vineyard, surrounded on all sides, except the water front, by Washington's holdings. He must have them. Then he would have gotten in all the Spencer 2500 acres. Triplett was willing to sell, but Penelope French and the Dulanys—that was another matter. Neither Mrs. French nor Dulany and his wife lived on the tract. They had a quarter there—an overseer with slaves—and the land fronted on navigable water. He seems to have known he could not buy it and so he proposed another scheme. He wrote to Dulany: "If there are Lands for which Mrs. French and you are disposed to barter your tract on Dogue-run; and these lands can be had upon reasonable terms; it will in the end be the same thing to me as a direct purchase."[39]

An agreement was finally reached by which Washington bought a tract on Great Hunting Creek near Alexandria and conveyed it to Elizabeth Dulany as devisee of Daniel French; and Dulany and his wife conveyed the land on Dogue Run to Washington.[40] Washington's instructions for drawing the deed are set out in a letter to his attorney, Charles Lee: "The original grant to Spencer and Washington comprehends all the land Mr. and Mrs. Dulany

---

[38]Daniel French of "Rose Hill" on the Franconia Road, Fairfax County, was a member of the Truro Vestry from 1744 to 1748. He was the contractor for Pohick Church but died in 1771 before completing the building, which was finished by his executor, George Mason. Washington noted in his diary that he attended the funeral. He married Penelope Manley, the sister of Harrison Manley, and left an only child, Elizabeth, who married Benjamin Dulany. The solid walls and good workmanship of Pohick Church are his memorial. His will is recorded in the Fairfax Will, Book C, pp. 134-136.

[39]*Writings*, Vol. 24, p. 69.

[40]*Ibid.*, Vol. 28, pp. 60-61.

Courtesy Virginia State Chamber of Commerce

Pohick Church (Page 157)

Home of William Ramsay, Fairfax and King Streets,
Alexandria, Virginia (Page 167)

Photographed by Frank W. Vedder

are to give for mine; and these are held by purchases from Richd. Osborne (the quantity I know not), Arbuthnot for 150 Acres; Manley for 68 acres; and John Posey for 136 Acres."[41] Washington agreed to pay Mrs. Penelope French a specified yearly rental for her interest in the tract. The deed of French and wife to Washington was recorded in the Fairfax Deed Book P, pages 318-328, on February 21st, 1785. It names the different tracts embraced, but does not give the acreage.

The deed from William Triplett, Edward Sanford and Margaret Sanford, his wife (formerly widow of Harrison Manley, surviving executors of Harrison Manley), to George Washington conveyed 142 acres, part of the patent granted to Nicholas Spencer and Col. John Washington.[42] The will of Harrison Manley is recorded in the Fairfax Will Book C, page 215.

Washington's Mill

As stated earlier, the original mill on the Mount Vernon estate was built on Dogue Run by Augustine Washington on land which stood in the name of his son, Lawrence. Lawrence in turn willed the estate to his wife Anne, for her life, and remainder to his infant daughter, and if the daughter should die without issue, then to his brother, George. The child survived her father, but died soon after. Anne Washington, Lawrence's widow, married George Lee. She and her husband made a deed to George Washington conveying the life interest of Anne Lee "in two parcels of land, one situated on Little Hunting Creek, the other on Dogue Creek . . . of which Lawrence Washington died seized, also one water Grist Mill." This was in 1752. Washington's *Diaries* show the mill was badly damaged in 1760 by a freshet; that a new mill was then under consideration, but apparently the existing one was repaired, as after the repairs were completed he made an entry that "all her works were decayed and out of order." The entries show that from December 1769 to July 1770 the mill was completely

[41] *Ibid.*, page 76.
[42] Fairfax D. B. Q, pp. 295-297.

rebuilt under the superintendence of John Ball, millwright, living at Cameron.[43]

"Across from the mill was a wharf where flat boats and small schooners were loaded with flour for England and the West Indies. Corn and other grains were ground as well as wheat. The mill did much grinding for farmers in the neighborhood, the toll exacted being one-eighth. . . Considerable difficulty was experienced in operating the Dogue Run mill due to variations in the supply of water. Floods in winter and spring and dry spells in summer were experienced. In 1757 Washington's miller, W. A. Poole, complained that he had been able to grind but little because 'she fails by want of water.' The lack of water was partly remedied in 1771 by turning the water of Piney Branch into the run."[44] This branch had previously flowed into Dogue Run below the millpond. Washington's will bequeathed to Lawrence Lewis and Eleanor Parke Lewis the Woodlawn tract "together with the Mill Distillery and all other houses and improvements on the premises." Major Lewis continued to operate the mill, probably until his death in 1839. In 1846 Woodlawn Plantation (and probably the mill) was bought by a group of Quakers. The mill building was standing until shortly before the Civil War. It gradually deteriorated and the stones were taken away for other uses until nothing remained but the foundation. "As plans were being developed for the Washington Bi-Centennial Celebration, interest was aroused in the restoration of the old mill." The Conservation and Development Commission of Virginia purchased a tract on Dogue Run including the mill site. Before the work of the restoration was begun, careful excavations were made and a thorough study was made of available documents, including letters from Lund Washington to George Washington and a Journal of Nicholas Cresswell who had visited the mill in 1774. "It was found that the Fortsmouth mill near Front Royal, Virginia, possessed intact a complete set of machinery of the same general period as the Washington mill." This was pur-

[43]Stetson. *Four Mile Run Land Grants*, p. 94 (note).
[44]*George Washington's Grist Mill.* An unpaged pamphlet distributed at the mill.

chased and installed in the restored Dogue Run Mill. A miller's cottage, duplicating the one used in Washington's day, has been built close to the mill. The mill has been leased from the Virginia Conservation Commission by the Future Farmers of America and is maintained and kept open to the public by that body, a national organization of farm boys studying vocational agriculture in public high schools, which owns a summer camp nearby.[45]

Mount Vernon since the death of Washington

Washington's will gave his widow a life estate in Mount Vernon and the Mansion House Farm. She died in May 1802. The estate then passed under the will to Bushrod Washington. He married Anne, daughter of Colonel Thomas Blackburn, of Rippon Lodge, Prince William County. They lived at Mount Vernon until Bushrod's death in 1829. They had no children. His means were limited, as the salaries paid to Supreme Court judges in those days were modest indeed. He had been appointed a Justice of the Supreme Court of the United States by President Adams. The hospitality he was obliged to maintain must have been a severe strain on his resources.

In 1824 Lafayette and his son, George Washington, came to Mount Vernon again, coming by steamboat from Washington, visiting first the tomb, which the Marquis entered alone and knelt for a long time over the sarcophagus in the old vault. He then took George in. He was met there by George Washington Parke Custis who addressed him: "Last of the Generals of the Army of Independence! At this awful and impressive moment, when forgetting the splendors of a triumph greater than Roman consul ever had, you bend with reverence over the remains of Washington, the child of Mount Vernon presents you with this token containing the hair of him whom while living you loved, and to whose honored grave you now pay the manly and affecting tribute of a patriot's and a soldier's tear,"[46] and Custis continued for ten or fifteen minutes

[45]This section is based on *George Washington's Grist Mill*, an unpaged pamphlet distributed at the mill.

[46]Custis, G. W. P. Recollections, p. 592.

in the same strain. Where Judge Bushrod Washington was does not appear. He may have been on circuit duty, and so escaped Custis' eloquence. He died in Philadelphia in 1829. His wife died a few days later. They were buried side by side in the old family vault (for the present vault was not built until 1831). His will divided the Mansion House Farm among his nephews and a niece. The home itself, the river front and the surrounding land of about 1228 acres was devised to John Augustine Washington, son of Bushrod's brother Corbin. This John Augustine took possession of the Mansion, but died in 1832. He devised all his property to his wife Jane, with power to divide it as she pleased among her children. She made a deed, recorded among the Fairfax Land Records in 1850, conveying the Mount Vernon estate to her eldest son, John Augustine Washington. She confirmed it by her will made in 1855. John Augustine Washington was the last private owner of Mount Vernon.

President Washington had large means and had been able to sustain the heavy expense of maintaining Mount Vernon. He took pride in the fertility of his farms, and gave them his personal attention. None of the subsequent owners had the means or ability to do this. When the second John Augustine acquired the Mansion, George Washington had been dead half a century. Much of what had been cultivated land had reverted to its wild state. Cedars, pines and undergrowth covered it. Had its last private owner possessed the means, it would have required a fortune to keep it in repair, and to entertain the numerous guests who still thronged it. He received various offers to purchase, but he refused. He held it that the United States Government or the State of Virginia might acquire it and care for it. Mount Vernon seemed doomed to decay and perhaps to disappear; to suffer the fate of the neighboring Hollin Hall of the Masons; West Grove of the Wests; Wakefield where Washington had been born; Society Hill of the Thorntons; Nomini Hall of the Carters, Leesylvania of the Lees, and others.

The salvation of Mount Vernon came from a Miss Anna Pamela Cunningham of South Carolina, an invalid of dauntless spirit. She began a crusade for funds to purchase Mount Vernon to be held by representative women in trust for the people of the United States. Her plan was to select a woman from each state of the Union as a regent. The Mount Vernon Ladies Association of the Union was chartered by the State of Virginia in 1856. The act provided for a Regent, and Vice Regents from each state. Miss Cunningham was the first Regent. The estate was exempted from taxation. Funds came from various sources, notably from Edward Everett, President of Harvard College, who travelled through the different states, delivering his oration on the character of Washington and devoting the proceeds to the purchase. In December 1859 the whole purchase price, $200,000 was raised and early in 1860 possession of two hundred acres delivered.

On the outbreak of the Civil War, John Augustine Washington joined the Confederate Army and was killed on September 13, 1861 in the battle of Cheat Mountain, West Virginia. The condition of the Mansion at the time of the purchase was deplorable. The great east portico was crumbling and was only prevented from falling by timbers hewed from the forest to reinforce the rotted columns. The wharf was strengthened and a small steamer was purchased for passenger service. It was from this source that the Association derived its first revenue. The house was painted and new cypress shingles put on the roof. In the War, both sides respected Mount Vernon, though the steamer which had carried visitors was taken over by Federal Government for transport service. In the years following the war the Association was so poor it was unable to pay a superintendent's salary and Miss Cunningham came to Mount Vernon and lived there, directing operations from 1868 to 1872 when ill health forced her to resign. During the succeeding years, some of the original furniture has been acquired and many duplicates procured. The restoration is now practically complete. The Mansion House, the outbuildings and the grounds present much the same appearance as they did when Washington died.[47]

A young westerner whom the author took to Mount Vernon said: "This is the most beautiful place I have ever seen."

[47]Paul Wilstach's *Mount Vernon* and Harrison Howell Dodge's *Mount Vernon* have supplied most of the facts of this section.

Chapter 13

Woodlawn

Woodlawn is situated on an eminence a little more than two miles west of Mount Vernon. It was a part of that estate in Washington's day and was called Gray's Hill. It overlooks the tidal estuary of Dogue Run, with the Potomac River and the hills of Belvoir in the distance. It was, as Washington wrote, "a most beautiful Site for a Gentleman's Seat." It was bequeathed by his will to Lawrence Lewis and Eleanor Parke Lewis, his wife. Eleanor, familiarly called Nelly, was Mrs. Washington's granddaughter, who, it will be recalled, was reared at Mount Vernon after her father's death. Nelly Custis had never known any other father, and Washington, having no children, gave her all the affection he would have given a child of his own. She grew up a beautiful and accomplished young woman. Washington was naturally grave and not given overmuch to laughter, but Nelly wrote of him: "I have sometimes made him laugh most heartily from sympathy with my joyous and extravagant spirits."

Miss Custis's exalted station and her charms attracted admirers. On March 22, 1798 Washington noted in his *Diary*: "Mr. Charles Carroll, Jun. and Mr. William Lee came to dinner." A note by the editor states: "This visit of young Carroll gave rise to talk in Annapolis that he was paying his addresses to Eleanor Parke Custis. George Washington Parke Custis, then a student at St. John's College, at Annapolis, wrote approving the match."[1]

Washington was none too well pleased by the news, for he wrote

[1]*Diaries*, Vol. 4, p. 273.

to Custis: "Young Mr. C—— came here about a fortnight ago to dinner, and left us next morning after breakfast. If his object was such as you say has been reported, it was not declared here; and therefore, the less said upon the subject, particularly by your sister's friends, the more prudent it will be until the subject develops itself more."[2]

In the meantime Lawrence Lewis had come to live at Mount Vernon to help Washington, who had written August 4, 1797 explaining his need: "As both your aunt and I are in the decline of life, and regular in our habits, especially in our hours of rising and going to bed, I require some person (fit and Proper) to ease me of the trouble of entertaining company, particularly of nights, as it is my inclination to retire (and unless prevented by very particular company, always do retire) either to bed, or to my study, soon after candle-light. In taking these duties (which hospitality obliges one to bestow on company) off my hands, it would render me a very acceptable service, and for a little time only, to come, an hour in the day, now and then devoted to the recording of some Papers which time would not allow me to complete before I left Philadelphia, would also be acceptable. . . ."[3]

Lawrence Lewis and Nelly Custis living in the same house soon fell in love. The General was fond of both and encouraged the alliance. His diary for February 22, 1799 contains this entry: "The Revd Mr. Davis and Mr. Geo. Calvert came to dinner and Miss Custis was married abt. Candle light to Mr. Lawe. Lewis."

As a wedding gift Washington announced that he had set aside two thousand acres, including part of his Dogue Run Farm, the grist mill and distillery, which they were to inherit on his death. At his request they remained at Mount Vernon to assist in entertaining the constant stream of visitors, though he urged them to start building at once, stating that it was unlikely that any act of theirs would cause his displeasure and thus cancel the provisions of the will.

---

[2]*Writings*, Vol. 36, p. 246.
[3]*Ibid.*, p. 3.

"Nelly and Lawrence Lewis resided at Mount Vernon until after the death of Mrs. Washington in 1802, when she wrote a friend, 'I live now in sight of Mount Vernon, and it is a continued source of uneasiness to reflect on lives past which can never be recalled.' But life went on and the Lewises became firmly established at Woodlawn Plantation—first in the wings of the intended house and then in the mansion when it was completed, about 1805. Nelly Custis, having been carefully trained by her grandmother, had developed into a cultured and accomplished woman, famous for her beauty, her wit, and charm. Painting, needlework, poetry and music were numbered among her talents, and these, together with her other social graces, were in turn transplanted to her own home and family circle. It was a considerable novelty, she admitted, to preside in a home of her own. There were eight children born to the Lewises—four girls and four boys. Two daughters were born while Nelly and Lawrence Lewis resided at Mount Vernon.

"The Mount Vernon tradition of hospitality and gracious living quite naturally took root at Woodlawn Plantation. Many of the Washington furnishings went to equip the great house of the Lewises. General Washington had left to Mrs. Washington all the household effects of Mount Vernon, most of which she divided among Nelly and the other three grandchildren. Many additional heirlooms passed to Woodlawn by bequest; still others were acquired by the Lewises at the private sales opened to the heirs. The proverbial traditions of the parent estate came to be associated with the new.

"The Lewises were on friendly terms with Washington officialdom of their time and entertained many famous people. The Marquis de Lafayette was a very special guest who came to pay his respects to 'Miss Nelly,' whom he had known as a child. Henry Clay, Zachary Taylor, Andrew Jackson and Millard Fillmore were particular friends. Visitors discribed the house as elegant and the entertainment lavish."[4]

---

[4]Woodlawn Plantation, Mount Vernon, Virginia. A folder prepared by the National Trust for Historic Preservation.

By the middle of the nineteenth century southern Fairfax suffered a depression. Many of the old families had deserted it. The McCartys had abandoned Cedar Grove and moved to Loudoun. The Mount Vernon estate of Judge Bushrod Washington was poorly cultivated, and many of the fields that George Washington had cultivated were abandoned and overgrown. George Mason's great Gunston estate was divided among his sons, or those of them who remained there, and their wealth was dissipated. Under such circumstances it was not strange that Lawrence Lewis purchased Audley in the lower Shenandoah Valley, where the Burwells, the Randolphs, the Pages and the Wormeleys had preceded him. He died in 1839 at Arlington and was buried at Mount Vernon. His widow then moved with her eldest son, Lorenzo, to Audley in Clarke County. In 1846 Woodlawn was sold to a group of Quakers. Nelly Custis Lewis died at Audley in 1852 and was buried at Mount Vernon. Catherine Prescott Wormeley once asked Mrs. Lewis if she had ever seen Washington lose his temper. Mrs. Lewis told her that she and her brother were sliding down the banisters at Mount Vernon, when Washington came out of a side room and boxed their ears. Miss Wormeley said that she always felt nearer to Washington after hearing that. From 1889 to 1901 Woodlawn was unoccupied and falling into ruins, when it was purchased and rehabilitated by Paul Kester, playwright. In 1905 it was purchased and extensively repaired by Miss Elizabeth M. Sharpe, from whom it passed in 1925 to Senator and Mrs. Oscar Underwood of Alabama. The Woodlawn Public Foundation, Inc. acquired the mansion in 1949. In 1951 administration of the Plantation was turned over to the National Trust for Historic Preservation in the United States. Much of the information as to the later history of Woodlawn has been taken from a folder issued by the National Trust for Historic Preservation.

Chapter 14

Pohick Church

Pohick Church is on the main road from Alexandria to Fredericksburg, six miles from Mount Vernon. The Colonial Church of Virginia was established by law and divided into parishes created by acts of the Assembly. One of these was Truro Parish, formed in 1732, and comprising all the present Fairfax and Loudoun Counties. It was named after the town of Truro in Cornwall, England. The existing brick church was begun in 1769 and completed in 1774. The contractor (styled undertaker) was Daniel French of Rose Hill. The consideration was the sum of eight hundred and seventy-seven pounds, current money of Virginia. French died before completing the contract and the final payment was made to his executors. The church superseded an earlier frame building two miles south of the present one and near Colchester.

Bishop Meade preserved a tradition which may or may not be true, but is interesting enough to reproduce here. "The Old Pohick Church was a frame building and occupied a site on the south side of Pohick Run, and about two miles from the present site which is on the north side of the run. When it was no longer fit for use, it is said the parishioners were called together to determine on the locality of the new Church, when George Mason, the compatriot of Washington, advocated the old site, pleading that it was the house in which their fathers worshipped and that the graves of many were around it, while Washington and others advocated a more central and convenient one. The question was left unsettled and another meeting for its decision appointed. Meanwhile Washington surveyed the neighborhood, and marked the houses and distances on a well-drawn map, and when the day of the decision arrived, met all the arguments of his opponent by presenting this paper, and thus carried his point." The story in the form the Bishop gave it cannot be accurate. The vestry and not the parishioners decided the location, but independently of its accuracy, Mason's position was untenable. When the old site was selected in the late seventeenth century, the population of the vicinity was sparse and centered mainly around the Occoquan. In 1769 the old site was convenient to Mason and a few other families, but distant from most of the parish members.

The *Vestry Book* recites the Act of the Assembly prescribing that the Sheriff of the County should summon the freeholders and housekeepers to meet and elect so many of the "most able and discreet persons of the Parish as shall make up the number of Vestrymen in said parish to twelve and no more." The vestrymen then became a closed corporation and, as vacancies occurred, chose their successors—"twelve lords of the parish," they were satirically called. Their duties were religious and secular. They fixed the amount of the tithes to be levied each year; engaged and paid the rector, erected churches and chapels as the need arose, provided the rector with a farm, or Glebe; provided for the poor of the parish, and processioned the roads; that is, fixed the boundaries of the lands of each proprietor on the public roads to prevent future disputes. The vestry elected two of their number as Church Wardens, whose duty it was to present to the Court of the County persons guilty of profanity, drunkenness, gambling, Sabbath breaking, failure to attend church, etc. The fines imposed by the courts went to the Wardens for the use of the Church,[1] but after the middle of the eighteenth century such prosecutions became rare.

The Vestry at the time the contract was made for building the new church consisted of Daniel French, Daniel McCarty, Edward Payne, George Washington, George William Fairfax, John Posey,

[1]*History of Truro Parish*, by Philip Slaughter, p. 28.

William Gardner and Tz. Ellzey. The building committee appointed to supervise the erection of the church was a notable one —the "Honble George Wm. Fairfax, George Washington, and George Mason Esqrs, Captn. Daniel McCarty and Mr. Edward Payne."

Two rectors served the church for fifty years: Charles Green and Lee Massey. Both were natives of the Colony. Green was recommended by Washington's father, Capt. Augustine Washington, in 1735. He went to England, was ordained by the Bishop of London, and became minister of the parish in 1736. He had formerly practiced medicine, and continued to prescribe for his parishioners thereafter. It appears that he attended both Washington and Mrs. Washington in sickness. In 1752 a brick house was built for him on his Glebe at Newington about two miles north of the church. In his later years he suffered from ill health. His will, probated in Fairfax in 1765, devised 3000 acres of land in Prince William, Fairfax and Loudoun counties to his wife, Margaret, which he advised her to sell, and return to her home in Dublin, Ireland.

His successor was the beloved Lee Massey (1732-1814). He studied law in the office of the well known lawyer George Johnston of Alexandria, and married his daughter. After the death of the Reverend Charles Green, Massey, at the solicitation of Washington, Mason and others of the congregation, took holy orders. He served Pohick until 1777. He developed an impediment of speech, which caused him to resign from the ministry. He then studied medicine but refused to accept fees for his services to the poor. He retired to his seat, "Bradley," on the Occoquan below Colchester, where he died in his eighty-eighth year and was buried in a private graveyard on his estate. In recent years his bones have been reinterred under the pulpit of his church.

Washington was elected a member of the Vestry in 1765 and was active in parochial affairs until 1775 when he left Mount Vernon to take command of the Continental Army. In 1772 he purchased a pew, No. 28, immediately in front of the chancel, for sixteen pounds, and subsequently acquired a pew back of it from his kinsman, Lund Washington. Col. George Mason purchased two pews "adjoining the south wall of the church." Others who purchased pews were George William Fairfax, Alexander Henderson, Martin Cockburn, Daniel McCarty, J. W. Coffer, William Triplett, and Harrison Manley.

The high pulpit with its sounding board and its stairs was located on the north side of the church, and the rector's pew was next to it. All the pews were large, oblong shaped, and could accommodate a dozen persons. Other pews were provided for Magistrates, Vestryman, Merchants, and Strangers and their wives. The Communion Table, enclosed by a railing, was at the east end of the church (as required by canon law), and on the wall above it the Altar Piece with the customary tablets containing the Lord's Prayer, the Creed and the Ten Commandments in gilt letters.

The new church had been finished only three years when its troubles began. The parish levy of 1776 was the largest ever collected, but it was the last ever levied, for in 1777 levies for the support of the old Colonial Church were suspended and afterward abolished by Acts of the Virginia Assembly. The clergy were thenceforth to be supported by voluntary contributions.[2] Many of the leading men were in the American Army. George William Fairfax was in England and was fated never to return to America. George Mason, while not unfriendly to Pohick Church, was one of the leaders in the movement to disestablish it and to take away its tithes. Lee Massey's disabilities prevented his preaching and there was no money available to pay his salary. Regular services were discontinued, though we hear of the eccentric Mr. Weems conducting occasional services. After the Revolution, Washington and perhaps others of the old congregation attended church in Alexandria. When Bishop Meade wrote of the church, many of the doors of the pews, including those of Washington and Mason, were gone; others, including those of George William Fairfax,

[2]*Ibid.*, page 93.

Martin Cockburn, Daniel McCarty, Edward Payne and the rectors, were still standing and their names legible. Although there was no regular minister after Lee Massey retired, occasional services were held for some years. Washington noted in his diary for Sunday Oct. 15, 1786, "Accompained by Majr. Washington, his wife, Mr. Lear, and Nellie and Washington Custis, went to Pohick Church," and another occasion in 1788 he went to Pohick Church on a Sunday.[3]

John Davis, the English tutor of the Ellicott children of Rockledge, Occoquan, wrote in his usual florid style: "About eight miles from the Occoquan Mills is a house of worship called Pohick Church, a name it claims from a run that flows near its walls. Hither I rode on Sunday and joined the congregation of Parson Weems, a minister of the Episcopel persuasion, who was cheerful in his mien that he might win men to religion. A Virginian churchyard on a Sunday resembles rather a race-course than a sepulchral ground; the ladies come to it in carriages, and the men after dismounting from their horses make them fast to the trees. But the steeples to the Virginia churches were designed not for utility but ornament; for the bell is always suspended to a tree. . . I was confounded on first entering the church at Pohick to hear,

'Steed threaten steed with high and boastful neigh.'

Nor was I less stunned with rattling of carriage-wheels, the cracking of whips, and the vociferations of the gentlemen to the negroes who accompained them."[4]

Weems had the impudence to call himself "Rector of Mount Vernon Parish." The lamp of Pohick was already fluttering; it was soon extinguished for many years. The last Vestry meeting for which we have evidence was held at Colchester in 1785.

During the Civil War the church was occupied and much abused by Federal soldiers. Today the restoration of the church is complete and the visitor sees it as it was in its prime. A brick wall surrounds

---

[3]*Diaries*, Vol. 3, pp. 125 and 436.

[4]Howe's Historic Collections—quoted by Rowland in *Life and Correspondence of George Mason,* Vol. 1, p. 115.

the church and graveyard, the latter well filled with graves. The vestry building whose erection was deferred by the Revolutionary War has been built. Sunday services are held, attended by a good congregation, and it appears to be a very active rural church. Best of all, its *Vestry Book*, about which Bishop Meade could learn nothing, was found by the Rev. Philip Slaughter and given to the church.

Courtesy Virginia State Chamber of Commerce

Christ Church, Alexandria, Virginia *(Pages 170 and 171)*

Courtesy Virginia State Chamber of Commerce

Gadsby's Tavern (Pages 174 to 177)

Chapter 15

Alexandria

No account of Washington's neighbors would be adequate which did not contain some account of the two towns with which he was most intimately connected, Alexandria and Colchester.

Alexandria lay at the south end of the six thousand acres patented by Robert Howsing in 1669. The land was soon transferred by him to John Alexander, the surveyor. In 1731 the Hunting Creek warehouse was built. It was operated by Hugh West and a tiny settlement grew up around it, named Belhaven, after the Scottish nobleman of the name. In 1749 the Assembly of Virginia passed an "Act for erecting a town at Hunting Creek Warehouse in the County of Fairfax." The Act recited that "it hath been represented to this present General Assembly that a town at Hunting Creek Warehouse on Potomack River would be commodious for trade and navigation and tend greatly to the ease and advantage of the frontier inhabitants."[1] The charter of Alexandria reads in part as follows: "Be it therefore enacted by the Lieutenant Governor, Council and Burgesses of this present General Assembly, and it is hereby enacted by the authority of the same, that within four months after the passage of this act, sixty acres of land, parcel of the lands of Philip Alexander, John Alexander and Hugh West, situate, lying and being on the south side of Potomac River, above the mouth of Great Hunting Creek and in the County of Fairfax shall be surveyed and laid out by the surveyor of said County . . . and the said sixty acres of land so surveyed and laid out shall

[1]*Landmarks*, Vol. 2, pp. 670-675.

be, and is hereby vested in the Right Honorable Thomas Lord Fairfax, the Honorable William Fairfax, Esq., George Fairfax, Richard Osborne, Lawrence Washington, William Ramsay, John Carlyle, John Pagan, Gerard Alexander and Hugh West of the said county of Fairfax, gentlemen, and Philip Alexander of the County of Stafford, gentleman, and their successors in trust for the several purposes thereinafter mentioned. . .

"And when the said town shall be so laid out the said Directors and Trustees shall have full power and authority to sell all the said lots by public sale or auction, from time to time, to the highest bidder so as no person shall have more than two lots, and when any such lots shall be sold, any two of such Trustees shall and may upon payment of the purchase money, by some sufficient conveyance or conveyances, convey the Fee Simple estate of such lot or lots to the purchaser or purchasers, and he or they, or his or their heirs and assigns, respectively shall and may forever thereafter peaceable and quietly have, hold, possess and enjoy free and discharged from all Right, Title, Claim, interest and demand whatsoever of the said Philip Alexander, John Alexander and Hugh West and their heirs and assigns of them respectively, and all persons whatsoever claiming by, from or under them or either of them.

"Provided, nevertheless, That the said Trustees and Directors after deducting sufficient to reimburse the charge and expense of surveying and laying out the said lots, shall pay or cause to be paid, to the said Philip Alexander, John Alexander and Hugh West all the money arising by the sale of said lots according to their respective rights therein. . ."

The Act next directs "that the grantee or grantees of every such lot or lots . . . shall within two years next after the date of the conveyance of the same, erect, build and finish on each lot so conveyed one house of Brick, Stone, or Wood well framed of the dimensions of twenty feet square and nine feet pitch, at the least, or proportionately thereto, if such Grantee shall have two lots contiguous, with a brick or stone chimney."

The Act provides for forfeiture of title for failure to comply with the condition of building one house or more; and that the Trustees shall use the proceeds of the resale of such lots for "such public use for the common benefit of the Inhabitants of the said Town as to them shall seem most proper."

A further provision is to the effect that on the death, or failure to act, of any Director or Trustee, the survivors may name a successor by an instrument in writing under their Hands and Seals. An earlier section provided that no wooden chimney should be built, or if built might be pulled down by the sheriff.

A final provision gave the town the name of Alexandria.

Who was the surveyor who laid off Alexandria? It is sometimes said that George Washington, then seventeen years old, was the official surveyor. John C. Fitzpatrick, the scholarly editor of Washington's *Writings* and *Diaries*, made the statement: "The map division of the Library of Congress has recently acquired a plan of Alexandria drawn by Washington in 1749 which shows that that youthful surveyor had the privilege of laying off the town site."[2] That there is a plat of the town in Washington's handwriting is undoubted, but it does not follow that he was the official surveyor. When Alexandria was laid off, the law required that any town should "be surveyed by the surveyor of said county" and the Act of the Virginia Assembly authorizing the establishment of the town specifically provided that the work should be done by the surveyor of Fairfax County.

The plat of the town is recorded in the earliest *Survey Book* of Fairfax County. It was attested by John West Jr. Washington's name does not appear on the plat. Probably John West was glad to have Washington's assistance, as his reputation as a surveyor had been established by his surveys in the Shenandoah Valley for Lord Fairfax.

The region around Alexandria soon turned from tobacco to wheat. Long canvas-topped wagons, filled with the grain, poured into the town from the neighboring country and from Frederick county. Flour mills were built, adding to the prosperity of the grow-

[2]*Diaries,* Vol. 1, p. 120 (note).

ing town. The same was true of Colchester, but on a smaller scale.

Thus, we find Washington writing to Carlyle and Adam on March 9, 1765: "As soon as Mr. Lund Washington returns from Fredk. I shall cause my Wheat to be delivered to your landing on Four Mile Run Creek, if Flats can get to it conveniently. . ."[3] The Four Mile Run Mill suffered the fate of Dumfries on Quantico Creek. The mill was located on the road from Alexandria to Georgetown, where it crosses the run. As late as the Civil War it is shown on a wartime map as Roach's Mill, but Four Mile Run had ceased to be navigable to that point long before then.

Washington built a house in Alexandria in 1769. The names of the streets of the town show the devotion of its founders to the Royal Family; King Street was then and is now the main street. Parallel to it are Duke and Prince on the south, and north of it are Cameron, Queen, and Princess streets. Running north and south are Fairfax, Royal, Pitt and St. Asaph. The last was named in honor of the Bishop of St. Asaph, who espoused the cause of the colonists in the Revolutionary War. The name of "Washington" Street needs no explanation. It was not a street of the originial town.

The chief concern of the new town was to establish a road to the Shenandoah Valley. The road then laid out was the Leesburg turnpike. Leesburg was not yet in existence. John Minor had an ordinary at the crossing of two roads where the future Leesburg was to be built. The road then led northwesterly through the Hillsborough Gap, and crossed the Blue Ridge at Vestal's (now Crampton's) Gap to Charlestown, now in West Virginia. The Little River Turnpike was laid off in 1802, to take the place of the Braddock Road. Its grades were less sharp than those of the latter road. The Little River Turnpike was continued, under another name, to Snicker's Gap. A prime concern of the founders of Alexandria was to secure overseas markets for its wheat. The Navigation Acts limited the trade of the colonies to England (which later included Scotland under the act of Union) and her West Indies islands. The merchants of the town sent their wheat to Baltimore and Philadelphia

---

[3]*Writings*, Vol. 2, p. 422.

as well as to Jamaica and the other British West Indies. In 1740 a public ferry was established from Hunting Creek warehouse on land of Hugh West to Fraziers Point in Maryland.[4]

The Fathers of Alexandria

William Ramsay, like John Carlyle, was born in Scotland, and like him settled first in Dumfries; from there they both moved to Alexandria, realizing astutely that the chances for mercantile success lay in Alexandria rather than in Dumfries. Ramsay bought lots forty-six and forty-seven on the southeast corner of King and Fairfax streets and built on lot 47. He served his adopted town in many capacities, as town overseer, census taker, postmaster, member of the Committee of Safety, colonel of the militia regiment, town trustee, gentleman justice, and crowned his civic career as Lord Mayor. As such he was given a gold chain and medal which styled him the Romulus of Alexandria. In 1773 he bought pew No. 20 in Christ Church for £33. He married Ann McCarty, daughter of Dennis McCarty of Cedar Grove. He was a signer of the Fairfax County Resolutions, passed in 1774, which urged the creation of a county militia to defend the colony from British aggression, and in the war that followed was a staunch adherent of the American cause. He died in 1785 in his sixty-ninth year. His will was probated in that year and recorded in the Fairfax *Will Book E*. His son, Colonel Dennis Ramsay, was a pallbearer at Washington's funeral.[5]

Washington noted in his *Diary*: "February 12, 1785. Received an Invitation to the Funeral of Willm. Ramsay Esqr. of Alexandria, the oldest Inhabitt of the Town; and went up. Walked in a procession as a free mason, Mr. Ramsay in his life being one, and now buried with the ceremonies and honors due to one."[6]

William Ramsay is buried in the graveyard of Christ Church.

[4]Virginia *Guide*, p. 193.
[5]Moore, Gay Montague. *Seaport in Virginia*, pp. 52-61 (hereafter cited as Moore).
[6]*Diaries*, Vol. 2, p. 342.

John Carlyle

John Carlyle was born in 1720 in Dumfrieshire, Scotland, and came to Dumfries, Virginia. Finding that Dumfries depended too much on the tobacco trade, he moved to Alexandria and speedily became the richest man in the town. He built the most imposing building there. Thomas Tileston Waterman's conjectural restoration shows a center building with two smaller buildings with two covered buildings joining them to the center building, much in the same fashion as the curved connecting buildings of Mount Airy in Richmond County.[7] The central building still stands and is operated as a museum.[8] In Carlyle's day the grounds extended to the river. When he died he owned probably as much land in Fairfax County as Washington did. He bought lot #41 and another lot adjoining it on which he built his house.[9] At different times he was a member of the firms of Carlyle and Adam and Carlyle and Dalton. Although he was a Presbyterian he subscribed to the building of Christ Church. He was married twice, first to Sarah, the daughter of the Honorable William Fairfax of Belvoir, and then to Sybil West. He and Washington were friends, and Washington's *Diaries* show visits by Carlyle to Mount Vernon and visits by Washington to Carlyle's house. Their friendship did not prevent controversies between them over the price of wheat, and over the proceeds of the sale of the brig *Ann and Elizabeth* in Jamaica, Carlyle claiming a half interest in the proceeds of the sale.[10] These were but passing clouds and did not affect their friendship.

Carlyle's crowded hour came in 1754 when General Edward Braddock with a fleet and two regiments of British regulars arrived at Alexandria. He made his headquarters at Carlyle's newly built house and called a meeting there of five colonial governors to consult on measures to assist him in the proposed campaign for the capture of Fort Duquesne; to provide him with militia, horses,

[7]Thomas Tileston Waterman. *The Mansions of Virginia*, facing p. 248.
[8]Davis, Deering, and others. *Alexandria Houses*, p. 52.
[9]Moore, p. 65.
[10]*Writings*, Vol. 3, p. 214.

wagons and provisions. An entry in the Fairfax Court records reads: "Mr. John Carlyle produced a commission from the Honorable, the Governor, under the seal of the Colony appointing him Commissary of provisions and stores for an expedition intended to the River Ohio, pursuant to which he took the oaths, according to Law, repeated and subscribed to the Test."[11] He was given the rank of Major. It was a hard task, but he fulfilled it with his accustomed energy.

In 1758 he was appointed to the lucrative office of Collector of His Majesty's customs for the South Potomac. In 1762 he was importing race horses and Madeira wines and other luxuries.[12]

He took over the unfinished work on Christ Church and died in 1780 at the age of sixty. He was buried in the graveyard of the Presbyterian Church in Alexandria. There is no stone over his grave, but a marker indicates the spot.

By his wife, Sarah Fairfax Carlyle, he had issue, Sarah, who married William Herbert, the Alexandria banker, and Ann Fairfax Carlyle, who married Henry Whiting. By his wife, Sybil West Carlyle, he had an only son, George William Carlyle, an officer in the Continental Army, who was killed at the age of seventeen at the battle of Eutaw Springs in 1781. John Carlyle's will devised most of his estate to his son, George William, and if he died without issue, then to be divided between his grandsons, John Carlyle Herbert and Carlyle Fairfax Whiting. Carlyle had a farm on the Alexandria and Leesburg pike, which was not conveyed to him in his life, but conveyed in 1784 to Carlyle Fairfax Whiting, who received it on division of the estate, made by the court of Fairfax County. He lived on the tract and gave it the name Morven.[13] It was a large frame house, used as a riding club in recent years. It was torn down several years ago in the development of Fairlington. A row of spruce trees marks the site.

---

[11]Moore, pp. 67, 69.

[12]*Ibid.*, p. 62.

[13]Four Mile Run Land Grants, p. 55.

Christ Church

It is not generally known that there was a frame building used for worship before the erection of the present church. Its date is shown by the parish records to have been 1753. "Local tradition is firmly entrenched that a Chapel of Ease stood on Pitt Street near Princess."[14] In 1765 the Vestry determined to build a handsome church in place of the little chapel that by this time had been outgrown. The architect was James Wren, a Fairfax man.[15] The contract was given to James Parsons for £600 stirling. The site chosen was at the head of Cameron Street. It was in a thick wood, which lay beyond the limits of the original town, but was included on the map of one of the additions. It is now in the heart of the city, surrounded by its beautiful yard and its overshadowing trees. Parsons failed to finish his work and the building came to a standstill. Colonel John Carlyle agreed to complete the building for an additional £220. In 1773 the church was accepted by the Vestry. The tower was completed and the bell hung in 1818. The Reverend Townsend Dade was the first rector. In 1770 the Vestry purchased a glebe of five hundred acres and three years later erected a glebe house or parsonage, with dairy, meathouse, barn, corn house and other outbuildings.

Washington purchased a pew. The entry is on a flyleaf of his *Diary* of 1773: "Sale of the Pews in Alexandria Church No 5 Col. G. Washington £36.10." The other purchasers noted on the flyleaf were "Mr. Townsend Dade," the rector, "Mr. Robert Adam, Mr. Robt. Alexander, Mr. Dalton, Mr. Thomas Fleming, Colo. Carlyle, Mr. William Ramsay, Messrs Jno. Muir & ca, Mr. Jno West Jr." For many years the churchyard was used as the town burying ground regardless of creed but in 1808 interments ceased in the churchyard and a small cemetery on Great Hunting Creek was established for the burial of church members. The oldest stone in the churchyard is in memory of Isaac Pearce, who died in 1771.

---

[14]Moore, p. 131.

[15]Waterman, *Mansions of Virginia*, p. 230.

The Reverend David Griffith succeeded Townsend Dade as rector and served until 1789. His successor was the Reverend Bryan Fairfax, Lord Fairfax, Baron of Cameron.

The next rector was the Reverend Thomas Davis, whose incumbency lasted from 1792 to 1811 and who conducted Washington's funeral. The Reverend William Meade, afterward Bishop of Virginia, and better known as the author of *Old Churches, Ministers and Families of Virginia*, was the most noted rector of the church. Washington's pew passed to George Washington Parke Custis of Arlington House. His daughter married Robert E. Lee. The pew is known as the Washington-Lee pew. It is the only square pew left in the church. Lee was attending service there when he received a note from Governor Letcher summoning him to Richmond. He was never to enter Arlington House again. There are white marble tablets on the east wall of the Church as memorials to Washington and Lee. Custis presented Washington's family Bible to the church.

In 1861 the Federal Army occupied the city, and used all the other churches as hospitals, but Christ Church was used for religious services, chaplains filling the pulpit. In 1866 the church was restored to the Vestry.

Dr. George Maclaren Brydon's *Virginia's Mother Church* tells the sad story of the confiscation of the colonial glebes after the Revolution, and their sale by the Overseers of the Poor, pursuant to acts of the Legislature of Virginia. A single glebe was saved to the Episcopal Church—the Glebe of Christ Church. In an opinion written by Justice Story in which Chief Justice Marshall concurred, the Supreme Court of the United States held that the acts of Virginia were confiscatory and could not affect the Glebe of Christ Church, which was then in the District of Columbia.[16]

The glebe was sold by the Vestry and the proceeds used to build the tower in front of the church.

---

[16]Terrett and others vs. Taylor and others. 9. Cranch USSC, p. 41.

Washington and Alexandria

Washington was fortunate in living near Alexandria. Planters living remote from towns had need to order their goods and farm implements from England or from the few cities of the province that grew up in the eighteenth century, and besides goods they needed society. This was the case with Madison, with the Byrds of Westover, the Harrisons of Lower Brandon and of Berkeley, Councillor Carter of Nomini and others. They met at the court-houses, the church, the races. For social life they had balls, suppers, horse races, barbecues, games. They whiled away the tedium of their lives on the lonely plantations by long visits, and other festivities. The wealthier planters went to Williamsburg for the sessions of the Assembly. They did not like life in towns and they thanked God there were none near them.

Washington combined the advantages and delights of country life with proximity to Alexandria. It was indeed his home town. His *Diaries* supply ample evidence of the advantages that its nearness afforded. Sometimes he went by road, on horseback or by wheeled conveyance, and occasionally by water. Thus he noted that on August 19, 1785: "After breakfast I accompained Colo. Humphreys by water to Alexandria."[17] The index to Fitzpatrick's edition of the *Diaries* has a column and a half devoted to Washington's connection with Alexandria. It became necessary for him to build a house, so frequently did he and his family spend the night there. He went to meetings of the Bank of Alexandria and of the Potomac Company; he was a director of both. On June 1st, 1797, he "went to Alexandria to settle some matters at the bank." A note by the editor states, "While in Alexandria . . . he received $100 dividend on stock of the Bank of Alexandria."[18] No money Washington received gave him so much pleasure. He was not peculiar in that respect. He went to balls and dances. On February 18, 1760 he noted, "Went to a Ball at Alexandria, where Musick and Dancing was the chief Entertainment. However in a convenient Room de-

[17]*Diaries*, Vol. 3, p. 107.
[18]*Ibid.*, Vol. 4, p. 257.

tached for the purpose abounded a great plenty of Bread and Butter. Some Biscuits with Tea and Coffee which the Drinkers could not Distinguish from Hot water sweetened. Be it remembered that pocket handkerchiefs served the purposes of Table Cloths and Napkins and that no Apologies were made for either. I shall therefore distinguish this Ball by the Stile and title of the Bread and Butter Ball."[19] Washington also attended celebrations of the anniversary of Independence, ratification of the Federal Constitution, with fireworks on these occasions. On November 21st 1785 he records: "Colo Harrison and Doctr. Craik left after Breakfast, and I went up to Alexandria with G. Washington to meet the Directors of the Potomac Comp. and to a Turtle feast (the Turtle being given by myself to the Gentlemen of Alexandria)."[20]

Washington had many friends in Alexandria. Besides those already named there were Mr. William Fitzhugh, Mr. Dulany, Colonel Charles Simms, Colonel Fitzgerald, Dennis Ramsay (a son of William Ramsay), Philip Marsteller, Doctor Brown, Dr. Dick, William Herbert, Colonel George Gilpin, and others. The *Diaries* show he visited them in Alexandria, and they visited him at Mount Vernon.

Washington as a Mason

Washington belonged to the Fredericksburg Lodge and afterward to the Alexandria Lodge. The buildings belonging to those Lodges are preserved. There are many references to Free Masonry in his letters, but there is only one to the Alexandria Lodge. It is:

"Mount Vernon, December 28, 1783

"Gentn. With pleasing sensibility I received your favor of the 26th, and beg leave to offer you my sincere thanks for the favorable sentiments with which it abounds.

"I shall always feel pleasure when it may be in my power to render Service to Lodge No. 39, and in every act of brotherly kindness

[19] *Ibid.*, Vol. 1, p. 126.
[20] *Ibid.*, Vol. 2, p. 445.

to the Members of it; being with great truth your affect. Brother, etc."[21]

The Alexandria-Washington Lodge of Masons was chartered in 1783. It stands on Cameron Street and Washington served as its first Worshipful Master. The Masonic Museum has many relics, including the high leather-covered library chair Washington presented and used as Master, and personal Masonic records.[22]

Gadsby's Tavern

This famous tavern was built in 1752 on lot 45, it is believed, by Charles Mason. It appears to have been called indifferently Mason's Ordinary and the Coffee House. Like all Alexandria lots, this lot contained half an acre, and was located on the corner of Royal and Cameron Streets. The Mason Ordinary did not occupy the whole of lot 45. It fronted on Royal Street but was not at the corner of Cameron. Between it and Cameron there was a vacant parcel, built upon in 1792 by a large building known as the City Hotel. Both are standing. The Mason house known for a century and a half as Gadsby's is a beautiful Georgian structure; the City Hotel (now joined to Gadsby's as a single whole) is a fine building but cannot be compared architecturally or in other ways to the sister building to the south. Mason died in 1756 but the tavern continued to be called by his name. He devised the house to his widow, who died in 1760.

For fifteen years, till the beginning of the Revolutionary War, John Carlyle operated the tavern in partnership with John Dalton. They had held it jointly in trust for Mrs. Mason's estate. Finally they bought it outright. John Wise purchased it from them. He held the property for thirty-three years; and then sold it. He also owned a tavern in Georgetown. It was during his ownership that the tavern attained its fame. The inhabitants of Alexandria have traditions of the famous persons who stopped there—George Mason, Benjamin Franklin, Governor Clinton of New York, but

[21] *Writings*, Vol. 27, p. 287.
[22] Virginia *Guide*, p. 196.

the person who stopped repeatedly at Gadsby's was Washington. His *Diaries* abundantly confirm this:

"April 5th, 1797. Went to Alexandria on business, ret'd in the afternoon."[23] A note by the editor quotes his Cash Memorandum Book. "Dinner &ca. at Gadsby's 15/."

"Jan. 15, 1798. I went to Alexandria to a meeting of the stockholders of that Bank. While in Alexandria stopped at Gadsby's." While there he probably ate that delicious canvasback duck that the tavern furnished. With its balcony for musicians, the tavern was well suited for a temporary theater. With Washington's fondness for the play, he was not apt to miss a chance to see one played in the nearby hostelry:

September 20, 1768—"Colo Burwell & ca. Went away to Belvoir, and (I) with Mrs. Washington and ye two childn. went up to Alexandria to see the Inconstant, or Way to Win him Acted." "21: Stay'd in Town all day and saw the Tragedy of Douglas Playd."[24]

At Gadsby's was celebrated the adoption of the Federal Constitution; here the Alexandria Assembly held its meetings and balls. After his retirement from the Presidency he had two birthdays; both were celebrated at Gadsby's: the first on February 12, 1798, the second Feby 11, 1799. Both are mentioned in his *Diaries*. The reference to the second is: "Went up to Alexandria to the celebration of my birthday. Many Manoeuvres by the Uniform Corps, and an elegant Ball and Supper at Night."[25]

On Lafayette's last visit to the United States in 1824 he visited Alexandria. In a "splendid barouche, drawn by four fine grays, with postilions dressed in white and blue sashes," he was escorted down Washington Street by "marines, fire companies, the Alexandria Battallion (1,500 men) all saluting, firing salvos, presenting arms,—two bands playing, a reception committee. . . A large arch

---

[23] *Diaries*, Vol. 4, p. 257.
[24] *Diaries*, Vol. 1, p. 292.
[25] *Ibid.*, Vol. 4, p. 298. Note: It appears that Alexandria had not then adopted the Gregorian calendar, dropping eleven days which had been approved by Act of Parliament, passed in 1752.

spanned the street, with smaller ones on the sidewalks. The columns were decorated with portraits of Washington and La Fayette."[26] At that time the tavern was in the occupation of Mr. Claggett, but a banquet in his honor was given there.

While the name of Gadsby is forever associated with the tavern, he never owned it. He leased it in 1796 from John Wise and by renewal of the lease was a tenant until 1808. His lease covered Gadsby's, known as the Coffee House and the City Hotel. He bought a farm in Fairfax County to keep his tavern table well supplied with meats, vegetables, and delicacies.

"There was always a fine stock of game, fish, oysters, terrapin, turkey and ham; Madeira, Port and brandy on hand for the traveler."[27]

John Gadsby proved a bird of passage in Alexandria. He was born in England and adopted the business of a caterer there. About 1816 he removed to Washington, where in 1836 he bought the Decatur house.

The original Assembly Room of the Tavern is now in the Metropolitan Museum of New York City but has been duplicated so that the room is essentially what it was in Gadsby's day. "Of unusual size, it is a magnificent example of the survival of a style for many years after the date of its greatest popularity. Openings are symmetrically located with walls panelled only to chair rail height. . ."[28]

The property is now owned by Gadsby's Tavern and City Hotel, Incorporated, in trust for Alexandria Post No. 24 of the American Legion, and is open to the public at certain times.

The death of the "female stranger," which has caused so much speculation throughout the years, occurred at Gadsby's Tavern. "All that is definitely known of the Female Stranger" has been related as follows:

"Mystery, romance and tragedy combine in the story of the

---

[26]Moore, p. 240.
[27]*Ibid.*, p. 102.
[28]Davis, Deering, and others. *Alexandria Houses*, 1750-1830, p. 45.

'Female Stranger,' who, with her husband, landed in Alexandria from a foreign ship in 1816. The lovely young woman, evidently of gentle birth, was ill with typhoid fever when she was brought to Gadsby's Tavern. The doctor and nurse who attended her were solemnly obligated never to disclose anything they might see or learn concerning their patient. When she died a few weeks later, her husband erected a handsome marble tomb, which may be seen in Saint Paul's Cemetery. . ."[29]

The table tomb standing on a slight eminence is clearly engraved with this inscription:

To the memory of a
FEMALE STRANGER
whose mortal sufferings terminated
on the 14th day of October 1816
Aged 23 years and 8 months.
This stone is placed here by her disconsolate
husband in whose arms she sighed out her
latest breath and who under God
did his utmost even to soothe the cold
dead ear of death.
How loved how valued once avails thee not
to whom related or by whom begot
A heap of dust alone remains of thee
Tis all thou art and all the proud shall be. . .

Several foreign travellers testified to the prosperity of the town in the post-revolutionary period: "In 1795, when Thomas Twining passed through Alexandria, he could comment: 'What most struck me was the vast number of houses which I saw building. . . The hammer and the trowel were at work every where, a cheering sight'. The effect of this was evident to the Duc de la Rochefoucauld in 1796: 'Alexandria,' he said, 'is beyond all comparison the handsomest town in Virginia and indeed is among the finest in the

[29]Lindsey, Mary. *Historic Homes and Landmarks of Alexandria, Virginia,* p. 42. (Printed by Newell-Cole Co., Inc., Alexandria, Va., 1953. Copyright, 1947).

United States'. In the same year Isaac Weld testified: 'Alexandria is one of the neatest towns in the United States. The houses are mostly of brick.' "[30]

In 1800 Alexandria ceased to be in Virginia. It was included in the territory ceded to the United States for the site of the Federal City. It was believed by Washington and many others that the new city would become the metropolis of the Union. Most Alexandrians shared this comfortable belief. But Congress left Alexandria to look out for itself, after passing an act in 1802 forbidding the erection of any public buildings south of the Potomac.

The Federal City grew slowly, and the Alexandrians found they had lost their suffrage and gained little in return. In 1846 Congress authorized a plebiscite to determine the future of the city. A large majority voted in favor of retrocession and the city returned to Virginia.

At the end of the eighteenth century, the industrial future of Alexandria seemed secure. There is a list in the handwriting of Councillor Carter of Nomini of the merchants doing business in Alexandria. It shows that the city's commercial influence extended down the Potomac River to the Chesapeake Bay. The peace following the Revolution seemed likely to give her the access to the British markets that war had interrupted. Her banks were ready to extend the credit needed by merchants to finance new enterprises bringing trade to the city. But this well justified hope proved delusive. As Alexandria had blanketed Colchester and Dumfries, Baltimore blanketed Alexandria. She was more centrally located, had a larger population and superior financial resources; above all, her overseas trade made her the queen of the Chesapeake. Her great Frederick turnpike, and much later, the extension of the Baltimore and Ohio Railroad to Winchester, crowned her victory. Alexandria tried to counter with the Little River turnpike, but that never got nearer the Shenandoah Valley than the Blue Ridge. When the era of railroads came, it was Alexandria's capital

[30]*Landmarks*, Vol. 2, p. 417.

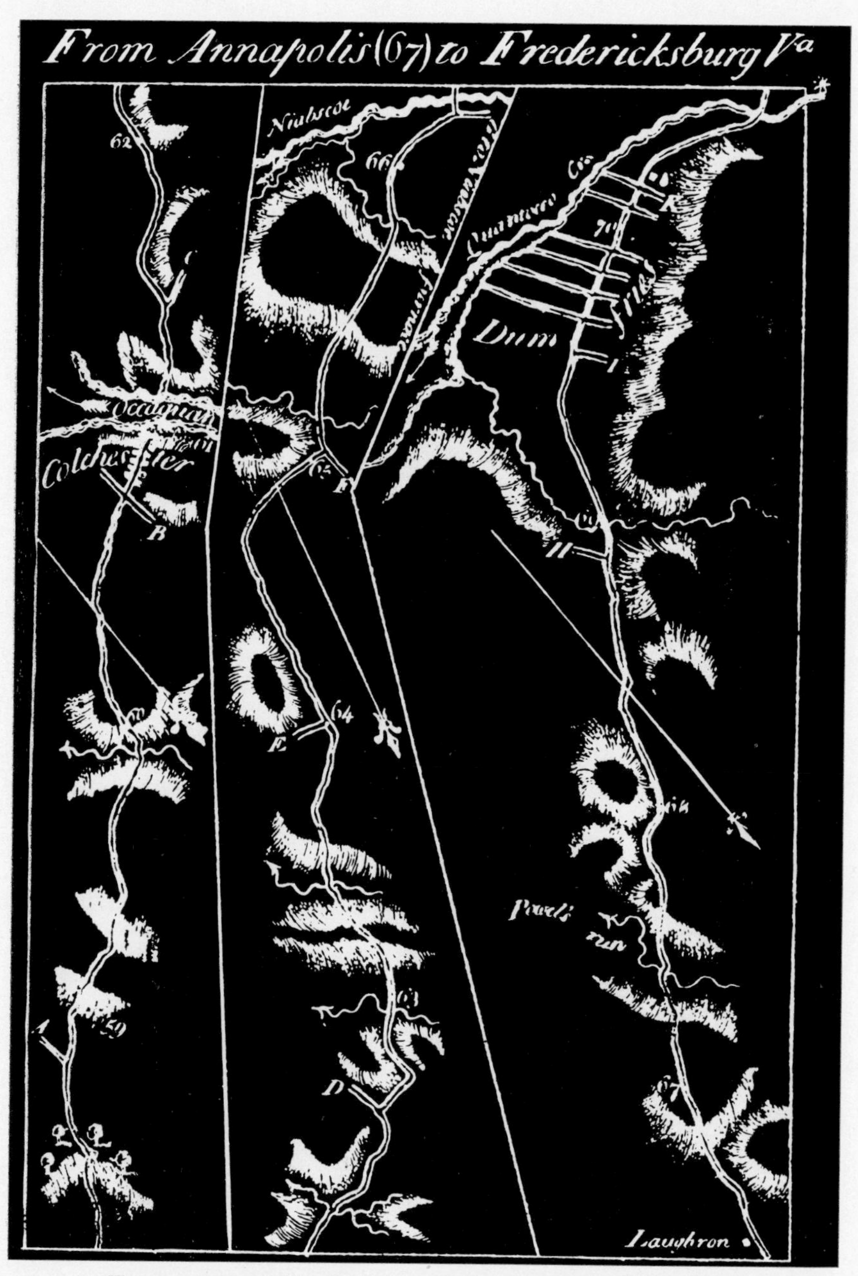

From Annapolis (67) to Fredericksburg, Virginia
(Pages 187 and 194)

(From Christopher Colles' Survey of the Roads of the United States of America. A.D. 1789.)

Fairfax Arms (Page 189)
Photographed by Mrs. Margaret B. Stetson

Belmont, Fairfax County (Pages 190 and 191)
Photographed by Mrs. Margaret B. Stetson

that financed the Orange and Alexandria Railroad (precursor of the Southern Railroad) and the Alexandria, Loudoun and Hampshire Railroad. The former achieved its object in establishing communications and bringing the trade of Central North Virginia to the little city by the Potomac, but the object of the latter, the tapping of the coal fields of Hampshire, was never realized. Long before that her finances had been well-nigh exhausted by the abortive effort to bring the Chesapeake and Ohio Canal Company across the Potomac River to strengthen her trade.[31] A reminiscence of that unfortunate venture long persisted in the name of "Aqueduct Bridge," given to the bridge (replaced by the present Key Bridge), when the canal's waters were carried over the Potomac on their way to Alexandria. The city fell back exhausted. Its brave efforts to retain its place in the sun had ended in failure. Its wharves were deserted. It drowsed in what seemed to be a long lethargy. The First World War awoke it. The Federal Government built merchant ships on her southern water front, or rather, employed private firms for that purpose. With the end of the war the project was abandoned. The impetus to industry given by the project outlived the death of the shipyards. "*Virginia: a Guide to the Old Dominion*" (page 195) says of the city's leading industries: "It has the second largest freight classification yards in America, . . . two large fertilizer plants; a plant for the construction and repair of refrigerator cars; chemical works; an automobile assembling plant; iron works; foundries; a shirt factory; a brick kiln; and a pottery."

Such industrialization would have destroyed the charm of most historic cities; not so, Alexandria. The factories and construction plants have been excluded from the historic sections of the city. The Georgian type of house, with its classic details, fluted pilasters, panelled rooms and dormer windows, continued to be built long after it had been abandoned in the country homes and the other cities of Virginia. It lasted through the first quarter of the nine-

[31]For this account of the Alexandria Railroads the author is indebted to Fairfax Harrison's chapter on Railroads in his *Landmarks of Old Prince William*, p. 593.

teenth century. This gives to the best eighteenth and early nineteenth century houses that grace and beauty that characterize them. Williamsburg is a model of the restoration of the eighteenth century. Alexandria cannot compete with her. She had no Rockefeller fortune. Unaided by corporate funds, she has accomplished her task of restoration with the money of her citizens and of those outsiders who have experienced her charm and have come to live there. She is second only to Williamsburg among the historic cities of Virginia in re-creating the life of the colonial age. She is connected with Mount Vernon by a scenic Boulevard along the Potomac River, said to have cost seven dollars a square foot. One irate Congressman exclaimed that George Washington would have turned in his grave if he had known what it cost. He would indeed.

Chapter 16

Colchester

Archdeacon Burnaby, shortly after Colchester was established, travelled from Williamsburg to Mount Vernon and relates the following incident:

"An occurrence happened to me in the course of this day's travelling, which, though it made a considerable impression upon me at the time, I should not have thought of sufficient moment to be recorded, had not the intellectual powers of the African negroes been frequently, of late, made the subject of conversation, both by the friends and opposers of the emanicipation of that unhappy race. In passing either Acquia, Quantico, or Occoquan rivers, I do not recollect which, I was rowed by an old gray-headed negro who seemed quite exhausted and worn down by age and infirmity. I inquired into his situation, and received for answer, that he had been a slave from his youth, and had continued to work for his master till age had rendered him unfit for service; that his master had then kindly given him a small piece of ground, and the profits of the ferry, which were indeed very inconsiderable, for his maintenance; and that with these means of subsistence he awaited the hour when it might please God to call him to another life. I observed that he must naturally wish for that hour, as it would release him from his present sufferings. His answer was, no; for he was afraid to die. On my questioning him, why he was afraid to die; whether he had any thing upon his conscience that gave him uneasiness; or whether he had not been honest and faithful to his master? He answered, yes; I have always done my duty to the best of my power: but yet I am afraid to die: and was not our Saviour himself afraid to die? The answer was so unexpected, and so far beyond what I supposed to be the intellectual capacity of the poor negro, that it sunk deep into my mind, and I was lost for a moment in silence."[1]

The stream referred to was the Occoquan, as that was the only place where it was necessary to ferry. Quantico or Aquia creeks could be forded easily by a man on horseback. The ferry at which he found the old slave was from the Prince William side to the Fairfax side of the Occoquan at the town of Colchester. George Mason of Gunston Hall owned the ferry. It is an instance of the kind treatment of his slaves that he gave him the profits of the ferry and a plot of ground.

By Act of the General Assembly of the colony passed in 1753 the town of Colchester was created. The act recited "that a town on Occoquan river, in the County of Fairfax, on the land of Peter Wagener, would be very convenient for trade and navigation, and greatly to the ease and advantage of the frontier inhabitants." It vested twenty-five acres of land belonging to Peter Wagener "in Peter Wagener, Daniel McCarty, John Barry, William Elzy, and Edward Washington, gentlemen, in trust."[2]

The trustees laid off the town and sold lots. Their deeds required, in accordance with the law, that the purchasers should "within two years next after the date of conveyance of the same, erect, build and finish on each lot so conveyed, one house of brick, stone, or wood, well framed, of the dimensions of twenty feet square, and nine feet pitch at the least. . . ." Each lot contained half an acre.

The method of vesting title in trustees continued in Maryland and Virginia until the nineteenth century, when legislation was enacted permitting small towns to be organized and governed by elected officers, such as mayors, town clerks, and police officials.

Colchester was laid off on a small scale. The plat of the town is recorded among the land records of Fairfax County, showing a

---

[1]Burnaby, pp. 66-67.

[2]Hening, *Statutes at Large . . . Virginia*, Vol. 6, p. 396.

triangular town with the apex pointing south, with forty-one lots, including the market place.

Although Colchester was located on navigable water, and had a tobacco warehouse, its prosperity depended upon the Colchester Road, which diverged from the Occoquan and turned sharply west and nothwest until it reached Williams', now Snicker's Gap. "In 1772 the Assembly recited it as one of the 'great roads' by which 'great numbers of waggons' came 'from the northwestern parts of the colony to the town . . . of Colchester.' "[3] The name "Colchester Road" has disappeared, but its location is shown on the map in Fairfax Harrison's *Landmarks of Old Prince William* (In pocket in back of volume 1.).

In the days of its prosperity Colchester was Major Peter Wagener's town. It was laid off on his land, his name leads the list of trustees, the town was his project. He was born in England, educated for the law and emigrated to Virginia in 1739. His father had been in the Colony as a clergyman, but had returned to England.

In 1750 Peter Wagener married the sister of Speaker John Robinson, one of the most important men in Virginia. It was a fortunate marriage, for the Robinson influence procured his appointment as clerk successively of Stafford, Prince William and Fairfax Counties.[4] He was a land speculator, holding title to nearly 30,000 acres.[5] He was on friendly terms with Washington. In 1769 it appears from Washington's *Diaries* that he spent parts of three days at Mount Vernon. On at least one occasion he dined with him at Colchester. In 1770 he was elected a member of the Truro Parish Vestry. He died in 1774. The inventory of his estate shows his personal property was valued at £1215.[6]

His son by the same name succeeded him as Clerk of Fairfax County, a position he held for many years, and also succeeded him

[3]Harrison, Vol. 2, p. 478.
[4]*Diaries,* Vol. 1, p. 309 (note).
[5]Freeman, Vol. 1, pp. 206, 207 (note).
[6]Fairfax County Inventories, C, 249.

as vestryman.[7] He married a daughter of Daniel McCarty. He is the Mr. Wagener named by Washington as a companion in fox hunting.

Lieutenant (later Captain) Wagener is supposed to have been a brother of Major Peter Wagener, founder of Colchester. He was with Washington in the skirmish in which Jumonville lost his life. He was also with Braddock, and Washington said that he distinguished himself by his bravery and coolness at the time of Braddock's defeat. Later he assisted in establishing forts for the defense of the frontier against the Indians.

Washington wrote to him: "From the great confidence I repose in your diligence, I have appointed you to a command on which much depends; and I doubt not you will see the work carried on with expedition."[8]

Washington was frequently named executor by people who had no claim upon him, the settlement of whose estates consumed much of his time. He was also named as an arbitrator in two controversies which took him to Colchester for many weary days. One was a dispute between Hector Ross of Colchester and James Semple of the Occoquan Mills. It appears that the other arbitrators were George Mason and Colonel Ludwell Lee of Bellevue, Stafford County. Thomson Mason and James Mercer were attorneys for the respective parties. It is not possible to state the nature of the controversy, but, with meetings now in Colchester and now in Dumfries, it consumed five days in August 1770 and a full week the following January before it was brought to a close.

The other arbitration on which Washington served was between John Graham and the estate of Allan Macrae. Both parties were Dumfries men, but some of the meetings took place at Colchester.

George Mason of Gunston Hall was more closely connected with Colchester than Washington, but as he kept no diary, our knowledge of his relations to the town consists of scanty allusions in his letters.

---

[7]Slaughter, Philip. *History of Truro Parish in Virginia*, p. 110.
[8]*Writings*, Vol. 1, p. 399.

Another Colchester man, Captain Cleon Moore, was elected to the Vestry of Truro Parish in 1781. He was an officer in the Continental Army and was badly wounded at the battle of Brandywine.

Dr. Slaughter in his *History of Truro Parish in Virginia* (edited by Goodwin) tells this amusing story about Colonel Moore: "During the Revolution he was stationed with a squad of men in the Northern Neck, without rations. Chancing to see a flock of geese, belonging to a Mr. Page, he 'impressed' them, except a gander, to whose neck he attached a piece of paper, containing nine-pence, with these lines:—

'My good Mr. Page,
'Be not in a rage,
'Nor think it a very great wonder;
'We have taken nine geese,
'At a penny apiece,
'And sent the money home by the gander.' "[9]

There was also a James Lawson of Colchester whom Washington must have known somewhat intimately, as on his way to Williamsburg in 1768 he, "with Mrs. Washington, Jacky and Patcy Custis, and Billy Bassett" spent the night at his house. On another occasion Mr. James Lawson came to Mount Vernon, was Washington's companion in a fox hunt and went away the next morning.

In 1781 on the eve of the siege of Yorktown, Washington wrote to Peter Wagener (the second), who was County Lieutenant of Fairfax as well as clerk of the Court, directing him to employ the militia of the county in repairing the road from Georgetown to the ford of the Occoquan that the wagons of the French and American armies might avoid the delay of ferrying at Colchester, and adding that the prompt discharge of this duty would probably excuse the militia from further service in the campaign.[10] The road so opened is still occasionally used. It crosses the Occoquan about five miles above the village of Occoquan.

---

[9]Slaughter. *History of Truro Parish*, pp. 116-117.
[10]*Writings*, Vol. 23, p. 109.

Whenever Washington went to Fredericksburg, or returned, he crossed the Occoquan by the ferry at Colchester. On March 26, 1772 he wrote "Sett off again and reached Colchester by nine Oclock, where I was detained all day by high Winds and low tide."[11]

The *Diaries* show that he frequently dined at Colchester and at times the Vestry of Truro Parish met there.[12]

While President, Washington undertook two journeys to show the presidency to the people of the United States. His first journey carried him as far north as New Hampshire. The second, took him south to Georgia, thus including all of the thirteen original states. On this latter journey he had a disagreeable experience at Colchester which he recorded in his *Diaries*:

"In attempting to cross the ferry at Colchester with the four horses hitched to the Chariot by the neglect of the person who stood before them, one of the leaders got overboard when the boat was in swimming water and 50 yards from the shore—with much difficulty he escaped drowning before he could be disengaged. His struggling frightened the others in such a manner that one after another and in quick succession they all got overboard harnessed and fastened as they were and with the utmost difficulty they were saved and the Carriage escaped being dragged after them, as the whole of it happened in swimming water and at a distance from the shore. Providentially—indeed miraculously—by the exertions of people who went off in Boats and jumped into the River as soon as the Batteau was forced into wading water—no damage was sustained by the horses, Carriage or harness."[13]

A few years later the ferry was replaced by a wooden toll bridge, making travel safer and easier. In his *Travels of Four Years and a Half in the United States of America (1798-1801)*, John Davis, the English tutor of Nathaniel Ellicott's children at Occoquan, wrote in his extravagant style: "After climbing over mountains,

---

[11] *Diaries*, Vol. 2, p. 56.
[12] *Writings*, Vol. 27, p. 341.
[13] *Diaries*, Vol. 4, p. 156.

almost inaccessible to human toil, you come to the junction of the Occoquan with the noble Potomac, and behold a bridge, whose semi-elliptical arches are scarcely inferior to those of princely London. . ."[14]

This bridge was built by Thomas Mason, son of George Mason of Gunston, who gave the name Woodbridge to his plantation on the Prince William side of the River. The house and the bridge are long since gone but the name survives in the present railway station of that name.

Alexandria and Dumfries betray their Scotch origin, but Colchester is English, named after the Essex city of that name.[15] The name of the English and American Colchester is pronounced as if it were Colechester. The houses of the Fairfax village were not built on the lots shown on the official plat recorded among the land records of Fairfax County. Christopher Colles' *Survey of the Roads of the United States of America,* published in 1789, shows that although the houses close to the Occoquan River may have been erected on the half acre lots of the plat, most of them were outside the subdivision and were on both sides of the road leading to the ferry. The ferry was older than the village. The ferry charges were prescribed by statute: in the Act of the Assembly passed in June, 1751, the ferrry charge: "on the river Occoquan in Prince William, for a man three pence, for a horse the same." There were also charges "for every coach, chariot or wagon and the driver thereof . . . for every hogshead of tobacco, for every head of neat cattle," and for sheep, lambs, or hogs.[16]

Colchester was on the post road, the most important in Virginia, by which the mail from the northern colonies reached Williamsburg and points south. There must have been an arrangement by which letters and newspapers could be left and collected there, for

[14]Rowland, Vol. 1, p. 113.

[15]The Baedeker *Handbook* on Great Britain, article on Colchester (pp. 484-5) states: there "stands the ruined *Balcon*, the principal Roman bastion, also called *King Cole's Castle*, from an association of Colchester with that hero of nursery rhyme." This perhaps accounts for the pronunciation.

[16]6 Hening's *Statutes*, pp. 19, 20.

a letter from George Mason, dated March 8th, 1789, asked the person to whom he wrote to "inform me by letter per post, directed to be left at the post office in Colchester."[17]

When the postal system of the United States was established sometime after 1789, Colchester had so decayed that no post office has ever been established there. The present inhabitants get their mail from Lorton. The records of the Richmond, Fredericksburg and Potomac Railroad Company show that in 1905, a freight station, called Colchester, was located at the Fairfax end of the railway bridge, and that it was abandoned in 1928.

When Colchester was founded, Dumfries and Alexandria had for five years "been launched on their respective careers, and were now vigorously seeking to demonstrate . . . that their markets afforded the true and only 'ease and advantage' of the same frontier inhabitants to which Colchester looked. As it happened, each of these towns had more men and stronger influence to back their challenge; and they succeeded in blanketing the town on the Occoquan. Although Colchester eventually became the headquarters of several Scots factors and down to the time of the Revolution continued to share in the exports of Old Prince William, at first of tobacco and then of flour, it remained . . . little more than a station on the Potomac Path where a journey might conveniently be broken, a pleasant place of congregational residence for lawyers and doctors who practised in both the adjacent counties, a resort for the meetings of the neighbouring planters, which was the more attractive because the local ordinary keepers maintained the high reputation of their tables and their wine cellars."[18]

After sleeping for more than a century and a quarter, Colchester shows signs of a revival. As the visitor drives through the railway underpass he sees a large sign—"COLCHESTER—Half Acre Lots —$1000. and up." There are ten or fifteen houses and a "Colchester Grocery Store." It is a pleasant little community, with a picturesque

[17]Rowland, Kate Mason. *Life of George Mason*, Vol. 2, p. 311 (hereafter cited as Rowland).

[18]*Landmarks*, Vol. 2, p. 425.

outlook on the river and the hills of Prince William beyond, but it is not the Colchester of old. No ships or schooners are loading with tobacco or wheat for the West Indies, or for New or Old England; no great wagons are bringing the produce of the Piedmont or the Shenandoah Valley. The sole industry appears to be fishing, and that more for pleasure than for profit. The small dock is always crowded on Sundays in pleasant weather and the river down towards Belmont Bay is dotted with small fishing boats. The roads are hard surfaced and automobiles are everywhere.

There is no church, but two miles north, on the site of the first Pohick Church, is Lewis Chapel, named from a prominent Methodist of the eighteenth century. It is the oldest site of a place of worship in Fairfax County, going back to 1696, and has an active Methodist congregation today.

The most famous of the old Colchester buildings remains. It is the Fairfax Arms, a frame building, flanked by two great free-standing stone chimneys. A sign in front of the house states: "Built in 1750." It is a story and a half structure, built on a high foundation overlooking the Occoquan River. It has five rooms with a fireplace in each, and a large cellar. The dining room is large, with wide fluted cupboards. The hand-hewn rafters testify to the building's age. It has been sympathetically and carefully restored, and until her recent death was owned by Mrs. A. H. Roberts.

It was of this ordinary that John Davis wrote in the early nineteenth century: "Every luxury that money can purchase is to be obtained at the first summons. . . . The richest viands cover the table . . . and ice cools the Madeira that has been thrice across the ocean. . . . Apartments are numerous and at the same time spacious . . . carpets of delicate texture cover the floors; and glasses are suspended from the walls in which a *Goliah* might survey himself."[19]

There is another old house nearer the river with large outside chimneys, but the building has been so changed that it has lost all semblance to its original appearance.

---

[19]Virginia *Guide*, p. 344.

Two miles below Colchester stands what is left of Belmont, home of two successive Edward Washingtons for more than seventy-five years. The house, which originally contained five rooms and cellar, was probably built by Catesby Cocke about 1730, when the first Prince William Courthouse was established on the Occoquan. He was clerk of Stafford, Prince William and Fairfax, ending his service for the last county in 1746. He married the daughter of John Graham, the leading merchant of Dumfries. He was living there when Washington made this amusing entry in his *Diary*: "Here I was informed that Colo. Cocke was disgusted at my house and left because he saw an old negro there resembling his own Image." As the entry was made in January, 1760, he was still living then.

The pedigree of this branch of the Washington family long puzzled genealogists. Lund Washington said of the Edward he knew: "Edward Washington lived a few miles from Colchester when I first went there to live in 1786. My Uncle Lawrence and I believed him to be a relative from his strong resemblance to the Family." Lund Washington was mistaken. Miss Cordelia Jackson has published an interesting account of Edward Washington, which establishes the fact that he was not related to George Washington's family or to Lund Washington's family, but was descended from a family of Irish Protestants. The American ancestor of the family emigrated to Westmoreland County before 1675 when his name appears on its records.[20] He resided there until his death early in the eighteenth century. His son, the second Edward Washington, moved to the part of Prince William afterwards embraced in Fairfax before 1737, and in 1742 purchased Belmont from Catesby Cocke. As noted, he was a trustee of Colchester. He died at an advanced age in 1792. His will, filed in Fairfax Courthouse, devised all his estate to his son Edward (1745-1813). This son was elected to the Vestry of Truro Parish in 1779 and again in 1784. He married Elizabeth Hough Sanford and left numerous issue. His will is recorded in Fairfax County.

---

[20]Jackson, Cordelia. *Edward Washington and His Kin.* Washington, D. C. Mimeoform press, 1934. 24pp.

Belmont was purchased by the present owners, the Haislip Family, about 1866. The father of the present Mr. Haislip (who was born on the place) finding most of the old house beyond repair, tore it down, except one end, which is one room deep, and replaced it by a comfortable frame building. The old part is a story and a half with dormer windows and a fine old chimney. It may well be the oldest house in Fairfax County. Back of the house the Occoquan widens out into shallow Belmont Bay. The house stands on rising ground and affords a fine view of the Bay and a glimpse of the hills in Maryland.

On Belmont Bay a short distance to the northwest was "Bradley," the seat of Lee Massey. The house is gone, but the old family graveyard remains, except that certain tombstones have been removed to the present Pohick Church.

Chapter 17

Dumfries

Dumfries and Alexandria were chartered by acts of the Virginia General Assembly passed on the same day, May 11, 1749.[1] The description of the land to be taken for Dumfries was: "60 acres belonging to John Graham situate . . . upon the head of Quantico Creek in the County of Prince William." The name Dumfries was given in honor of John Graham's old home in Scotland. The trustees and directors named in the act were John Graham, Peter Hedgman, William Fitzhugh, George Mason, Joseph Blackwell, Richard Blackburn, and Thomas Harrison. In its early years the town enjoyed great prosperity and grew faster than Alexandria. It outgrew its original sixty acres and additional lands were added to it by successive acts of the Assembly. It was pre-eminently the town of the Scottish tobacco merchants, as shown by the names Graham, McCrea, Dunlop, Scott, Murray, Douglas, Gordon, Glassford, and others.

In 1752 a brick church for the parish of Dettingen was built in the town, superseding an earlier frame church. Both buildings were known as the Quantico Church. The vestry of the parish, in November, 1748, consisted of Benjamin Grayson and Anthony Seale, church wardens, Richard Blackburn, Valentine Peyton, Lewis Renno, John Baxter, Isaac Farguson, Robert Wickliff, Bertrand Ewell, William Tibbs (Tebbs?), John Diskin, Charles Ewell.[2] The rector of the church at the time Dumfries was founded was the Reverend

[1]Harrison. *Landmarks,* p. 670.
[2]Dettingen Parish Register quoted in Groome. *Fauquier during the Proprietorship,* p. 157.

James Scott, the younger brother of the Reverend Alexander Scott, rector of Aquia Church.

In 1759 after the county of Fauquier had been carved out of Prince William, the county seat was removed to Dumfries.

New roads for the trade of the back country were laid off or improved. The principal one, called the Dumfries Road, crossed the Blue Ridge at Ashby's Gap. A tobacco inspection house on Quantico Creek had been authorized and built in 1732, but after the town was established, private warehouses in which to store the tobacco awaiting inspection, were built by the Grahams and others.

"The Lees, the Turbervilles, the McCartys, the Brents, and the Fitzhughs drove thither in their chariots and chairs for balls and tea-drinkings."[3] The accommodation of these gentry and travellers required an inn or ordinary, and a handsome one was built, first known as "Williams' Ordinary, later as Love's Tavern and still functioning as the Stage Coach Inn. Its two red brick stories—between high basement and hip-roof—are ornamented with white stone quoining up the front two corners and with splayed flat arches of stone heavily keyed over each window. Built-in chimneys rise in pairs at both ends, high above eaves that protect a cornice set with modillions. . . Notables undoubtedly stayed here and undoubtedly banqueted and danced at parties held in the spacious dining room."[4]

Washington must have stopped at the ordinary many times on his trips to and from Fredericksburg, Williamsburg and Richmond. The distance from Mount Vernon to Fredericksburg was too great to be covered in a single day. His diaries mention only two private homes where he stayed overnight—Mr. McCrea's when travelling in his chariot with Mrs. Bassett, and then he sent his horses "to the tavern"; and again when he reviewed the Independent Company in 1775 and "dined and lodged at Mr. Leitch." This was Andrew Leitch, a merchant. On all other occasions, whether alone or with friends or relatives, he records lodging, breakfasting and

---

[3]Harrison. *Landmarks,* p. 388.
[4]Prince William *Guide Book,* p. 91.

dining in the town. His expense accounts show he stayed at a place of public entertainment for travellers.

Christopher Colles' Road Map of the United States shows the original layout of Dumfries. The north and south street is presumably the present Main Street (the only one left). The cross streets running east and west to Quantico Creek where it was once navigable were named King, Prince, Duke, Hedgman, Graham, Walker, Clark, Whisky, Fairfax, Market. No trace remains of any of them except Fairfax on the west side as it runs into the Manassas Road.

Shortly after the Revolution, silt began to clog Quantico Creek and eventually prevented ships from reaching the Dumfries wharf. Commerce dwindled and the sea-borne trade finally ceased. John Graham, founder of the town, lived to be an old man, dying in 1787—long enough to see his town decaying. Dumfries, however, did not give up without a struggle. Efforts were made to build new towns at the mouth of the Creek and to dredge and clear its channel. Nothing came of the enterprises.

Bishop Meade, writing of the town in the eighteen thirties, says: "Dumfries itself once the mart of that part of Virginia, the scene of gayety and fashion, the abode of wealthy merchants from Scotland . . . is now in ruins." The population, once exceeding two thousand, had sunk in 1806 to about three hundred, according to a traveller passing through it, though it still had the courthouse and jail. In 1789 the legislature of Virginia established a system of Superior Courts, intermediate between the county courts and the Supreme Court of the State, and such a court was authorized at Dumfries for Fairfax, Prince William, Fauquier, and Loudoun, but the system did not continue long. In 1822 the County Court House was moved to Brentsville. In his *Landmarks of Old Prince William,* Fairfax Harrison quotes Miss Ewell as writing: "At one time there were forty widows in the reduced number of inhabitants." Dumfries seemed about to suffer the fate that overtook Jamestown, and Colchester, but that was not to be. It was on the main route south from Washington to Richmond and until the advent of the railroads

Old Tavern—Dumfries (Page 193)
Photographed by Mrs. Virginia S. Harris

Henderson House (Page 196)
Photographed by Mrs. Virginia S. Harris

Courtesy Virginia State Chamber of Commerce

Gunston Hall (Page 202)

the mail and travellers generally passed through it. With the establishment of the Marine Base at Quantico and the hard-surfacing of Virginia roads, Dumfries has staged a modest revival.

Several frame buildings from the eighteenth century still survive on the main street, among them the office of the Tobacco Inspector. Back of the Stage Coach Inn, the home of Foushee Tebbs—a notable brick house—survived until its walls were destroyed by a storm in 1933, though it had ceased to be inhabited for many years. At its rear is Grayson's Hill where William Grayson (1736-1790) maintained a home and farm. He was the most eminent citizen of Dumfries. As an aide to Washington, he participated in many of the battles of the Revolution. Later he was a member of the Virginia Legislature, and of the Continental Congress. He opposed the ratification of the Federal Constitution, fearing the domination of the Northern States, but he and Richard Henry Lee were elected as Virginia's first United States Senators. Grayson County honors his memory.

Alexander Henderson

Alexander Henderson was born in Scotland in 1738. He came to Virginia in 1756 and settled as a merchant in Colchester. He was a vestryman in Truro Parish from 1765 to 1785,[5] and purchased pews nos. 22 and 23 in the new church. He attended the ball given by Washington to celebrate his election as burgess in December 1768. The *Diaries* record that he went home with Washington the following night and joined in a fox hunt the next day.[6] While not active in politics he took such a decided part against the Mother Country that he thought it prudent during the Revolutionary War to retire to his farm in Fairfax County.

In March 1785, as one of the Commissioners of Virginia, he stayed several days at Mount Vernon while attending the meetings in Alexandria "for settling the Jurisdiction of Chesapeak Bay and the Rivers Potomack and Pocomoke between the States of Virginia and Maryland." The other Commissioners from Virginia

---

[5]Slaughter. *History of Truro Parish,* pp. 108, 122.
[6]*Diaries,* Vol. 1, p. 301.

were George Mason, Edmund Randolph, and James Madison. Those for Maryland were Major Jenifer, Thomas Johnson, Thomas Stone, and Samuel Chase.[7]

Shortly afterwards Henderson removed to Dumfries, where he established a flourishing store, and then set up branch stores in Colchester, Occoquan and Alexandria. He may thus claim to be the founder of the chain store in America.[8]

He represented Prince William County in the General Assembly of 1798. His home in Dumfries was begun about 1785 and is notable for the molded tops of its brick chimneys. The porch shown in the photograph is probably a later addition to the house as built by Henderson. "In the forest on the land that once belonged to the Hendersons lonely graves are marked by a double tombstone inscribed to the memory of Alexander Henderson, 'who was born on the river Clide near Glasgow in Scotland' and died in 1815 'in the 78th year of his life'; and of Sarah Henderson 'consort of Alexander Henderson', who died in 1816 'aged about 64 years'."[8]

They left six sons and four daughters: one, Richard, was an eminent lawyer of Leesburg. Another, Archibald, was General and first Commandant of the Marine Corps. Alexander Henderson's descendants, the Nevitts still worship in Pohick Church.

The Ewells

The first member of the Ewell family in Virginia was Charles Ewell (1665-1722) who, it is said, came under contract to build the capitol at Williamsburg. He later settled in Lancaster County, where he married Mary Ann Bertrand, daughter of a Huguenot clergyman. He left two sons, Charles and Bertrand. Both of them moved to the neighborhood of Dumfries. Bertrand (1715-1795) was Surveyor of Prince William County. He was a vestryman of Dettingen Parish in 1748.

This second Charles Ewell (born 1713) built Bel Air about 1740. Washington knew him and described him as a "man of af-

[7] *Ibid.*, Vol. 2, pp. 352-353.
[8] Prince William *Guide*, p. 93.

fairs." As noted above, one of his daughters, Marianna, married Dr. James Craik. He was prominent in secular and religious circles; was interested in the development of iron mines on Neabsco Creek, and associated with his brother-in-law, John Ballendine, in the development of iron mines on the Occoquan. A joint stock company was organized for the purpose, but the scheme came to nothing. He appears to have died before 1767.[9] A Captain Charles Ewell who served under Washington in the Revolution in the First Virginia State Regiment in 1778 belonged to this family, but whether a son of Charles or Bertrand does not appear.[10]

Charles Ewell left a son Jesse Ewell (1771-1847). Probably due to the decline of Dumfries, Jesse Ewell removed his home to the upper part of Prince William County where good farming land was to be found under the shadow of the Bull Run Mountains. He named his house Edgehill and in the burial plot nearby lie four generations of Ewells. His son, the second Jesse Ewell, built not far away a frame building named Dunblane.

His daughter Fannie married Mason Locke Weems (Parson Weems), author of the well-known life of Washington. Weems was born in Maryland and died in Virginia. In middle age he made long visits at Bel Air and is buried in the family graveyard there. His lives of Washington and Francis Marion, the patriotic partisan leader from South Carolina, were very popular, but as Bishop Meade says, "You know not how much of fiction there is in them."[11]

The first Jesse Ewell of Bel Air and Edgehill had a brother Thomas Ewell, who married a daughter of Benjamin Stoddert, first Secretary of the Navy, whose home still stands in Georgetown, D. C. He had four sons, of whom the best known were Benjamin Stoddert Ewell (1810-1894), President of the College of William and Mary, who became a Colonel in the Confederate Army; and Richard Stoddert Ewell (1817-1872), a Major General and later a Lieutenant General, in the Confederate Army. He lost a leg in the second

[9]*Ibid.*, p. 105.
[10]*Writings,* Vol. 12, p. 375.
[11]Meade, Vol. 2, p. 235.

battle of Manassas and was carried to the home of his cousin at Dunblane.[12] Ewell was a character. In the regular Army of the United States he had been a captain, and on entering the Confederate service he "modestly asserted that in two decades of service in the cavalry he had learned all about commanding fifty dragoons and forgotten everything else." It did not take him long to remember what he had learned at West Point, for he was Stonewall Jackson's brilliant and trusted division commander in Jackson's famous Shenandoah Valley campaign. Although he admired his chief, he insisted privately that Jackson was crazy, possibly referring to Jackson's habit of concealing advance notice of his plans from his most trusted subordinates. Douglas Southall Freeman describes him as "an excellent cook, though a chronic dyspeptic, and despite a lisp, was voluble. Completely bald, and with bulging bright eyes, he was likened by some to an eagle, and by some to a woodcock. When he spoke he put his head on one side, and as likely as not he swore."[13] When his wound had sufficiently healed he rejoined the army and remained in service until the end of the war. During the war he married a Mrs. Brown and introduced her at their wedding reception as "my wife, Mrs. Brown."

Bel Air is situated about seven miles northwest of Dumfries. Stone gateposts bearing the name Bel Air mark the entrance from the main road. A long shady lane leads to a second pair of stone gateposts, and continues through open fields to the rounded hill on which the house is located. The mansion is of red brick, a story and a half above a high basement, with thick walls and joists of hewn timber. It is set between end chimneys, one of which is exceptionally wide. Surrounded by its ample acres, now in use as a farm, the house has an air of solidity and repose. It was for many years the property of the late George C. Round of Manassas. The present owners are Mr. and Mrs. William E. S. Flory.

[12]Prince William *Guide,* p. 195.
[13]*Lee's Lieutenants,* Vol. 1, p. 347.

Chapter 18

George Mason and His Circle

George Mason's home was situated on a peninsula originally called Doeg Neck and later Mason's Neck, surrounded on three sides by water. The Masons, the Bronaughs, the Cockburns, the Masseys lived in this Neck, and were thus a community, somewhat apart from the rest of Fairfax County. They met with a wider circle at church, at the county court and at other public gatherings, but for daily society depended much on each other.

The first Mason to settle in Doeg Neck was George Mason, grandfather of the builder of Gunston. He was the son of George Mason, a Royalist immigrant who came to Virginia before 1658 and lived in the Accokeek region of Stafford County some thirty miles below Dogue (or Doeg) Neck. There had been an Indian war in 1676 and the frontier country along the Occoquan was not completely pacified when George Mason's grandfather established his residence in this Neck above the Occoquan. It was still an outpost toward the end of the seventeenth century, occupied by the Doeg and Necostin Indian tribes. The Doegs, in particular, had a bad reputation with the colonists. The method of protection adopted by Governor Nicholson was the appointment of rangers to patrol the lands above the settlements, and to keep an eye on the roving Indians. The George Mason of that period was County Lieutenant and he had been appointed commander-in-chief of the Stafford Rangers. The band was composed of a Lieutenant and eleven men with horses, arms, etc.

A journal of one of their trips has been preserved. It gives us our first glimpse of the Mount Vernon region at the time of its earliest settlement by the white men.

"A Journall of our Ranging, Given by me, David Strahane, Lieut. of the Rangers of the Pottomack.

"June 9th 1692: We ranged on Ackoquane and so back of the Inhabitants and thence South. We returned and discovered nothing.

"Jun 17th: We Ranged over Ackoquane and so we Ranged Round Puscattaway Neck and ther we lay that night.

"And on the 18th came to Pohike and ther we heard that Capt. Masone's Servt. man was missing. Then we went to see if we could find him, and we followed his foot about half a mile, to a house that is deserted, and we took the track of a great many Indians and we followed it about 10 miles, and our horses being weary, and having no provisions, we was forced to returne.

"June the 26th: we Ranged up to Jonathan Mathew's hs. along with Capt Masone, and ther we mett with Capt. Houseley, and we sent over for the Emperour, but he would not come and we went over to the towne, and they held a Mascomacko (council) and ordered 20 of their Indians to goe after the Indians that carried away Capt. Masone's man, and so we returned.

"July the 3d: We Ranged up Neapsico and so back of the Inhabitants, &c.

"July 11th: We Ranged up to Brent-towne and ther we lay &c The 19th: We ranged up Ackotink and discovered nothing &c So we Ranged once in the week till th 20th of Septbr.; then we marched up to Capt. Masone's and ther we met with Capt Houseley and his men, and so we drawed out 12 of our best horses, and so we ranged up Ackotink and ther we lay that night.

"Sept the 22d: We ranged due north till we came to a great Runn that made unto the suggar land and we marcht down it about 6 miles and ther we lay that night.

"Sept the 23rd: We marcht to the suggar land and the 24th we ranged about to see if we could find the trace of any Indians but we could not see any fresh sign. The 26th marcht to Capt. Masone's and there I dismissed my men til the next march."[1]

"Ackoquane" is the Occoquan. "Pohike" is Pohick. Puscattaway (Piscataway) Neck is between Mount Vernon and Alexandria though the main village of the Piscataway Indians was in Maryland on Piscataway Creek south of Fort Washington, where the "Emperour" lived. The "suggar land" was along Sugarland Run, west of Dranesville. Sugar maples have long disappeared from the region.

The George Mason who established himself on Dogue Neck died in 1716 and was succeeded by his son of the same name who was the father of the celebrated George Mason. This second George Mason succeeded his father as County Lieutenant and was elected a member of the House of Burgesses in 1718. Like his ancestors he patented land in Virginia but unlike them he acquired land in Charles County, Maryland. He married Ann Thomson and by her had three children who lived to maturity. While crossing the Potomac his sailboat upset and he was drowned in 1735. His eldest son was George Mason, author of the Virginia Bill of Rights. He was born in 1725. As his father died without leaving a will, George inherited all of his land. This included the Chickamuxon Plantation in Charles County, Maryland, the Dogue Neck plantation, then containing about four thousand acres, and the Occoquan Plantation, later called Woodbridge, from which there was a public ferry crossing the Occoquan River to Dogue Neck. On his father's death the widow and her children returned to the Dogue Neck Plantation in the then Prince William County.

Practically nothing is known of George Mason's early education. One of his guardians was John Mercer of Marlborough, who has been mentioned as the early legal adviser of Washington. He had married George Mason's aunt, Catherine Mason. He was not only a lawyer of distinction, but was the owner of one of the best libraries in Virginia. Young Mason enjoyed the benefit of this library, and must have profited from his close association with him. In 1750 he

---

[1]Harrison. *Landmarks,* Vol. 1, pp. 84-85. (From Cal. Va. State Papers, Vol. 1, p. 44.)

married Anne Eilbeck of Charles County, Maryland. She was sixteen and he was twenty five. Five sons and four daughters were born of the union.[2] It must have been soon after his marriage that he projected the building of Gunston, as he felt the need of a home other than his mother's residence, though the mansion was not completed until 1758. It received its name from the old home in Staffordshire, England, the residence of his maternal ancestors, the Fowkes. The outbuildings of Mount Vernon have survived and are a part of its charm. Gunston Hall was once surrounded by similar outbuildings. They are gone. Besides the main building, the box walk and a great well are all that remain. Mason himself probably dictated the size of the building and the arrangement of the rooms, but he wisely left the interior to William Buckland, who came from London to Virginia in 1755 under an indenture with Thomson Mason, a brother of George, especially to assist in the construction of the house.

"Of the interior, Buckland, who at first was primarily a carver, created rooms of outstanding richness and beauty with door and window trim unparalleled in elaboration in Virginia. These he derived or adapted from the great style books of the period."[3] The work of building and finishing took three years, 1755-1758.

Mason, like Washington, had wide interests, but they were both primarily farmers, devoted to the cultivation and development of their estates. The recollections of Mason's son, General John Mason, written in old age, preserve an account of Gunston Hall as it was in his boyhood and youth. Some extracts from his narrative are given here:

" 'To the west of the main building were first the schoolhouse, and then at a little distance, masked by a row of large English walnut trees, were the stables. To the east was a high paled yard, adjoining the house, into which opened an outer door from the private front, within, or connected with which yard, were the kitchen, well, poultry houses, and other domestic arrangements; and beyond

[2]Rowland, Kate Mason. *Life and Correspondence of George Mason,* Vol. 1, pp. 52-58. Hereafter cited as Rowland.

[3]Waterman. *Mansions of Virginia,* p. 226.

it on the same side, were the corn house and granary, servants houses (in those days called negro quarters), hay yard and cattle pens, all of which were masked by rows of large cherry and mulberry trees. And adjoining the enclosed grounds on which stood the mansion and all these appendages on the eastern side was an extensive pasture for stock of all kinds running down to the river, through which led the road to the Landing, emphatically so called, where all persons or things water borne, were landed or taken off, and where were kept the boats, pettiangers and canoes of which there were always several for business transportation, fishing and hunting belonging to the establishment. Farther north and on the same side was an extensive orchard of fine fruit trees of a variety of kinds. Beyond this was a small and highly fenced pasture devoted to a single brood horse. . . .

" 'The heights on which the mansion house stood extended in an east and west direction across an isthmus and were at the northern extremity of the estate to which it belonged. This contained something more than five thousand acres, and was called Dogue's Neck (I believe after the tribe of Indians which had inhabited this and the neighboring country), water-locked by the Potomac on the south, the Occoquan on the west, and Pohick Creek (a bold and navigable branch of the Potomac) on the east, and again by Holt's Creek, a branch of the Occoquan, that stretches for some distance across from that river in an easterly direction. The isthmus on the northern boundary is narrow and the whole estate was kept completely enclosed by a fence on that side of about one mile in length running from the head of Holt's to the margin of Pohick Creek. This fence was maintained with great care and in good repair in my father's time, in order to secure to his own stock the exclusive range within it, and made of uncommon height, to keep in the native deer which had been preserved there in abundance from the first settlement of the country and indeed are yet there (1832) in considerable numbers. The land south of the heights and comprising more than nine tenths of the estate was an uniform level elevated some twenty feet above the surface of the river, with the exception of one extensive marsh and three or four water courses, which were accompanied by some ravines and undulations of minor character—and about two thirds of it were yet clothed with the primitive wood; the whole of this level tract was embraced in one view from the mansion house. In different parts of this tract and detached from each other, my father worked four plantations with his own slaves, each under an overseer; and containing four or five hundred acres of open land. The crops were principally Indian corn and tobacco; the corn for the support of the plantations and the home house, and the tobacco for sale. There was but little small grain made in that part of the country in those days. He had also another plantation worked in the same manner, on an estate he had in Charles County, Maryland, on the Potomac about twenty miles lower down, at a place called Stump Neck.

" 'It was very much the practise with gentlemen of landed and slave estates in the interior of Virginia, so to organize them as to have considerable resources within themselves; to employ and pay but few tradesmen and to buy little or none of the coarse stuffs and materials used by them, and this practise became stronger and more general during the long period of the Revolutionary War which in great measure cut off the means of supply from elsewhere. Thus my father had among his slaves carpenters, coopers, sawyers, blacksmiths, tanners, curriers, shoemakers, spinners, weavers and knitters, and even a distiller. His woods furnished timber and plank for the carpenters and coopers, and charcoal for the blacksmiths; his cattle killed for his own consumption and for sale supplied skins for the tanners, curriers and shoemakers, and his sheep gave wool and his fields produced cotton and flax for the weavers and spinners, and his orchards fruit for the distiller. His carpenters and sawyers built and kept in repair all the dwelling-houses, barns, stables, ploughs, harrows, gates &c., on the plantations and the outhouses at the home house. His coopers made the hogsheads the tobacco was prized in and the tight casks to hold the cider and other liquors. The tanners and curriers with the proper vats &c., tanned and dressed the skins as well for upper as for lower leather to the full amount of the consumption of the estate, and the shoemakers made them into shoes for the negroes. A professed shoemaker was hired for three or four months in the year to come and make up the shoes for the white part of the family. The blacksmiths did all the iron work required by the establishment, as making and repairing ploughs, harrows, teeth chains, bolts &c., &c. The spinners, weavers and knitters made all the coarse cloths and stockings used by the negroes, and some of finer texture worn by the white family, nearly all worn by the children of it. The distiller made every fall a good deal of apple, peach and persimmon brandy. The art of distilling from grain was not then among us, and but few public distilleries. All these operations were carried on at the home house, and their results distributed as occasion required to the different plantations. Moreover all the beeves and hogs for consumption or sale were driven up and slaughtered there at the proper seasons, and whatever was to be preserved was salted and packed away for after distribution.

" 'My father kept no steward or clerk about him. He kept his own books and superintended, with the assistance of a trusty slave or two, and occasionally of some of his sons, all the operations at or about the home house above described; except that during the Revolutionary War and when it was necessary to do a great deal in that way to clothe all his slaves, he had in his service a white man, a weaver of the finer stuffs, to weave himself and superintend the black weavers, and a white woman to superintend the negro spinning-women. To carry on these operations to the extent required, it will be seen that a considerable force was necessary, besides the house servants, who for such a household, a large family and entertaining a great deal of company, must be numerous—and such a force was constantly kept there, independently of any of the plantations and besides occasional drafts from them of labor for particular occasions. As I had during my youth constant intercourse with all these people, I remember them all and their several employments, as if it was yesterday. . .'

"There are said to have been five hundred persons on the estate, including the several quarters. And Colonel Mason is reported to have shipped from his own wharf at one time twenty-three thousand bushels of wheat."[4]

In 1773 while Mason was still under fifty years old his wife died, after a marriage lasting twenty-three years. Washington's diaries show that a funeral service for her was held at Pohick Church on April 27th, 1773 as he noted: "Mrs. Calvert, Mrs. Washington and my Wife went to hear Mrs. Mason's Funeral Ser." On May 3d, "Went by the Church to Colo. Mason's where I dined. Returned in the Afternoon."[5] The visit to Gunston was evidently a condolence call.

Writing to his cousin, George Mercer, who was in England in 1778, Mason said: "About four years ago I had the misfortune to lose my wife. To you who knew her and the happy manner in which we lived, I will not attempt to describe my feelings. I was scarce able to bear the first shock. A depression of my spirits and a settled melancholy followed from which I never expect or desire to recover."

He remained a widower for seven years and then married Sarah Brent, daughter of George Brent of Woodstock. Considering the urgent need of a helpmate to care for his young children, and to assume the management of his home, it was a tribute to the memory of his first wife that he should have waited so long. George Brent was a Roman Catholic, but the marriage ceremony was performed by the Rev. James Scott, rector of Dettingen Parish, whose church was at Quantico, near the bride's home. There was no issue born of the marriage.

Mason, like Washington, had varied interests. He drafted the Fairfax County Resolutions in 1774. He was a Burgess for Fairfax County from 1758 to 1761; a delegate to the Virginia Convention of 1775; a Vestryman of Truro Parish from 1749 to 1785 and during that time was several times Church Warden, and with Washington and others a member of the committee to supervise the construction of the new Pohick Church. The contractor, Daniel

---

[4]Rowland, Vol. 1, pp. 99-102.
[5]*Diaries,* Vol. 2, p. 109.

French, died before completing his contract, and Mason, as his executor, finished the work. He purchased two pews in the church for fourteen pounds eleven shillings and eight pence each.[6]

Wealth in Virginia in Mason's day was chiefly landed wealth. Opportunities for speculation in other ways were few. Loaning money on mortgages was the principal way of investing surplus funds. The Fairfax Deed Books show several such loans made by him. Like John Mercer and George Washington, he acquired back lands in Loudoun and Frederick Counties and in what is now Kentucky, but he also made large investments in his home county of Fairfax. He bought Analostan Island; once called Mason's Island, and now Roosevelt. He acquired the land of the Awbreys on the adjoining Virginia shore and succeeded in their ownership of the ferry to Georgetown. He took title to large tracts in the neighborhood of Fairfax Courthouse, still called Mason's Commons. He was a trustee of the towns of Dumfries and Alexandria, and purchased a lot in the last-named town, but he did not seek political life. In a letter to his neighbor and friend, Martin Cockburn from Williamsburg, in 1774, he wrote: "I begin to grow heartily tired of this town, and look to be able to leave it sometime next week." At this time he had been a burgess for only a single term. If an emergency arose in which he thought his services were needed he would accept office. He was fifty years old and would have preferred to live in retirement and manage his plantation and his business affairs, but this was not to be.

In the letter to James Mercer above referred to, he told how he came to enter public life again:

"In the summer of '75 I was, much against my inclination dragged out of my retirement by the people of my county, and sent a delegate to the General Convention in Richmond, where I was appointed a member of the first Committee of Safety, and have since at different times been chosen a member of the Privy Council and of the American Congress, but have constantly declined acting in any other public character than that of an independ-

[6]Slaughter. *History of Truro Parish,* p. 82.

ent representative of the people in the House of Delegates, where I still remain from a consciousness of being able to do my country more service there than in any other department; and have ever since devoted most of my time to public business to the no small neglect and injury of my private fortune; . . ."[7]

His public career, on which his fame rests, had just begun. Virginia had revolted; the colonial government had been destroyed. A new government based on new principles must be formed. He had been elected to the Virginia Convention of 1775 and was reelected to that of 1776. He was chiefly instrumental in drawing the Virginia Constitution of 1776; he was the author of the famous Virginia Bill of Rights. Jefferson drew on it for the introductory clauses of the Declaration of Independence. It also contained statements of principles embodied in the first ten amendments to the Constitution of the United States.

All men "are by nature equally free and independent, and have certain inherent rights, of which, when they enter into a state of society, they cannot by any compact deprive or divest their posterity." These rights, Mason asserts, are "the enjoyment of life and liberty, and the means of acquiring and possessing property, and pursuing and attaining happiness and safety." All power, he says "is vested in and consequently derived from the people . . . magistrates are their trustees and servants and at all times amenable to them." "That when any Government shall be found inadequate or inimical to these principles a majority of the community has the right to alter or abolish it." The freedom of the press is "one of the great bulwarks of liberty and can never be restrained but by despotic governments. . . . In all cases the military should be under strict subordination to, and governed by the civil power. . . . All men are equally entitled to the free exercise of religion according to the dictates of conscience." These are commonplace today, but how many know that they owe their first enunciation, in America, at least, to the philosopher of Gunston Hall?

By this time, his former dislike for holding office had so far abated

[7]Rowland, Vol. 1, p. 298.

that he served as a representative of Fairfax County from 1776 to 1787. During the Revolutionary War, George Rogers Clark, with Virginia troops, had taken the British forts in the country lying north and northwest of the Ohio River, and Virginia laid claim to this vast territory. Maryland refused to ratify the Articles of Confederation until Virginia relinquished its claim. In 1780 Mason outlined the plan which was subsequently adopted for ceding to the Federal Government Virginia's claim to the back lands, comprising the future states of Ohio, Indiana, Illinois, Michigan and Wisconsin.

During the Revolutionary War, Washington and Mason saw little of each other. The importance Washington attached to Mason's views and information is shown by his letter written from his camp at Middlebrook in 1779:

"Though it is not in my power to devote much time to private corrispondences, owing to the multiplicity of public letters (and other business) I have to read, write, and transact; yet I can with great truth assure you, that it would afford me very singular pleasure to be favoured at all times with your sentiments in a leizure hour, upon public matters of general concernment as well as those which more immediately respect your own State. . . ."[8]

In 1787 Mason was one of the Virginia delegates to the convention in Philadelphia which framed the Federal Constitution. He was an able debater and took an active part in its discussions. He opposed the compromise which permitted the slave trade to continue until 1808. Like Washington and many prominent Virginians of his day, he favored the gradual abolition of slavery. The provision permitting the slave trade to continue until 1808 was designed to induce South Carolina to ratify the Constitution. He objected strenuously to the large powers vested in Congress by the proposed Constitution. These powers, he believed, encroached on the sovereignty of the individual states. He therefore refused to sign the Constitution and returned to oppose its ratification by

[8]*Writings,* Vol. 14, p. 299.

the Virginia Convention. He was joined by Patrick Henry and Richard Henry Lee.

Under the leadership of Madison, backed by the approval of Washington, the Convention ratified the new Constitution.

Mason's opposition was not fruitless, however. As a delegate in Philadelphia he had pressed for inclusion in the Constitution of the substance of the Virginia Bill of Rights. He was unsuccessful there, but in its ratification by the Virginia Convention, amendments were recommended embodying much of Mason's Bill of Rights and such amendments were adopted by the several states concurrently with the adoption of the Constitution itself. Throughout his political career Mason advocated strengthening local government, at the expense of the central government. The old friendship between Washington and Mason was strained by their difference of opinion over the adoption of the Constitution and Washington referred to him as his "quandam friend." Notwithstanding his known sentiments Mason was appointed a senator from Virginia. He declined. It may have been the gout from which he had suffered for many years or it may have been his longing for retirement. He died in 1792. Washington, writing to James Mercer shortly after Mason's death, said: "and I will also unite my regret to yours for the death of our old friend and acquaintance Colo. Mason."

When his long friendship with Mason and the warm sentiments of his previous letter are recalled, his regrets for "our old friend and acquaintance" seem perfunctory and suggests that Washington could not forgive Mason's opposition to the adoption of the Federal Constitution.

Mason's biographer records one specimen of his wit. He was a candidate for the Virginia Assembly. His opponent declared that the people of Fairfax knew that Colonel Mason's mind was failing, to which he replied that when his adversary's mind failed nobody would ever discover it.

His native state has not forgotten him. On the north side of the Capitol Square in Richmond is Crawford's equestrian statue of

Bel Air, Prince William County (Pages 196 to 198)

Photographed by Mrs. Virginia S. Harris

Rockledge 1758, Occoquan, Virginia (Pages 217 and 218), Wm. Buckland, Architect

Photographed by Mrs. Virginia S. Harris

Photographed by Dementi, Richmond

George Mason (Pages 210 and 211)

One of the six Virginia Patriots on pedestals surrounding the equestrian Statue of Washington in the Capitol grounds at Richmond

Washington and below are six bronze figures surrounding it; one of them is the statue of George Mason.

Gunston Hall was conveyed by its last private owner, Mr. Louis C. Hertle, to the State of Virginia and is now open to the public.

Martin Cockburn

George Mason's nearest neighbor was Martin Cockburn, son of Dr. James Cockburn of Jamaica. The Cockburn home was "Springfield." It was a long, low frame building, looking out on Pohick Bay. A notice of him is given in Kate Mason Rowland's *Life of George Mason:*

"It is related of Martin Cockburn, George Mason's friend and neighbor, that it was while travelling in this country, a youth of eighteen, with his father that he met Miss Bronaugh and fell in love with her. His father promised that if he would wait until he was of age he should have his bride. The three years of probation over, the lover returned to claim the lady, but finding that she could not be prevailed on to go so far from her family as the West Indies, he purchased a place near her relatives in Virginia, where he and his wife lived in the quiet enjoyment of rural life to an advanced age. The Rev. Lee Massey, his brother-in-law, said of Mr. Cockburn and his wife that they were the only couple he believed who had lived fifty years together without a moment's disturbance of their domestic harmony, so entire was their mutual affection. Martin Cockburn was a fine scholar, as well as a courteous and amiable gentleman. . . ."[9]

He was elected a member of Truro Vestry in 1770 and continued to serve until 1779. He was church warden for the years 1772 and 1773. He purchased a pew in the new church. He was not active in politics but his sympathies in the struggle against England were with the colonists. He was a signer of the Fairfax County Resolutions in 1774. Throughout his life Mason showed a warm affection for him. He usually signed his letters to him: "Your affectionate friend and servant." In recommending Cockburn, he wrote: "He

[9]Rowland, Vol. 1, p. 96.

was regularly bred to business in a very capital house in London, and I know no man whose attachment to the American cause, or whose integrity, diligence and punctuality can be more thoroughly confided in." Cockburn and his wife were childless. "Springfield" was left to Mrs. Cockburn's relatives, the Masseys; and Mrs. Nancy Triplett, a daughter of the Rev. Lee Massey, was the last one of the family to live there. Martin Cockburn's nephew, Admiral Sir George Cockburn, commanded the British fleet, in the War of 1812, which was repulsed before Fort McHenry at Baltimore. Another relative, Sir Alexander Cockburn (1802-1880), was Lord Chief Justice of England.

The Bronaughs

Above the Cockburns, but fronting on Pohick Bay, lived the Bronaughs of New-Town. They were cousins of George Mason. The most prominent member of the family was Jeremiah Bronaugh, who had married a daughter of the second George Mason and was seated on his lands before 1733. He was sheriff of Prince William County and became one of the Justices of Fairfax Court when that County was organized. He was a member of the Truro Vestry from 1733 to 1744 and again from 1747 to 1750, when he died, apparently intestate, as there is an inventory of his estate in Fairfax, but no will. He was living at New-Town in 1737, as Robert Brooke's Map of the Potomac shows the house of Mrs. Brenaud there.[10]

The Bronaugh of George Mason's adult years was his son, William Bronaugh. He was a Captain of the Virginia Militia and served under Washington at Great Meadows and received bounty land on the Ohio River about which he and Washington had some correspondence, and he dined at Mt. Vernon.[11]

"New-Town, the old Bronaugh place, where Mrs. Cockburn and Mrs. Massey spent their girlhood, has passed away utterly; the very name of it is unknown in the neighborhood at this day, and recent owners of the land have ruthlessly ploughed up the old

[10] *Landmarks,* facing p. 419.
[11] *Diaries,* Vol. 2, p. 127.

graveyard, one of the old tombstones having been left leaning against a tree in one of the fields."[12]

The McCartys of Cedar Grove

The McCarty family, which was intimate both with Washington and Mason, was descended from Daniel McCarty of Westmoreland County who was Speaker of the House of Burgesses, and who married Ann Lee Fitzhugh, widow of William Fitzhugh of Eagles Nest. She was the only sister of Thomas Lee, builder of Stratford.[13] In the next generation his son, Col. Dennis McCarty, moved to the part of Prince William County, later Fairfax, and established his residence at Cedar Grove, across the narrow Pohick Bay from the Dogue Neck property of the Masons. This Dennis was elected a member of the Vestry of Truro Parish on its creation in 1732 and served until 1741. He was a member of the Prince William County Court. His daughter Ann married William Ramsay, the first Mayor of Alexandria. He died about 1744, and was succeeded in the ownership of Cedar Grove by his son, Captain Daniel McCarty, who was a trustee of the town of Colchester and married the daughter of its founder, Peter Wagener. He is often mentioned in Washington's *Diaries*. They were frequent companions in fox hunting. In 1772 "Colo Mason and Captn McCarty dined at Mount Vernon. Mason went away after dinner but McCarty stayed all night." In 1786 occurs the entry: "Mrs. Washington, Kitty Washington, Miss Ramsay, Mr. Shaw and myself went to Colo. McCarty's to the funeral of Mrs. Peers (one of his daughters)." She was the wife of Valentine Peers, of the firm of Fitzgerald and Peers of Alexandria. Daniel McCarty served on the Vestry of Truro Parish from 1749 to 1785; was one of the notable building committee, to supervise the building of the new Pohick church, and purchased a pew adjoining that of the rector.

In 1767 when the old Glebe land of 385 acres was sold by the

---

[12]Rowland, Vol, 1, p. 111.
[13]Armes, Ethel. *Stratford Hall,* p. 371.

Vestry it was purchased by Daniel McCarty for 322 pounds, Virginia currency. It was adjacent to his Cedar Grove estate.[14]

In 1777 the Vestries of the established church were deprived of the authority to levy tithes for the payment of ministers or for the maintenance and care of the church buildings, but until 1784 they were continued as parish officials with the duty of caring for the poor and the orphans. Lee Massey had resigned as rector of Truro Parish. In that year McCarty wrote to Washington notifying him of a vestry meeting to be held at Colchester. Washington had never formally resigned as vestryman but had bought a pew in Christ Church, Alexandria. Regular services at Pohick were no longer held. Washington replied that he no longer considered himself a vestryman, but made suggestions about appropriating money for the relief of the needy. McCarty had been a vestryman nearly forty years and it speaks eloquently of his devotion to Pohick that he continued his interest in that church in its decadence. He died in 1792. His will is recorded in the Fairfax Will Book E.

The McCartys owned a large plantation along Sugarland Run, west of Dranesville. It had been acquired by Daniel McCarty of Westmoreland in 1709 and was still in their possession in 1797 when Washington exchanged letters with McCarty's son, Daniel, about the exchange of this plantation for some of Washington's land on the Ohio. Nothing seems to have come of the proposal. This son married Sarah, daughter of George Mason.

"Cedar Grove" is described in Rowland's *Life of George Mason:*

" 'Cedar Grove', the McCarty place, like all those we have named, has gone out of the family of its original owners. It is beautifully situated on Pohick Creek, and is a low, rambling frame building, now much out of repair though still habitable. Its lovely water views, from its commanding position on high ground almost entirely surrounded by the creek, are its chief atraction now, but in former days, with its lawns, its orchards, and its shrubberies, it must have made a delightful residence. The family burying-ground at 'Cedar Grove' is, perhaps, a half mile from the house, in a dense grove of

[14]Slaughter. *History of Truro Parish,* pp. 61, 93.

oaks and poplars. Bending back the thick branches in this Druid-like solitude, and stooping over fallen trees, one finds three graves, with their gray, moss-covered stones, marking the spots where rest Dennis McCarty and his grandson, Daniel McCarty, with the wife of the latter, who was a daughter of Colonel Mason. Col. Daniel McCarty, the elder, the friend and contemporary of George Mason, was buried at 'Mount Airy', another family seat of the McCartys."[15]

The old house has since been destroyed. The estate is now included in the Fort Belvoir Reservation.

Richard Chichester

Richard Chichester was born in Lancaster County in the Northern Neck, his mother being a Ball. In 1766 he married a daughter of Daniel McCarty and moved to Fairfax where he established himself at Newington, near the present Accotink railroad station. He was repeatedly at Mount Vernon, where he sometimes joined Washington in fox hunts. Washington acted as godfather for one of his children, Daniel McCarty Chichester. Though living near Pohick Church his name does not appear in the list of vestrymen or other officers, nor did he hold any county office. One of his sons married Ann, daughter of George Mason. Early in his presidency Washington wrote to Dr. Craik that he expected Richard Chichester and Martin Cockburn would follow blindfolded the lead of George Mason in his opposition to the new government. As Cockburn was Mason's neighbor and intimate friend, and as Chichester was related to Mason by marriage, there was nothing surprising about this. Washington could not have expected either should be enthusiastic but he was just entering upon his administration and it displeased him that his old neighbors should not approve the new government. His letter to Dr. Craik was, of course, confidential. His displeasure was not communicated to Cockburn or Chichester.

Chichester's will was proved in the Fairfax County Court in September, 1796 and recorded in Will Book G. He was survived

[15]Rowland, Vol. 1, p. 111.

by his widow, Sarah, daughter of Daniel McCarty, by sons Doddridge Pitt Chichester and Daniel McCarty Chichester, and by daughters and grandchildren. It was to these sons, apparently, that Washington sent a sharp note forbidding them to hunt deer upon his land.

When the town of Providence (now Fairfax) was incorporated by act of the Virginia Assembly in 1805, Daniel McCarty Chichester was named one of its trustees, so presumably he no longer lived at Newington. Unlike many of the old families, the Chichesters have continued to live in Fairfax County and have been prominent in law, medicine and politics.

The Tripletts

The first of this family to appear on the Fairfax records was Francis, whose will is recorded in 1758, in Will Book B, and names, among others, sons Thomas and William. The family home was at Round Hill on the back (now the Telegraph) road adjoining on the south Lund Washington's estate of Hayfield. William was a Vestryman of Truro from 1776 to 1785 and, with Thomas Withers Coffer, purchased pew No. 5 in the Pohick Church. Thomas Triplett served in Washington's regiment in the French and Indian War. He was a man of some prominence in his neighborhood, and was one of those invited by Mrs. Washington to the funeral of the General.[16] Washington visited him repeatedly and went on numerous fox hunts with him, and he was repeatedly at Mount Vernon. In 1773 the "two Mr. Tripletts, Mr. Manly and Mr. Peake, all came to Dinner, and Mr. Thomas Triplett stayed all Night."[17] This Thomas was a Justice of the Peace and served on the County Committee of Safety of Fairfax in 1774.[18] It is possible that some of William Triplett's work can be seen at Mount Vernon today: "March 27-1760: Agreed to give Mr. William Triplett £18 to build two Houses in the Front of my House

[16]Slaughter. *History of Truro Parish,* p. 119.
[17]*Diaries,* Vol. 2, p. 103.
[18]*Ibid.,* Vol. 1, p. 142 (note).

(plastering them also), and running wall for Pallisades to them, from the Great house and from the Great House to the Wash House and Kitchen also."[19]

Round Hill stood in a dilapidated condition until about twenty-five years ago. It was across the road from the Truro glebe.

Occoquan

Before Dumfries, Alexandria or Colchester were towns, there was a considerable commercial development at the falls of the Occoquan. Robert Brooke's Map of the Potomack shows that before 1737 there was a small community there, as the houses of Mr. Brenaud, Mrs. Cofer,[20] Mr. Catesby Cock, Mr. James Baxter, and Mr. Grensden are shown on his map. The location of the first Pohick Church (two miles away) was probably dictated by its nearness to this community. In 1759 the Merchants Grist Mill was built below the falls. It was destroyed in 1924, but its massive stone walls still remain. The first Prince William Courthouse was located at Woodbridge nearby. Occoquan, it seemed, was destined to become the metropolis of Prince William, but it missed its chance and when the town of Colchester was established on the Occoquan in 1753 it was located on the Fairfax side. It was not until 1805 that an act of the Legislature created the town of Occoquan. Its situation in a narrow, rocky valley was unfavorable to the growth of a considerable town. The bridge over the river here was built in 1795 by Nathaniel Ellicott pursuant to an act of the General Assembly authorizing the erection of a toll bridge.[21] Until the building of the present high bridge at Woodbridge, U.S. Highway No. 1 passed by the Ellicott Bridge through Occoquan.

In the center of the village, but somewhat back from the main street, on the side of a steep hill, stands a much older house—Rockledge . . . "a two story rock house, with dormers, built in 1759

[19]*Ibid.*, p. 142.

[20]"Mrs. Cofer" was probably the mother of Thomas Withers Coffer, Vestryman of Truro (1765-1784). There is a short biographical note on him in Goodwin's *History of Truro Parish.*

[21]Prince William (American Guide Series), p. 79.

by John Ballendine on designs by Mathew Buckland. Under the gabled roof runs a fine denticulated cornice. With window panes that time has made iridescent, and a crane swinging in the huge kitchen fireplace, Rockledge preserves the fine qualities of its builder."[22]

The house passed through the ownership of three notable men in the eighteenth century. Ballendine established a flour mill and iron works at the falls of the Occoquan. He planned a stock company to improve the navigation of the upper Potomac and interested Washington in the project. He went to England to get subscriptions. Although he did not succeed, it was the beginning of the "Potomack Company" to which Washington later was to devote his energies.[23] Ballendine's affairs on the Occoquan, perhaps due to his attention to his canal projects, forced him to borrow money from John Semple of Charles County, Maryland, who took over his Occoquan Mills and succeeded him in the ownership of Rockledge. He died in 1773 leaving a will probated in Prince William County. About the end of the eighteenth century the ownership of the mills passed to the Quaker, Nathaniel Ellicott. It was he who employed the young Englishman, John Davis, as a tutor for his children. Occoquan, Davis wrote: "consists only of a house built upon a rock, three others on the riverside and a half dozen log huts scattered at some distance. Yet no place can be more romantic than the view of Occoquan to a stranger, after crossing the rustic bridge which has been constructed by the inhabitants across the stream. He contemplates the river urging its course along mountains that lose themselves among the clouds; he beholds vessells taking on board flour from the mills, and others, deeply laden, expanding their sails to the breeze; while every face wears contentment, every gale wafts health, and echo from the rocks multiples the voices of the waggoners calling to their teams."[24]

---

[22]Virginia *Guide*, p. 344.

[23]*Diaries*, Vol. 1, p. 363.

[24]*Four and One Half Years in the United States*, by John Davis, quoted by Fairfax Harrison in his *Landmarks*, pp. 429-430.

More than half a century ago a flat-bottomed steamer carried excursionists from Washington thirty miles down the Potomac and ten miles up Belmont Bay to the village. The long river trip was tedious, but it was repaid by a walk of a mile along the Occoquan, tumbling and swirling over great rocks, and across on the Fairfax side precipitous hills (not mountains as Burnaby and Davis called them) added to the romantic view. The silting of the Occoquan destroyed the flour trade of the village and the sails that delighted Davis have vanished, but the river and its wooded hills are still beautiful.

Chapter 19

Ravensworth

On October 1st, 1694 the proprietors of the Northern Neck granted to William Fitzhugh a tract of 19,996 acres lying in the part of Stafford County subsequently included in Fairfax County.[1] The land lay inward from the Potomac River. The metes and bounds given in the patent show that it included Accotink Creek, parts of Pohick Creek, Back-lick Run and Holmes Run. A line of its northern boundary is Four Mile Run, near its source, now in Falls Church. It was the largest grant of land in Fairfax County. The patent recites an earlier grant in 1686 which had been lost.

The patentee was Col. William Fitzhugh, of Bedford, on the Potomac River, then in Stafford County, but now in King George. He was born in England in 1651 and died at his residence in Virginia in 1701. He was a lawyer of repute, a member of the Stafford County Court for many years, and accumulated much land. His personal property included costly silverware and portraits. He was what was unusual in Virginia of his day—a Tory in politics and a high churchman in religion. Copies of much of his correspondence with his London agent have been preserved and are now in the archives of the Virginia Historical Society. He was interested in diverting the emigration of the French Huguenots to Virginia and secured a small party of them as tenants on his Ravensworth plantation, where he set them to raising tobacco. By his will, proved in Stafford County,[2] he divided "His Accotink dividend" (Ravens-

---

[1]Northern Neck Land Grants, Vol. 2, p. 14.
[2]Stafford County Will Book, Liber Z, folio 92.

worth) equally between his two eldest sons, William of Eagle's Nest and Henry of Bedford. At some subsequent date a division of the tract was made between William, who died in 1714, and Henry, who was born in 1687 and died in 1758. The line of division was apparently the "Braddock Road" running from Alexandria to Centerville, Henry Fitzhugh taking the part north of the road and William or his heirs taking the part south. Presumably the division was made by a survey, but there is no record of it in the Fairfax, Prince William or the Stafford Records. The original patent does not designate the tract as Ravensworth. It was not until 1724 that the name appears on the records and then as describing an adjoining tract as bordering on Ravensworth (Northern Neck A—208).[3]

In the late eighteenth century the owner of the southern half of the Ravensworth plantation was William Fitzhugh of Chatham, great-grandson of William Fitzhugh the emigrant.[4]

Chatham is supposed to have been built about 1765. It is opposite Fredericksburg and overlooks the Rappahannock and the town. Set amidst its terraced gardens, with its outbuildings still intact, it is as beautiful as when built, with the added charm of age.

This William married Ann Bolling Randolph. Washington and Mrs. Washington visited him when in Fredericksburg, and he visited repeatedly at Mount Vernon, as Washington's *Diaries* show. He was a patron of the turf and laid off a racecourse east of his house. Washington valued his judgment of horses, for in 1798, when war with France seemed impending, he wrote to Fitzhugh asking if he could sell him or recommend a riding horse—"knowing that you are a good judge of the parts and general symmetry of a horse of figure."[5]

Fitzhugh offered to give Washington a doe for his deer park.

---

[3]Cited in *Landmarks of Old Prince William,* p. 195.

[4]The descent of William Fitzhugh of Chatham, born 1743, from William Fitzhugh the emigrant is given in Eubank, H. Ragland. *Historic Northern Neck of Virginia* as (1) William Fitzhugh of Bedford, emigrant; (2) William Fitzhugh, his eldest son; (3) Henry Fitzhugh of Eagle's Nest; (4) William Fitzhugh of Chatham.

[5]*Writings,* Vol. 36, p. 390.

In thanking him Washington asked that the doe be kept at Chatham until he had enclosed the deer park at Mount Vernon.

While a man of means, Fitzhugh felt the strain and expense of constant entertaining. He is reported to have said he had so many visitors that they turned his home into a tavern and ate him out of house and home.[6] So toward the close of the century, he sold Chatham to Major Churchill Jones and moved to Ravensworth to obtain quiet and peace. This vast plantation was no longer a wilderness outpost.

Fairfax County had become a well settled community with seaports at Alexandria and Colchester. A rolling road called the Ravensworth Road, leading to Colchester, afforded access to tidewater for the shipment of its tobacco and other products. The Braddock Road passed through it. By Act of the General Assembly, Benoni Price had established an ordinary on this road on the "land of William Fitzhugh, gentleman."[7] It had become a profitable quarter, managed by agents. Fitzhugh advertised Chatham for sale in the Philadelphia papers in 1796,[8] but nothing came of this as he subsequently sold it to Major Jones. He evidently kept an eye on his Ravensworth plantation, as Washington noted in his diary of August 8, 1786, "Mr. Fitzhugh of Chatham and Mr. Robert Randolph came here from Ravensworth."[9] The last entry in the diaries mentioning Fitzhugh is dated July 1st 1797 and styles him "of Chatham."[10]

As Fitzhugh purchased a house in Alexandria in 1799, he probably moved to Ravensworth at the same time. The Alexandria house is No. 607 Oronoco Street and is still standing. It was later occupied by Anne Carter Lee and is known as the Robert E. Lee house.[11]

William Fitzhugh died at Ravensworth and is buried in the

[6]Goolrick, John T. *Fredericksburg,* p. 64.
[7]*Landmarks of Old Prince William,* p. 324.
[8]*Diaries,* Vol. 2, p. 427 (note).
[9]*Ibid.,* Vol. 3, p. 105.
[10]*Ibid.,* Vol. 4, p. 279.
[11]Davis, Dorsey, and Hall. *Alexandria Houses,* p. 88.

small family burying ground, where there are four marble obelisks of identical design; one "Sacred to the memory of William Fitzhugh, born September 4th, 1741, died December 18th, 1809." Beside it is the tomb of his wife, Ann Fitzhugh, born May 15th, 1747, died August 10th, 1805.

The will of William Fitzhugh, dated September 3d, 1805, reciting himself, formerly of Chatham, but now residing in Alexandria, was however (with two codicils) admitted to probate in Fairfax County in December 1809 (Will Book J no. 1, page 244). It devised to his daughter Mary L. Custis, land in Westmoreland County, and confirmed to his daughter Ann Randolph Craik part of the Ravensworth tract containing about 800 acres. She was the Nancy Craik, wife of George Washington Craik, and daughter-in-law of Dr. James Craik, often mentioned in Washington's *Diaries*.

The residue of his estate he devised to his infant son, William Henry Fitzhugh, "with the hope that he will make a proper use of it, that he will prove himself a good and virtuous man, an affectionate brother and a friend to all good men." This son spent his short life at Ravensworth, dying at the age of thirty-eight. He married Anna Maria Sarah Goldsborough of Talbot County, Maryland. His will, dated March 21st, 1829, requested that he be interred in the family graveyard "with as little parade as possible" and that three monuments—very simple pyramids—be erected to his father, his mother and himself.

He devised the main part of his Ravensworth estate to his wife, Anna Maria Fitzhugh, for her life and in remainder after her death to his niece, Mary Ann Randolph Custis. His will was proved in the Fairfax County Court and is recorded in Will Book Q, No. 1, pages 57 and 243. The inscription on his tomb reads: "Sacred to the Memory of William Henry Fitzhugh, born March 9th, 1792, died May 21st, 1830." Beside it is the tombstone of his wife, Anna Maria Sarah, "born November 15th, 1796, died October 17th, 1874."

His sister, Mary Lee Fitzhugh (1788-1853), at the age of sixteen, married George Washington Parke Custis and became shortly afterwards the mistress of the newly completed Arlington Mansion. Custis and his wife had an only daughter, Mary Ann Randolph. In 1831 she married Robert E. Lee. She survived her illustrious husband and died in 1873. The life tenant of the will of William Henry Fitzhugh thus survived the remainder-man, Mary Ann Randolph Lee, by less than a year. It does not appear that Mary Ann Randolph Lee ever visited Ravensworth after the beginning of the Civil War. Whether the widow of William Henry Fitzhugh continued to occupy the mansion during the Civil War is not known, but she is buried there and the chances are she returned after the War. If so she was the mistress of the house in 1869 and 1870 when General Lee made two short visits there. In July 1869 he came to Alexandria to attend the funeral of his brother, Sidney Smith Lee. In Dr. Freeman's *R. E. Lee* the first visit is described thus: "In melancholy mood, he went from the Mansion House, Alexandria, to Ravensworth, rested a day or two in its pleasant shade, and wandered about the well-beloved old house. At the door of the room in which his mother had died, he paused, almost overwhelmed by memories. 'Forty years ago', he wrote to his wife, 'I stood in this room by my mother's death-bed! It seems now but yesterday!' "[112]

The following summer, he went again to Ravensworth and stayed about a week. His health was failing, the weather was hot, and he then returned to his home in Lexington where he died in 1870.

General Lee's mother, Ann Carter Lee, was buried at Ravensworth in the family graveyard, but her body was subsequently re-interred in the Chapel of Washington and Lee University at Lexington.

In 1867, General Lee's son, William H. F. Lee (who had commanded a division of cavalry in the war), married Mary Tabb Bolling in Petersburg. The marriage was a brilliant affair, the bride having ten bridesmaids, and the groom attended by the same

[112]Freeman, *R. E. Lee,* Vol. 4, p. 434.

number of friends. Lee and his sons were present, but Mrs. Lee's health prevented her being there.[12]

On the death of Anna Maria Fitzhugh in 1874 the Ravensworth estate, then comprising over eight thousand acres, became the property of Mrs. Lee's sons and daughters. They partitioned it by deeds recorded in the Fairfax County Deed Book R-4, pages 453 to 464, to which is attached a plat of the land. General W. H. Fitzhugh Lee (Rooney Lee) received the mansion house and five hundred and sixty-three acres, thus perpetuating the Fitzhugh name in the ownership for his lifetime. He spent the remainder of his life there as a gentleman farmer. He was elected a member of the House of Representatives, and told this amusing story of his campaign. He asked each man he encountered in his tours, "How is your wife?" One of the persons to whom he put the question answered, "She is dead." Meeting the same man again and not recognizing him, he put the same question, and got the answer, "She is still dead."

He died in 1891 leaving a will devising all his estate to his wife, Mary Tabb Bolling Lee, for her life and after her death to be divided between his two sons, Robert E. Lee, Jr. and George Bolling Lee. The widow died about 1900. Robert E. Lee, Jr. died in 1922, leaving his half interest in Ravensworth to his wife, Mary M., for her life or widowhood, and in remainder to his brother, George Bolling Lee. On the death of the widow the title to Ravensworth became vested in Dr. George Bolling Lee. He was a surgeon living in New York City, and the farm was entrusted to a manager. It was during his ownership that the mansion was burned.

His will, dated in 1944, a copy of which is filed in the Clerk's Office of Fairfax County, devised the residue of his estate to trustees for the benefit of his wife, Helen Keeney Lee, who is still living. She has recently returned to Ravensworth, and is living in a frame house near the site of the former mansion. All that is left of the mansion is an outbuilding and a large brick barn.

---

[12]Freeman. *R. E. Lee,* Vol. 4, p. 339.

Ravensworth formerly contained a valuable collection of Custis, Fitzhugh, Lee, and Bolling portraits, which fortunately were removed before its destruction. These have been entrusted to the custody of the Virginia Historical Society by Mrs. Helen Keeney Lee, and are now hung in Battle Abbey in Richmond.[13]

Custis Lee and Ravensworth

George Washington Custis Lee, oldest son of General Lee, graduated from West Point and like his father entered the Engineer Corps of the Army. He succeeded his father as President of Washington College, renamed Washington and Lee. He was a man of scholarly tastes, modest and self-effacing. Realizing he was not a success as a university executive, he made several attempts to resign, but it was not until 1897 that the trustees accepted his resignation. The $150,000 he had received from the United States government for his quitclaim deed to Arlington put him in comfortable circumstances; and he retired to Ravensworth, at that time the home of his brother's widow, Mrs. Mary Bolling Lee, and her son, Robert E. Lee, Jr. There he led a quiet life, receiving few visitors other than his two sisters, Miss Mary and Miss Mildred Lee. His days were spent in the garden and around the farm, and he took great interest in the farmers and the servants. His evenings were spent in the library reading, mostly scientific books dealing with engineering. He remained unmarried, and the sixteen years he lived there were the happiest of his life. He died in 1913 and his remains were laid in the family chapel beside those of his father.[14]

Ossian and Oak Hill

As stated above, the will of William Fitzhugh, the immigrant, devised the Ravensworth tract to be divided between his two older sons, William and Henry, and on division Henry received the northern half. This son, known as Captain Henry Fitzhugh (1686-

---

[13] *Virginia Magazine of History and Biography,* Vol. 57, no. 2, p. 205. April 1949.

[14] "George Washington Custis Lee." By Jas. Lewis Howe. *Virginia Magazine of History and Biography,* October 1940.

Oak Hill, Fairfax County (Pages 228 to 229)
Photographed by Mrs. Margaret B. Stetson

Adams-Payne House, near Munson Hill, Fairfax County, Virginia (Pages 232 and 233)
Photographed by Mrs. Margaret B. Stetson

Wren House, Shreve Road near Dunn Loring, Virginia (Pages 233 and 234)
Photographed by Mrs. Margaret B. Stetson

1758), married Susanna Cooke. They left issue, Major Henry Fitzhugh (1723-1783), who married Sarah Battaille. Lund Washington was Henry Fitzhugh's manager for his part of Ravensworth before he entered Washington's employ at Mount Vernon at the beginning of the Revolution. Major Henry Fitzhugh was still residing in Stafford, now King George, County, and it is believed he never moved to his Ravensworth plantation. His will was proved in King George County on June 5, 1783. He left his lands in Fairfax County called "Ravensworth" to his sons, Nicholas, Richard, Mordecai, Battaille, and Giles. A plat of the division is recorded in Fairfax Courthouse, Deed Book A-2, folio 186, in which it is recited he left a will devising a life estate to his wife and a remainder to his children as joint tenants. One object of the partition was to convert the joint tenancy into estates as tenants in common. Nicholas was allotted 1062 acres, which he divided into an upper and lower tract. He was a man of some importance. He was a member of the House of Delegates from Fairfax County for the years 1790, 1791, and 1802. He was appointed a judge of the Circuit Court of the District of Columbia (which then included Alexandria).

Washington was well acquainted with both Major Henry and his son Nicholas. The latter dined and stayed all night at Mount Vernon in 1798, and he was there again in 1799.[15] About a month before his death, Washington visited his land on Difficult Run, and on his way "dined at Mr. Nicholas Fitzhugh's." This was probably at Ossian.

Judge Nicholas Fitzhugh married Sarah Washington Ashton.[16] In 1804 he conveyed to Dr. David Stuart part of the tract of Ravensworth "on Accotinque Run lying north of the road from Centerville to Alexandria, containing 831 ¼ acres, part of the lands devised to said Nicholas by his father, Henry Fitzhugh and upon which the said Nicholas lately resided." The consideration was 13,854 Spanish milled dollars.[17] This was the tract that Stuart named Ossian.

---

[15] *Diaries,* Vol. 4, pp. 275, 298, 316.
[16] Compendium of American Genealogy, Vol. 5.
[17] Fairfax County Deed Book E-2, folio 289-291.

The will of Nicholas Fitzhugh, proved in 1815, devised to his sons, Augustine, Edmund, Burdett, Henry William, Charles, and Laurence, "the residue of my lower tract out of which I sold to Doctor Stuart 831 acres" and several hundred additional acres contiguous to the residue. These parcels probably included the Oak Hill tract. His will was proved and admitted to record in Alexandria County (then in the District of Columbia) where the testator then lived, and a certified copy transmitted to the Court of Fairfax County. The descendants of the Fitzhughs continued to live at Oak Hill for many years after his death.

In the sixties the owner of Oak Hill was David Fitzhugh. It is said in the neighborhood that he left Oak Hill "the day the 'Yankees' crossed the Potomac and took refuge in Culpeper and he never returned."

His will, made in 1861 and proved in Fairfax County in March 1868 (Will Book A-2, folio 343), devised to his sister, Ann F. Battaille, "the farm on which I now reside," subject to the life estate of his sister Maria in the said property, about 900 acres.

In 1889, Nancy T. Battaille deeded her share, which included Oak Hill, to William Watt for $900 being "all that tract or parcel of land in the County of Fairfax designated at Lot no. 1 upon the plat of the partition of the real estate of which Ann F. Battaille died seized . . .," except ten acres previously sold to Jonas Ayres. (Liber H-5, folio 559).

After the death of William Watt, his son, Egbert T. Watt, and his wife, Grace Watt, sold this property (50 acres and the dwelling) to the present owners, Edward F. Howrey and his wife Jane G. Howrey. The deed, dated June 24, 1935, is recorded in Fairfax Deed Book H no. 5, folio 559.

Oak Hill has been admirably restored by the present owners. The house is situated on a gentle eminence a short distance west of County road 650 (known as Wakefield Chapel Road) running from the Braddock Road to the Little River turnpike. The inscription "Oak Hill" is on the brick gateposts at the entrance to the private road leading through the woods to the house. Nearer the house the road is lined with English box.

Oak Hill and Ossian are built on the same plan (and possibly had the same builder). But Ossian is two rooms deep and Oak Hill one. The traditional date assigned for the building of both is about 1730, but this seems much too early. Fairfax County was not created until 1742, Alexandria was laid off in 1749, and Colchester several years later. Belvoir was built by William Fairfax in 1741 and Gunston by George Mason in 1758. It is improbable that such substantial houses as Ossian and Oak Hill were built so far from the Potomac River at so early a date. There may have been overseers' houses on these tracts before 1780.

Mr. Egbert Watt, who has spent most of his life in the neighborhood, recalls that Miss "Dolly" Fitzhugh, daughter of William Fitzhugh of Cool Spring, used to visit his family at Oak Hill, and she told him that it was built about 1780 for an eighteen year old Fitzhugh bride. He did not remember her name. That is probably the approximate date of Oak Hill and Ossian. Cool Spring, another old Fitzhugh house built some distance west of Oak Hill, is no longer standing.

The End of Ossian

Ossian will probably not be standing much longer, as a New York corporation purchased the property at the end of 1954 from the estate of the late Senator Joseph Little Bristow of Kansas who died in 1944. It is said that the plan is to construct 2000 houses on the 900 acres purchased, and that the house is in too bad repair to be worth saving. This is a misfortune from the historic point of view. The old house has been standing for about 175 years. Washington visited it when it was the home of the Fitzhugh family. In the early part of the 19th century it was the home of Dr. David Stuart. Early in the 20th century it was purchased by Senator Bristow. During his ownership, appropriate plantings were made of box and other shrubs to enhance the beauty of the natural setting. As seen from the Braddock Road across the fields sloping gently to the crest of the hill the house presents a lovely picture against a background of great oak trees.

Belvoir, Abington, Lund Washington's Hayfield, and Ravensworth of the Fitzhugh Lee family were burned. Ossian may be deliberately torn down. Mount Vernon, Gunston Hall, and Woodlawn still stand and are protected from the depredations of modern progress. All lovers of Colonial Virginia must regret the failure of Ossian to have such protection.

The Ravensworth Rolling Road

From the time that John Rolfe raised the first tobacco in Virginia the problem of getting it to England arose. The tobacco was prized into hogsheads and rolled on board the ships. They were rolled by the sailors, or, when the tobacco had to be rolled some distance, by slaves or indentured servants. As almost all the early plantations lay close to navigable water, getting the tobacco to the ship was not difficult. But by the end of the seventeenth century many of the settlements were farther inland and the distance the hogsheads had to be rolled was too great to push them as heretofore. The method adopted was to place an iron bar through the center of the hogshead to which shafts were attached so it could be drawn by horses or oxen. For this purpose many former bridle paths were improved and widened and became known as rolling roads.

The Virginia authorities collected a tax on tobacco exported. At first this tax was paid when the tobacco was placed on board the ship, or at the wharf, where private sheds, called rolling houses, were built to shelter it in case the amount was too large to roll on shipboard at one time. As the export of tobacco became more extensive and was the chief export crop of the Colony, acts were passed regulating the trade. These culminated in the tobacco inspection act of Governor Gooch in 1730, providing for inspection warehouses, called "Agents houses" and the rejection of poor tobacco. On the tobacco stored the agent issued demand notes, which were negotiable and accepted in payment of all public charges. This act varied only in detail from the one passed in 1713 under Governor

Spottswood, which had been disallowed by the Crown for political reasons. To Governor Gooch credit is due for his persistence in getting it re-enacted, but Governor Spottswood was responsible for the original idea of using the certificates as currency payable for public dues.

Under the Act of 1730, through the influence of the McCartys and the Fitzhughs, a warehouse was established on McCarty lands on Pohick Bay at the foot of the already existing Ravensworth rolling road. This road ran from the Braddock Road southeasterly along the ridge between Pohick and Accotink Creeks. The "back road" from Great Hunting Creek crossed it at Pohick Church making a convenient connection with Colchester when it was established. The existence of the rolling road indicates there was tobacco sufficient for export raised on the Ravensworth Estate, and that quarters had been established.

It has been many years since tobacco was raised in Fairfax County, but the old road from the Braddock Road to Shirley Highway is still marked "Rolling Road." It is at present a hard-surfaced road, designated as Fairfax County road number 638. The woods through which it runs are of secondary growth, and the country is still sparsely settled. Only one farm is seen from the road. Part of the road is bordered on the east by a military reservation. There are indications that new subdivisions are planned.

Chapter 20

Other Neighbors

William Adams

William Adams was the son of Gabriel Adams, who was a member of the Truro Vestry in 1732 and 1733. His will was proved in Fairfax in 1750 and is recorded in the Fairfax Will Book A. He named as executors his sons Gabriel and William.

This William was sheriff of Fairfax County in 1767 and charged with collecting the parish levy for the upper part of Truro Parish, which included the part where the Falls Church was located.[1] He seems to have been an active member of the Old Falls Church as Washington's Ledger has an entry 1770: "By Mr. William Adam for my subscription toward decorating the Falls Church £1."[2] He had a mill where the Columbia Pike crosses Holmes Run. The ruins of a stone mill are there yet, which may be the ruins of his mill. His home tract, however, lay southwest of the present Munson Hill and within sight of the Alexandria-Leesburg road. It adjoined on the southwest a tract of 790 acres patented by his father[3] which Washington subsequently acquired and incorporated in his Four Mile Run tract. Washington surveyed his land several times. A copy of his last survey appears in the author's *Four Mile Run Land Grants*. A corner of his land is shown as "in Mr. W. Adams old field." It was his custom when surveying this tract to call the adjoining proprietors to avoid future disputes about the lines between his and their properties. In his last survey in 1799 he made an entry

[1]*Diaries,* Vol. 1, p. 388 (note).
[2]*Ibid.,* p. 369 (note).
[3]Northern Neck Land Grants, Liber C, folio 136.

in his diary: "Apr 4th Recommenced to survey at the upper end where we left off, in Company with Colo. Little, Captn Terrett and Mr. William Adams."[4]

William Adams died in 1809 and his will, dated March 7, 1806, was admitted to probate in Fairfax County, Will Book (Sup. Court) pages 5 to 7. He devised to his son Wesley Adams his dwelling house and plantation. At some time either before or after the Civil War the house and adjoining land passed to the Payne family and it is generally known as the Payne house. The house was originally a story and a half. Within the last twenty-five years a second story was added. The old brick walls are now covered with white clapboarding. It is pleasantly situated in a small grove of trees. The present owner is Mr. Donald Macleay.

James Wren and the Falls Church

James Wren was the only builder living in Fairfax County in the eighteenth century who can be justly styled an architect as well as a builder, and as an architect he is praised by Thomas Tileston Waterman in his *Mansions of Virginia.* He was paid forty shillings for plans furnished the Vestry of Truro for Pohick Church.[5] He also drew the plans for Christ Church, Alexandria, and he was architect and builder of Falls Church in Fairfax County. Not much is known of him. In 1753 he married Catherine, daughter of Charles Brent.[6] He was a Justice of the Peace for Fairfax County, and a Trustee of the stillborn town of Turberville in 1798, which was laid off near the Little Falls of the Potomac.[7] He must have married a second time for in his will dated March 9th 1808 and recorded in Will Book K no. 1, page 367 of the Fairfax records he devised to his wife Sarah, a life estate in "the tract whereon I live on," with remainder to his son John. His small but lovely house is still standing, a short distance from the railway station of Dunn

[4]*Diaries,* Vol. 4, p. 301.
[5]Slaughter, *History of Truro Parish,* p. 70.
[6]Overwharton Parish Register, cited in *Virginia Magazine of History and Biography,* April 1926, p. 182.
[7]Harrison, *Landmarks,* p. 666.

Loring. Like the Adams-Payne house it has been weatherboarded to protect its brick walls, but unlike it, it remains as Wren built it. At some time in the nineteenth century it must have been acquired by the Darne family, as it is still known by that name in the neighborhood.

The Falls Church

The present church is the successor of an earlier one built in 1733 at the crossroads near Michael Reagan's. The crossroad was formed by the intersection of the present Alexandria and Leesburg Road with a road leading to the Little Falls of the Potomac. The church was not built on Michael Reagan's land, but on the land of John Trammell, who subsequently made a deed for two acres to the Vestry of Truro Parish. The church continued to be in Truro until 1765 when Fairfax Parish was carved out of Truro. Christ Church, Alexandria and Falls Church were in the new parish. The first regular rector was the Rev. Charles Green who had charge of Pohick, Christ Church and Falls Church. The present church was planned while the wooden church near the crossroads was still in Truro Parish. The evidence is an entry in the Vestry Book of Truro: "At a Vestry held at the Falls Church March 28th 1763. Present Henry Gunnell, William Payne Jun, Church Wardens, John West, William Payne (sen), Charles Broadwater, Thomas Wren, Abra. Barnes, Danl. McCarty, Robert Bogges and Geo. Washington, Vestrymen. Who being there met to examine into the state of the said Church greatly in decay and want of repairs, and likewise whether the same should be repaired, or a new one built, and whether at the same place or removed to a more convenient one—Resolved it is the opinion of this Vestry that a new church be built at the same place."[8] The order went on to direct advertisements for bids for building a Brick Church with a gallery. This was in 1763. Two years later and before the present building was completed the new Fairfax Parish was created by an Act of the Virginia Assembly, out of part of Truro. Washington was a Vestryman of Fairfax Parish

---

[8]Slaughter, *History of Truro Parish*, pp. 34, 35.

for a few months only, when the line between Truro and Fairfax was altered by another Act of the Assembly and Washington's estate was restored to Truro. He had no further official connection with Falls Church. It is of record, however, that he and George William Fairfax, as Church Wardens, signed the advertisement in 1764 calling for bids on the new building.[9] After the building of the new church, the Rev. Townsend Dade was rector of both Christ Church, Alexandria and the Falls Church. He was succeeded by the Rev. David Griffith, who in turn was succeeded by Bryan Fairfax. Washington's correspondence and his *Diaries* contain no evidence that he ever attended services at the brick church. He did, on one occasion at least, attend service in the old church. In 1760 there is an entry: "Set out for Frederick to see my Negroes that lay ill of the Small Pox. Took church in my way to Coleman's where I arrived about sun-setting."[10] The church that he took in on his way must have been the wooden church near Michael Reagan's. There is a tradition that he occasionally attended service at the present church. That may be, but his correspondence and his diaries do not mention it. With the disestablishment of the church in Virginia, the Falls Church fell on evil days. Tithes for the support of the ministers and for the maintenance of church buildings were abolished. The congregations were untrained in voluntary contributions.

Writing to a correspondent in 1786, Washington told him of the condition of Pohick Church and added: "A Church above this, formerly under the same ministry is, I believe, unprovided; but of what Religion the people thereabout *now* are, I am unable to say. Most probably a medley, as they have had Methodist and Baptist preachers of all kinds among them."[11]

Writing of its condition in 1827 Bishop Meade states: "It was deserted as a house of worship by Episcopalians about forty years ago. About that period, for the first, and it is believed for the last

[9] *Ibid.*, p. 36.
[10] *Diaries*, Vol. 1, p. 159.
[11] *Wrtings*, Vol. 28, p. 527.

time, it was visited by Bishop Madison. Since then it has been used by any who were disposed to occupy it as a place of worship; and the doors and windows being open, itself standing on the common highway, it has been entered at pleasure by travellers on the road and animals of every kind."[12] He further states that some years later, students from the Theological Seminary near Alexandria conducted occasional services there. "This led to its partial repair," the expense chiefly borne by Henry Fairfax, of Ash Grove, grandson of Bryan Fairfax. The church went through a trying experience in the Civil War, being used as a hospital, and later as a stable; but in compensation, the Federal Government expended thirteen hundred dollars in repairs. The thriving town of Falls Church has grown up around the church since the Civil War, and it is now in a prosperous condition. Under the leadership of its present rector, the Rev. Francis J. Hayes, a large parish house has been recently erected. In its quiet grove in the center of a busy town, this survival of the eighteen century is an island of repose. Its durable walls and its simplicity of design are a tribute to its architect and builder, James Wren.

Colonel Charles Broadwater

Another Fairfax man with whom Washington was thrown in close contact in the earlier part of his career was Charles Broadwater. He was the son of Captain Charles Broadwater, a merchant mariner, who had established himself on the south side of Great Hunting Creek in the decade between 1720 and 1730. A tobacco warehouse was directed to be built on his land. None appears to have been erected, as a later Act of Assembly passed in 1732 transferred the warehouse to Simon Pearson's land on the north side of the creek "as more convenient." He was elected a member of the Truro Vestry in 1732,[13] but died in 1733. He patented several tracts of land in the present Fairfax County, on one of which he is said to have settled. He left two sons, Charles and Guy. His son Charles served in the French and Indian War, for in 1756, Washington

[12]Meade, Wm. *Old Churches and Families of Virginia,* Vol. 2, pp. 257-258.
[13]Slaughter, p. 120.

"received an express from Captn Broadwater at the Gap of the Short Hills (Hillsborough) informing me that himself and the Captns. Ramsay, Minor and Hamilton with abt 100 Men were at this place; that he had received dispatches to hurry on the Militia and desir'd to know wht number shoud be sent."[14] Presumably he continued in the service until danger to Virginia had been removed. He was a Vestryman of Truro from 1744 to 1765. As previously noted, Fairfax Parish was created in 1765. As Broadwater was in the new parish, he was a member of its vestry in 1765, in 1775, and again in 1787, and presumably attended the Falls Church. He was also prominent in local politics. For many years he was one of the Justices of the Fairfax County Court.

In 1774 he was a candidate for election to the House of Burgesses as a colleague of Washington. The latter wrote to Bryan Fairfax urging him to run (which Bryan declined to do), and adding, "I entreated several gentlemen at our church yesterday to press Colo. Mason to take a poll, as I really think Major Broadwater, though a good man, might do as well in the discharge of his domestic concerns as in the capacity of a legislator."[15] In saying this Washington violated his own maxim: "I never say anything of a Man that I have the slightest scruple of saying *to him*."

Broadwater was elected a Burgess at the election and was also delegate to the Virginia Convention in March 1775 with Washington. Washington left for the Continental Congress and in July of the same year Broadwater and George Mason were elected. In December of the same year Broadwater alone represented Fairfax.

A part of his political success may have been due to the fact that he came from the western part of the County where there were fewer men of prominence. It is natural to suppose that the Hutchinsons, the Gunnells, the Hunters, the Jenkinses, were jealous of the monopoly of county offices enjoyed by the Fairfaxes, Washington, Mason, the Wests and the Alexandria men, George Johnston, John Carlyle, Thomison Ellzey and others.

---

[14] *Writings,* Vol. 1, p. 345.
[15] *Ibid.,* Vol. 3, p. 227.

About 1790 Major Broadwater seems to have retired to his home and estate of "Springfield," on the old Courthouse Road, near Vienna, where he died in 1806. His house stood until about thirty years ago, when demolished to make way for several modern houses. The graves of the family still remain. The Fairfax County Chapter of the Daughters of the American Revolution have erected a white marble headstone over his grave, inscribed "Colonel Charles Broadwater, Colonial Service, died 1806."[16]

The Blackburns

Colonel Thomas Blackburn, so frequently mentioned in Washington's diaries and correspondence, was the son of Richard Blackburn (1702-1757) who built Rippon Lodge on the Potomac Path, a few miles north of Dumfries. His tombstone there with a long inscription can still be read. He was a friend of the Honorable William Fairfax and of Lawrence Washington. His son Thomas (1740-1807) married a daughter of the Rev. James Scott, rector of the Quantico Church, and was chosen a trustee of Dumfries in 1774 and of Centerville in 1792. Washington often stopped at Rippon Lodge on his way to Williamsburg and Richmond and sometimes spent the night there.[17] Bushrod Washington married his daughter, Julia Ann. Washington received an invitation to the wedding, but sent his regrets.

"Monday, October 10, 1785. Genl. and Mrs. Washington present their compliments to Colo. and Mrs. Blackburn; are much obliged to them for their kind invitation to the Wedding on Thursday. They would attend with pleasure, but for the indisposition of the latter; and the particular engagement of the former which confines him at home this week, and obliges him to attend the Board of Directors at Georgetown, the Great Falls, etc. the beginning of next.

"The Genl and Mrs. Washington will always be happy to see

[16] Robert Lee Haycock. "Career of Col. Charles Broadwater of Fairfax County, Va."—*Virginia Magazine of History and Biography*, July 1939.

[17] *Diaries*, Vol. 2, p. 188; Vol. 3, p. 365.

the young couple at Mount Vernon."[18] Bushrod and his wife, and Richard Blackburn and Miss Polly Blackburn, son and daughter of Col. Thomas Blackburn, were visitors at Mount Vernon.[19]

Rippon Lodge is situated on Neabsco Creek within sight of the Potomac River. Brick gateposts mark the entrance from U. S. Route 1.

An interesting feature of the house, which has been the subject of much speculation as to its use, is a brick tunnel from the cellar to a now wooded ravine. Only two explanations deserve serious considerations. That it was the means of escape from Indians is improbable, as the Indians had disappeared from that region by 1725, the approximate date of the building of the house. The most likely explanation is that it connected Rippon Lodge with another house which stood on the estate.[20] This view is substantiated by a sketch made in 1796 by Benjamin H. Latrobe, who had visited there.

Rippon Lodge was purchased some thirty years ago by the late Wade H. Ellis, a descendant of Colonel Blackburn. It was restored, enlarged and beautified by him. About two years ago his widow sold it to Commander Richard Blackburn Black, a descendant of the original builder, who is now retired from the U. S. Navy.

Bush Hill

This eighteenth century house is situated on a slight ridge south of Back Lick Run (an affluent of Great Hunting Creek). It is about a mile and a half northeast of the village of Franconia, Fairfax County. The approach to it is through a long wooded lane, which crosses the Richmond, Fredericksburg and Potomac Railroad by an overpass. The tradition in the Gunnell family, the present owners, is that the house was built about 1762.

The first owner of the tract on which Bush Hill was built, shown on the Fairfax records, was John West, whom Washington called "Colo. West." He was a member of a prominent Fairfax family;

[18]*Writings,* Vol. 28, p. 292.
[19]*Diaries,* Vol. 3, pp. 145, 148; Vol. 4, p. 3.
[20]Garden Club of Virginia. *Homes and Gardens in Old Virginia.* Rev. 1950, p. 57.

was a vestryman of Truro Parish, a burgess from Fairfax County and a merchant in Alexandria. His second marriage was with his cousin Margaret, widow of William Henry Terrett, and daughter of Simon Pearson.[21] By her he had an only son, Roger. His will, proved in Fairfax County on August 18, 1771, bequeathed to his son Roger "my new Quarter containing 458 acres of land lying on the main road where Conner Maguire now teaches school."[22] The location of this 458 acres appears from the deeds of Roger West, one to Charles Lee conveying a parcel of land which had been devised to him by his father "lying on the north side of the back lick creek of Holmes Run."[23]

His second deed is more precise. It is from Roger West to James Hendricks, dated December 10th 1787 and recites "that John West was in his lifetime seised in fee of a tract situate and lying on both sides of Holmes Run, otherwise called back lick run containing 440 acres or thereabouts, and by his will devised the same to said Roger," and that "sd. Roger has sold that part of the tract lying on the north side of sd run to Charles Lee, and by this deed does bargain and sell all the rest of the tract which lies on the south side of sd run (describing it by metes and bounds) to said Hendricks."[24]

It appears that on January 25, 1789, James Hendricks, John Hendricks and Kitty executed a mortgage conveying this land to Benjamin Stoddert, Josiah Watson, and William Hartshorne, and being unable to pay the debt secured, James Hendricks joined with the trustees in conveying the land to John Richter.[25] By deed dated October 6, 1791 Richter conveyed said land to Josiah Watson of Alexandria.[26] Watson was probably the party secured by the mortgage and put the title temporarily in Richter's name. He did business under the name Josiah Watson and Co. Washington had business dealings with him. In 1786, "sent Major Washington to

[21]Harrison, *Landmarks of Old Prince William,* p. 138.
[22]Fairfax County Will Book D-25.
[23]Fairfax County Deed Book R, p. 106.
[24]*Ibid.,* Q, p. 515.
[25]*Ibid.,* T, p. 330.
[26]*Ibid.,* p. 486.

town on business, where he and Mr. Lund Washington engaged to Mr. Watson 100 Barrls of my Flour, to be delivered next week at 32/ pr Barrl."[27]

Writing to his manager, Anthony Whiting, in 1793 about his tobacco, Washington told him that "Mr. Watson sometime ago wanted to buy it."[28] Other letters of Washington's refer to bills of exchange given by Watson and a bond to Thomas Colvill's estate on which he was liable.

On August 16, 1797 Josiah Watson conveyed the "Bush Hill" estate containing 354 acres to Richard Marshall Scott.[29] Scott was a man of consequence in his day. In the organization of the Federal Government he applied for the position of Collector of Revenue for the port of Alexandria, apparently with the backing of Richard Henry Lee. In reply Washington wrote that Charles Lee would certainly be a candidate for the post, and suggested that Scott should receive the Collectorship of Dumfries.[30] This appointment was accepted by Scott. Later he made his home at Bush Hill, and kept a long diary, now in the possession of the Gunnell family. His son, Richard Marshall Scott, Jr., succeeded in the ownership of the estate and married Miss Virginia Gunnell, who lived to an advanced age.

The will of the second Richard Marshall Scott, dated December 19, 1855 and proved in Fairfax County, January 21, 1859, (Will Book Z, no. 1, pages 119 to 121) devised to his "dear wife Virginia" all the residue of his estate "to be disposed of as she may deem proper." He constituted her executrix and requested her to make every effort to keep the residence of Bush Hill in the family so that it should descend on her death to their son, Richard Marshall Scott.

In the poverty that fell on that part of Fairfax County after the Civil War the widow was unable to meet the taxes and other expenses, and in 1870 deeded the property to her brother, Dr. Francis

[27] *Diaries*, Vol. 3, p. 55.
[28] *Writings*, Vol. 32, p. 356.
[29] Fairfax County Deed Book A-2, p. 198.
[30] *Writings*, Vol. 30, p. 369.

M. Gunnell,[31] who had been Surgeon General of the Navy during the Civil War. In 1891 he conveyed the tract to another brother, Dr. James S. Gunnell.[32] In 1910 Dr. Francis M. Gunnell, in a deed reciting that he is a devisee of Dr. James S. Gunnell, conveyed "Bush Hill" to his nephew, Leonard C. Gunnell.[33] At the same time Leonard C. Gunnell took a quitclaim deed from Richard Marshall Scott, III.[34] Mr. Gunnell made Bush Hill his residence. On his death the ownership passed to his son, Bruce C. Gunnell, the present owner, who has built a home on the tract nearer the public road, and has rented the Bush Hill mansion to a private school.

---

[31]Fairfax County Deed Book M-4, p. 14.
[32]*Ibid.*, L-5, p. 65.
[33]*Ibid.*, I-7, p. 79.
[34]*Ibid.*, p. 78.

Courtesy Virginia State Chamber of Commerce

The Falls Church (Pages 234 to 236)

Courtesy Publishers Homes and Gardens in Old Virginia

Rippon Lodge (Pages 238 and 239)

Bush Hill (Pages 239 to 242)

Photographed by Mrs. Margaret B. Stetson

Chapter 21

Washington and the Revolution

Washington was one of the seven delegates from Virginia to the First Continental Congress, which met in Philadelphia in September 1774. It was the first meeting of Americans in common council, with delegates from all of the colonies except Georgia.

The Congress sought a redress of grievances, but still did not consider independence. But sentiment was changing rapidly.

The Second Continental Congress met in Philadelphia in May 1775. The Virginia delegation included Peyton Randolph, Richard Henry Lee, George Washington, Benjamin Harrison, Thomas Jefferson and Carter Braxton.

The question of the hour was—should Congress declare for independence or still seek a reconciliation with Great Britain. Washington's mind was made up: he was for independence, and to show his stand he appeared in the uniform of a Colonel of the Virginia Regiment of the French and Indian War. Before the Declaration of Independence was signed Washington was far away. "On this day" (June 15, 1775) "George Washington, Esquire, was unanimously elected General and Commander-in-Chief of all the forces raised, or to be raised by the United Colonies."[1] He replied:

"Mr. President: Tho' I am truly sensible of the high Honour done me in this Appointment, yet I feel great distress from a consciousness that my abilities and Military experience may not be equal to the extensive and important Trust: However, as the Congress desires I will enter upon the momentous duty, and exert every power I Possess In their Service for the Support of the glorious

[1] Journals of the Continental Congress.

Cause: I beg they will accept my most cordial thanks for this distinguished testimony of their Approbation.

"But lest some unlucky event should happen unfavorable to my reputation, I beg it may be remembered by every Gentn. in the room, that I this day declare with the unmost sincerity, I do not think my self equal to the Command I am honoured with.

"As to pay, Sir, I beg leave to Assure the Congress that as no pecuniary consideration could have tempted me to have accepted this Arduous employment (at the expence of my domestt. ease and happiness) I do not wish to make any proffit from it: I will keep an exact Account of my expences; those I doubt not they will discharge and that is all I desire."[2]

His modesty was not feigned. His past military experience had been the command of a regiment of Virginia provincials, engaged mainly in protecting the frontier from Indian raids. Now he would be pitted against British generals with long military training, leading regulars with combat experience. Two days after his appointment he wrote to his wife.

"My Dearest: I am now set down to write to you on a subject, which fills me with inexpressible concern, and this concern is greatly aggravated and increased, when I reflect upon the uneasiness I know it will give you. It has been determined in Congress, that the whole army raised for the defence of the American cause shall be put under my care, and that it is necessary for me to proceed immediately to Boston to take upon me the command of it.

"You may believe me, my dear Patsy, when I assure you, in the most solemn manner that, so far from seeking this appointment, I have used every endeavor in my power to avoid it, not only from my unwillingness to part with you and the family, but from a consciousness of its being a trust too great for my capacity, and that I should enjoy more real happiness in one month with you at home, than I have the most distant prospect of finding abroad, if my stay were to be seven times seven years. But as it has been a kind of des-

[2]*Writings,* Vol. 3, pp. 292, 293.

tiny, that has thrown me upon this service, I shall hope that my undertaking it is designed to answer some good purpose. You might, and I suppose did perceive, from the tenor of my letters, that I was apprehensive I could not avoid this appointment, as I did not pretend to intimate when I should return. That was the case. It was utterly out of my power to refuse this appointment, without exposing my character to such censures, as would have reflected dishonor upon myself, and given pain to my friends. This, I am sure, could not, and ought not, to be pleasing to you, and must have lessened me considerably in my own esteem. I shall rely, therefore, confidently on that Providence, which has heretofore preserved and been bountiful to me, not doubting but that I shall return safe to you in the fall. I shall feel no pain from the toil or the danger of the campaign; my unhappiness will flow from the uneasiness I know you will feel from being left alone. I therefore beg, that you will summon your whole fortitude, and pass your time as agreeably as possible. Nothing will give me so much sincere satisfaction as to hear this, and to hear it from your own pen. My earnest and ardent desire is, that you would pursue any plan that is most likely to produce content, and a tolerable degree of tranquillity; as it must add greatly to my uneasy feelings to hear, that you are dissatisfied or complaining at what I really could not avoid.

"As life is always uncertain, and common prudence dictates to every man the necessity of settling his temporal concerns, while it is in his power, and while the mind is calm and undisturbed, I have, since I came to this place (for I had not time to do it before I left home) got Colonel Pendleton to draft a will for me, by the directions I gave him, which will I now enclose. The provision made for you in case of my death will, I hope, be agreeable.

"I shall add nothing more, as I have several letters to write, but to desire that you will remember me to your friends, and to assure you that I am, with the most unfeigned regard, my dear Patsy, your affectionate, &c."[3]

---

[3]*Writings,* Vol. 3, pp. 293-295.

A few days later he sent her a short note:

"My Dearest: As I am within a few minutes of leaving this city, I would not think of departing from it with out dropping you a line, especially as I do not know whether it may be in my power to write again till I get to the camp at Boston. I go fully trusting in that providence, which has been more bountiful to me than I deserve and in full confidence of a happy meeting with you some time in the fall. I have no time to add more as I am surrounded with company to take leave of me. I return an unalterable affection for you which neither time or distance can change my best love to Jack and Nelly and regard for the rest of the family; conclude me with the utmost truth and Sincerety, Yr. entire."[4]

After Washington's death, Martha Washington destroyed all letters of her husband to her, except these two. She did not propose that the world should know what passed between them. Amidst his many trials during the war Washington had the comfort of his wife's company during most of its winters. She was with him at Cambridge in 1775 and 1776; at Morristown, New Jersey, in 1776 and 1777; at Valley Forge in 1777 and 1778; in the highlands of the Hudson during most of the remaining winters.

It is no part of the plan of this book to attempt an evaluation of Washington as a general. The English-Canadian historian Goldwin Smith has given us a noble and truthful characterization of Washington's services at that time.

"Washington was to the confederacy all in all. Without him it would have been ten times lost, and the names of the politicians who had drawn the country into the conflict would have gone down to posterity linked with defeat and shame. History has hardly a stronger case of an indispensable man. His form, like all other forms of the revolution, has no doubt been seen through a golden haze of panegyric. We can hardly number among the greatest captains a general who acted on so small a scale and who, though he was the soul of the war, never won a battle. In that respect Carlyle, who

---

[4]*Writings,* Vol. 3, pp. 300-301.

threatened 'to take George down a peg or two,' might have made good his threat. But he could not have stripped Washington of any part of his credit for patriotism, wisdom, and courage; for the union of enterprise with prudence; for integrity and truthfulness; for simple dignity of character; for tact and forbearance in dealing with men; above all for serene fortitude in the darkest hour of his cause and under trials from the perversity, insubordination, jealousy, and perfidy of those around him severer than any defeat."[5]

Dr. Freeman's *George Washington* gives a detailed and critical account of Washington's generalship and of his difficulties during the war. His correspondence and orders given in Fitzpatrick's edition of the *Writings of Washington* show his endless troubles with a constantly depreciating currency, with supplies and ammunition, with desertions, with failures of regiments to re-enlist, or continue in service beyond the expirations of their terms, with jealousies among officers, his patience and expostulations with a helpless, incompetent Congress. It was not until after the bitter winter at Valley Forge that Washington, with the help of Baron von Steuben, forged an army capable of meeting the English army on equal terms, as the battle of Monmouth showed. It is not only Washington who is seen "through a golden haze." The whole war is popularly seen through a denser haze. The Stamp Act and the claim of the British Parliament to lay internal taxes upon the colonies met with a united and determined opposition, but when it came to war to back up resistance, the situation was different. Most of the leaders of public opinion and a majority of the people favored such a course, but there was a formidable Tory opposition, and Tory units such as Simcoe's Rangers joined the English armies. As the British armies successively evacuated Boston, Philadelphia, Charleston, Savannah and New York, thousands of English sympathizers followed them. Today their descendants form the backbone of the population of New Brunswick, Nova Scotia and Ontario. Their ideal of a united British Empire, though a lost cause, was not an unworthy one.

---

[5]Smith, Goldwin. *The United States,* pp. 96, 97.

Between these two warring adversaries was a large fluctuating population which favored the Americans when they were in the ascendancy and the English when they seemed to be winning. While Washington's army was in dire straits at Valley Forge, the Quaker farmers were selling their produce to Howe's army in Philadelphia. The Civil War in our country, or the War between the States, as the Southerners prefer to call it, was fought with an energy and devotion far beyond that displayed by the average man or woman in the Revolutionary War. In the North there was the grim determination to conquer at all costs and in the South the heroic resolve to achieve independence or fight to the bitter end.

During the war Washington was brought into contact with many foreign officers—with Baron von Steuben, Du Portail and Lafayette before the French alliance, and with Chastellux, Rochambeau, the Chevalier de la Luzerne after the alliance. Steuben was appointed Inspector General of the Continental Army. He drew up a manual of tactics, which, with some changes, was adopted by Washington. His great services at Valley Forge have been mentioned. Du Portail was the competent self-effacing French engineer. But it was Lafayette that Washington loved. We shall have occasion to mention Lafayette again.

Washington corresponded with Rochambeau, Chastellux and Luzerne in cordial terms during the war and after peace was made. Of the American Generals he seems to have been fondest of Greene and Knox. It is said that he wished Greene to be his successor if he should be killed or disabled, and Greene's campaigns in North and South Carolina in 1780 and 1781 indicate that his judgment was sound.

It is pleasant to record that after his difficulties and perplexities, Washington's military career closed with his greatest triumph. In 1781 he felt that something must be done to offset the British successes in the South. He was considering a joint American and French attack on New York City, the center and stronghold of the British forces in America. This required the co-operation of the small French fleet at Newport. The plan was difficult enough in any event, but Barras, commander of the fleet, declined to risk his forces until reinforced by the larger French fleet in the West Indies, so the plan had to be abandoned. Then came startling news recorded in his diary. (Washington kept no diaries from 1775 until 1781 when he resumed them.)

"August 14th 1781. Received dispatches from the Count de Barras announcing the intended departure of the Count de Grasse from Cape Francois with between 25 and 29 Sail of the line and 3200 land Troops on the 3d Instant for Chesapeake Bay. . . ."[6] Lord Cornwallis having failed, through opposition of Lafayette and Wayne, to conquer Virginia, had fortified himself at Yorktown. If de Grasse could maintain temporary supremacy at the Virginia capes it would be possible to capture his army. Instantly the plans of Washington and Rochambeau were changed and the allied armies started for Virginia. They passed through Philadelphia, the Americans on one day, the French on the next. "The French troops, beautifully uniformed in white broadcloth, with different colored facings, for the several regiments, were the best appointed soldiers in the world. Moreover they had a brass band. . . The uniformed men marching in perfect time, the beautiful flags, the music of the band, made up such a scene as Philadelphia had never before seen. The French passed in review before the Continental Congress, members of which took off their hats to Washington and Rochambeau."[7]

"I left this city for the head of Elk to hasten the Imbarkation at that place, and on my way (at Chester) received the agreeable news of the safe arrival of the Count de Grasse in the Bay of Chesapeake."[8] Washington had sent out circulars to collect all possible shipping at the head of Elk (Elkton) to transport the army down the Chesapeake Bay, and thence up the James River to Jamestown. The baggage trains were to make the journey by land.

---

[6]*Diaries,* Vol. 2, pp. 253-254.

[7]H. J. Eckenrode. (Pamphlet). *Story of Campaign and Seige of Yorktown.*

[8]*Diaries,* Vol. 2, p. 258.

"Judging it highly expedient to be with the Army in Virginia as soon as possible, to make the necessary arrangements for the siege and to get the Materials prepared for it, I determined to set out for the Camp of the Marq's de la Fayette without loss of time and accordingly in Company with the Count de Rochambeau, who requested to attend me, and the Chevr. de Chastellux set out on the 8th. . ."[9]

"Sept. 9th I reached my own Seat at Mount Vernon where I stayed until the 12th."[10]

It was the first time he had seen it since May 4, 1775 when he left for the Continental Congress.

While Washington was at Mount Vernon, the vitally important question of the control of the sea had been settled. On September 5th, Admiral Graves' fleet from New York arrived off the Virginia Capes. Compte de Grasse was ready to fight but he wanted more sea room and sailed out into the ocean. An indecisive battle took place, but several of the English ships were so damaged that Graves returned to New York and De Grasse re-entered the Chesapeake Bay. There a welcome sight greeted his eyes. Barras had arrived from Newport with eight ships. He had now such strength that the British fleet dare not attack him, and Cornwallis was left to his fate. Washington and Rochambeau had now some 16,000 men, including the soldiers and marines from the fleet. Cornwallis had about 8,000 men.[11]

On October 17th Cornwallis proposed negotiations for a surrender. The representatives of both sides met at the Moore house, about a mile down the river from Yorktown and agreed upon terms. The house is still standing. It is included in the Colonial Parkway and belongs to the United States. The British marched out from their works to the field of surrender, the Americans lining one side of the road, the French the other. The flags of the

---

[9]*Ibid.*, p. 259.
[10]*Ibid.*, p. 260.
[11]Eckenrode. *Campaign and Seige of Yorktown*, p. 41.

British were cased and their fifes played the tune, *The World Turned Upside Down*. Cornwallis was sick at heart and sent General O'Hara to deliver his sword, which was immediately returned.

Mr. Paul Leicester Ford in his *True George Washington* relates that after the surrender, Cornwallis and his principal officers were entertained at dinner by Washington. At this dinner, so a contemporary account states. "Rochambeau, being asked for a toast, gave, The United States. Washington gave the King of France, Lord Cornwallis, simply, The King, but Washington, putting that toast added, 'of England', and facetiously, 'Confine him there and I'll drink him a full bumper'." After the surrender the Continental Army returned to the Hudson. The French army spent the winter in Williamsburg. The Governor's Palace was used as a hospital and was accidentally burned. On the wall of the Arcade back of the Wren building of the College of William and Mary, there is a large inscription giving the names and regiments of the French officers and soldiers who lost their lives in the siege of Yorktown.

Hostilities virtually closed with the surrender at Yorktown but more than two years were to pass before Washington returned to Mount Vernon to live. The American army stayed at its posts on the Hudson. The period that followed was a difficult one. Both Congress and the public felt the war was practically over and their efforts could be relaxed. Washington hoped so too, but in the meantime the army must be kept ready for action. "The enemy talk loudly, and very confidently of Peace; but whether they are in earnest," he wrote to Chastellux, who was still in America, "or whether it is to amuse and while away the time till they can prepare for a more vigorous prosecution of the War, time will evince."[12] Sir Henry Clinton had been recalled and Sir Guy Carleton put in command in New York City. Washington transmitted to Congress a copy of the letter received from him and Admiral Digby, commander of the British fleet, proposing preliminary negotiations. This was in August, 1782. In December of the same

[12] *Writings*, Vol. 24, p. 496.

year the French army was recalled and Washington wrote to Rochambeau:

"Newburgh, December 14, 1782.

"I cannot, My dear Genl., permit you to depart from this Country without repeating to you the high sense I entertain of the Services you have rendered America, by the constant attention which you have paid to the Interests of it.

"By the exact order and discipline of the Corps under your Command, and by your readiness, at all time, to give facility to every measure which the force of the Combined Armies was competent to.

"To this testimony of your Public character I should be wanting to the feelings of my heart, was I not to add expressions of the happiness I have enjoyed in your private friendship. The remembrance of which, will be one of the most pleasing Circumstances of my life."[18]

And on the same day he wrote in even warmer terms to Chastellux:

"Newburgh, December 14, 1782.

"My dear Chevr: I felt too much to express anything, the day I parted with you; A Sense of your public Services to this Country, and gratitude for your private friendship, quite overcame me at the moment of our seperation. But I should be wanting to the feelings of my heart, and should do violence to my inclination, was I to suffer you to leave this Country, without the warmest assurances of an affectionate regard for your person and character. . . .

"I can truly say, that never in my life did I part with a Man to whom my Soul clave more sincerely than it did to you. My warmest wishes will attend you in your voyage across the Atlantic; to the rewards of a generous Prince, the Arms of Affectionate friends, and be assured that it will be one of my highest gratifications to keep up a regular intercourse with you by Letter.

[18]*Ibid.*, Vol. 25, pp. 427, 428.

"I regret exceedingly, that our circumstances should withdraw you from this Country before the final accomplishment of that Independence and Peace which the Arms of our good Ally has assisted in placing before us in so agreeable a point of view. Nothing would give me more pleasure than to accompany you in a tour through the Continent of North America at the close of the War, in search of the National curiosities with which it abounds, and to view the foundation of a rising Empire. I have the honr etc."[14]

The Marquis François Jean de Chastellux had served in the Seven Years' War before he came to America with Rochambeau; he was also an author, a member of the French Academy, and a cousin of Lafayette.[15] He was born in 1734 and died in 1788.

It was at Newburgh that Washington called his principal officers to meet him early in 1783, to soothe their justifiable discontents over arrears of pay due them. There occurred the incident so often quoted. As he was about to read his address he said: "Gentlemen, you will permit me to put on my spectacles, for I have not only grown gray, but almost blind in the service of my country."

While a Proclamation of Peace was issued by Congress on April 11, 1783, there were many details to be attended to; the exchange of prisoners; the evacuation of New York City; the transportation of six thousand loyalists to Nova Scotia.

And when the war was over and the British Army about to sail, he wrote Sir Guy Carleton with simple unaffected courtesy his sincere wish "that your Excellency with the Troops under your Orders, may have a safe and pleasant passage."[16] There was no rancor in George Washington.

It was not until Dec. 23, 1783 that Washington resigned his commission at Annapolis. His letter ended with these words: "Having now finished the work assigned to me, I retire from the

---

[14]*Writings,* Vol. 25, pp. 428, 429.
[15]*Petit Larousse*—note on Chastellux.
[16]*Writings,* Vol. 27, p. 254.

great theatre of Action, and bidding an affectionate farewell to this August body (Congress) under whose orders I have so long acted, I here offer my Commission, and take my leave of all the employments of public life."[17] He then drew his Commission from his pocket and handed it to the President of Congress. On Christmas eve he was at Mount Vernon.

[17] *Ibid.*, p. 285.

Chapter 22

"A Private Citizen . . . on the Banks of the Potomac"

There are no existing diaries for 1782-1783, nor from January to September 1784. In this last month there is an entry: "Having found it indispensably necessary to visit my Landed property West of the Apalachean Mountains . . . I set out myself in company with Doctor James Craik." Dr. Craik's son, George Washington Craik, and Washington's nephew, Bushrod Washington, accompanied them. The doctor was one of Washington's most devoted friends. He was with him in the French and Indian War and the Revolutionary War. As he was his friend, neighbor and doctor, it seems appropriate to give a short account of him.

Dr. James Craik

James Craik was born near Dumfries in Scotland in 1730. He was educated as a physician at the University of Edinburgh. He came to Virginia in 1750 and subsequently resided in Winchester for several years. He participated in the campaign of Great Meadows and Fort Necessity, as he is known to have been "the Surgeon" in Washington's list of his officers and subalterns. Presumably he served Braddock's army for he was still a surgeon in the Virginia Regiment when Washington wrote to him in 1755.[1] By 1760 he moved to Charles County, Maryland, where his home, La Grange, built in 1765, is still standing near La Plata. In 1760 he married Marianne Ewell, daughter of Captain Charles Ewell of Bel Air,

[1] *Writings,* Vol. 1, p. 255.

Prince William County, Virginia, by whom he had six sons and three daughters.

In 1777 Washington procured his appointment as Assistant Director General of the Hospital for the Middle Department of the Army, which covered the territory from the Hudson to the Potomac. Throughout the war he was attached to Washington's Military Headquarters. He served in the Yorktown Campaign. In 1783, at Washington's request, he moved to Alexandria. His residence, No. 210 Duke St., still stands. His trip with Washington in 1770 down the Ohio and up the Kanawha has been mentioned. Washington's letter to him in 1784 inviting him to be his companion in a second trip to his western lands is printed in Fitzpatrick's edition of his *Writings* (Vol. 27, page 437). This trip will be described later. After he moved to Alexandria he was a constant visitor at Mount Vernon both as friend and as physician, and Washington repeatedly visited the doctor in Alexandria. A typical entry in his diary is: July 20, 1798: "Went up to Alexa. with Mrs. Washington and Miss Custis, dined at Doctr Craik's, retnd in ye aftn."

What Washington thought of Dr. Craik's ability is shown by a letter of July 3, 1789: "The habits of intimacy and friendship in which I have long lived with Dr. Craik, and the opinion I have of his professional knowledge, would most certainly point him out as the man of my choice in all cases of sickness. I am convinced of his sincere attachment to me and I should cheerfully trust my life in his hands."[2]

As is well known, he attended Washington in his last illness. Later he wrote of it: "I, who was bred among scenes of human calamity, and had so often witnessed death in its direct and most awful forms, believed that its terrors were too familiar to my eyes to shake my fortitude; but when I saw this great man die it seemed to me as if the bonds of my nature were rent and the pillars of my country's happiness had fallen to the ground."[3]

---

[2]*Ibid.,* Vol. 30, p. 351.

[3]Hon. R. Walton Moore. (Pamphlet). *Dr. James Craik.*

His last years were spent at Vaucluse, (spelled Vauxcleuse on the gateposts now in front of the house), near the Episcopal Theological Seminary, where he died in 1814 at the age of 84. His eldest son he named George Washington Craik. His physical vigor lasted until the end of his life. He frequently walked from Vaucluse to Alexandria and back, a distance of at least five miles. In a sketch of him he is described as being toward the end, "a stout, hale, cheery old man, perfectly erect, fond of company and children, and amusing himself with light garden work." The Honorable Walton Moore in the pamphlet quoted says: "I like to think of him as a country physician of that group who then and in less remote days excelled all others in the simple self-sacrificing service of humanity."

He is buried in the churchyard of the old Presbyterian Meeting House in Alexandria. Washington contributed to the education of his son. In his *Diary* for August 31, 1785, there is an entry: 'This day I told Doctor Craik that I would contribute one hundred dollars pr. ann. as long as it was necessary, to the Education of His Son, George Washington, either in this Country or in Scotland."[4]

Washington's primary object was, as stated, to visit his western lands, to collect rents from his tenants, to see if squatters had encroached upon them, but he had another object, "to obtain information of the nearest and best communication between the Eastern and Western Waters." On the way he stopped at the Berkeley Warm Springs, which he now called "Bath," and contracted for building a house on his lot. The party then proceeded to Gilbert Simpson's. Simpson was Washington's agent and partner in the ownership of certain of his lands. He had built a mill for Washington in 1776 on The Youghiogheny. There he was visited by Captain David Luckett, the Continental officer commanding the garrison at Fort Pitt, and other officers. They confirmed "the reports of the discontented temper of the Indians" on the Ohio, and Washington decided to abandon that part of his proposed trip.

[4]*Diaries,* Vol. 2, p. 410.

As he wrote to Jacob Read: "My trip to the Westward, was less extensive that I intended. The Indians, it was said, were in too discontented a mood, for me to expose myself to their insults, and as I had no object in contemplation which could justify any risk, my property in that Country having previously undergone every species of attack and diminution, that the nature of it would admit. To see the condition of my lands which were nearest, and settled and to dispose of those which were more remote, and unsettled, was all I had in view."[5]

Washington had already visited his holdings on the Ohio and Great Kanawha in 1770 in company with Dr. Craik. He put off a second visit until the Indian trouble should be settled. He was destined never to see those lands again. While President he had no time to go so far. After he retired from that office, he had no inclination. As he said, "And further than twenty miles from Mount Vernon I never expect to go."[6]

He made Simpson's his headquarters. He brought quite a party with him. Besides Dr. Craik, young Craik and young Washington there were three servants, six horses, a wagon and luggage. He and Simpson settled accounts. He received rents collected. He sold at auction his half interest in the partnership property; received some cash and £146 in bonds and notes. These matters being attended to, he went after the squatters.

"September 19, 1784: Being Sunday, and the People living on my land, *apparently* very religious, it was thought best to postpone going among them till tomorrow. . ." There were thirteen of them and before interviewing them he visited each of their parcels and made notes of the amount and quality of the land each occupied and his improvements—over four hundred acres in all. He called them to meet him.

"I told them I had no inclination to sell; however, after hearing a great deal of their hardships, their Religious principles (which

---

[5]*Writings*, Vol. 27, p. 485.

[6]He actually went to Philadelphia when war with France seemed imminent, and to Harpers Ferry on Potomac Canal business.

Home of Dr. James Craik, 210 Duke Street, Alexandria, Virginia *(Page 256)*

Photographed by Alexandria Studio

Courtesy Virginia State Chamber of Commerce

George Washington—Houdon Statue (Page 267)

had brought them together as a society of Ceceders) and unwillingness to separate or remove; I told them I would make them a last offer. . ."[7] Who "Ceceders" were, Washington did not tell if he knew. His last offer was "25 S. per Acre, the money to be paid at 3 annual payments with interest, or to become Tenants upon leases of 999 years." The bold frontiersmen were not awed by the late Commander-in-Chief of the Continental Army and decided to stand suit.

On their way back, Washington and the whole party kept together until they reached the neighborhood of Winchester when they separated, Dr. Craik returning to Alexandria, while Washington went up the Shenandoah Valley to "Mr. Thomas Lewis's (near Staunton), from whose office I wanted some papers to enable me to prosecute my ejectments against those who had possessed themselves of my Land."[8] The land in question was apparently a part of Captain John Posey's bounty land which he had sold to Washington. Ejectment suits were filed and the squatters ejected.[9] By the time he reached home he estimated he had travelled 680 miles, and well as he knew Virginia, he had missed the right road twice from Culpeper Courthouse to Colchester, due to faulty directions, and on one of these occasions had to employ a guide.

When Washington returned to Mount Vernon after the Revolutionary War, the exterior of his mansion looked much as it does today, but the improvement and beautification of the grounds had hardly begun. In October 1785 he noted in his diary: "Finished levelling and Sowing the lawn in front of the Ho. intended for a Bolling Green—as far as the Garden Houses."[10] This was the two-acre lawn in front of the west side of the house. Around it were the Serpentine roads and walks. The editor of the *Diaries* describes them in this way.

"The Serpentine Road enclosed the great lawn on the west of

[7] *Diaries*, Vol. 2, p. 297.
[8] *Ibid.*, p. 313.
[9] *Ibid.*, p. 299 (note).
[10] *Ibid.*, p. 429.

the Mansion House. It consisted of a large circular road from the front, or west door, of the Mansion, and from each side of this circle an undulating carriage drive swept outward to swing around and meet at the gate leading from the Mount Vernon grounds to the Alexandria highway; bounding the far side of the serpentine at its western limits, were mounds on which grew weeping willows, so grouped as not to interfere with the view of the distant woods from the mansion house."[11]

These roads or walks, as Washington indifferently called them, he lined with a great variety of trees, mostly transplanted or grafted; some from other parts of his estate; many gifts from his friends and admirers. There were Linden trees sent by Governor Clinton of New York: "Received from Genl. Lincoln 3 young Spruce Pine and two of the fir and Hemlock in half Barrells."[12]

"Finished laying out my Serpentine roads. Dug most of the holes where the trees by the side of them are to stand, and planted some of the Maples, which were dug yesterday, and some of the Aspans, which had been brought here on Wednesday last"—this in Februray, 1785.

Other trees and bushes that he grafted and planted include, Holly, Tulip, Oak, Balsam, Mulberry, Crab, Magnolias. He mentioned Hemlock scions which he brought home from the estate of his neighbor, Martin Cockburn: "28 in number in the shrubbery."[13]

"I also removed from the Woods and the old fields several young trees of the Sassafras, Dogwood and Red bud to the shrubbery on the No. side of the grass plot."

He also had a Botanical Garden (which is reproduced at Mount Vernon today). There he planted Chinese seed given him by Mr. Porter and Dr. Craik, but they seem to have died. A favorite tree for transplanting was the honey locust.

He had also what he called his "Wildernesses." These were

---

[11]*Ibid.*, p. 336.
[12]*Ibid.*, p. 387.
[13]*Ibid.*, p. 349 (note). "Washington seems to have called young root saplings scions."

natural forests to the north and south of the Serpentine Road, but he took good care to "search" for "the sort of Trees, I shall want for Walks, groves, and Wildernesses." The *Diary* of 1785 tells of building north and south ha ha walls. The editor of the *Diaries* says of them: "The ha ha walls were a method of permitting the grazing cattle and sheep to appear on the landscape and at the same time hold them at a distance from the house. They converted the lawn into a series of flat terraces and both the walls and the terrace effect was invisible from the house." The walls were brick, and the ground had to be slightly undulating to produce the illusion.

In the next year, 1786, Washington enclosed a paddock for deer on the east slope of Mount Vernon between the Mansion House and the river. Something over eighteen acres was enclosed by a post-and-rail fence,[14] though it seems afterward to have been enlarged. Governor Benjamin Ogle of Belair, Maryland presented him with six fawns from his park of English deer, for which Washington wrote him a polite letter.[15]

Before Washington died, however, the fence was destroyed and the deer roamed the woods with the wild deer of the neighborhood. In recent years, the deer paddock has been stocked again with some deer, and an iron fence has replaced the original post-and-rail fence.

In 1784 Washington wrote to the Chevalier de Chastellux: "I am at length become a private citizen of America, on the banks of the Patowmac; where under my own Vine and my own Fig-tree, free from the bustle of a camp and the intrigues of a court, I shall view the busy world in the calm light of mild philosophy, and with serenity of mind, which the Soldier in his pursuit of glory, and the Statesman of fame, have not time to enjoy. I have not only retired from all public employments; but I am retiring within myself and shall tread the private walks of life with heart felt satisfaction."[16]

---

[14] *Ibid.*, p. 481 (note).
[15] *Writings*, Vol. 28, p. 221.
[16] *Ibid.*, Vol. 27, p. 314.

He wrote of "retiring within myself," but that was possible only within limits. A connection between the headwaters of the Potomac and the tributaries of the Ohio had been his lifelong dream. Back in 1770 John Ballendine and John Semple, then of Occoquan, had interested him in the subject of canals about the obstructions and around the falls of the Potomac. Ballendine had commenced but never finished a canal around the Great Falls of that river. On his second journey with Dr. Craik to his western lands, he had made extensive inquiries about the best portage from the upper Potomac to the headwaters of the Monongahelia, the Cheat and the Youghiogheny Rivers. So when a bill was introduced in 1784 in the Virginia Assembly to charter a Potomack Company, he put his influence behind it and it was passed. The Company was to be managed by a President and Board of Directors who were to receive private subscriptions, and with the proceeds open the river to navigation by flatboats. Obstructions were to be removed and shallow canals to be cut around the falls.[17] A similar act of the Maryland Assembly was procured. Washington was elected President. Subscription offices were opened in Richmond, Alexandria, Annapolis, Georgetown, Frederick and Winchester.[18] In 1785, Washington and several of the Directors left Georgetown to examine the obstructions and to point out a mode for the improvement and extention of the navigation. They were provided with canoes, and near the Shenandoah River were met by Mr. James Rumsey, the manager of the company. They engaged laborers. From Harpers Ferry they descended the river, taking notes of the places where the channel could be deepened and cleared of rocks. Canals were found necessary at Great and Little Falls. At Great Falls the party broke up and Washington returned to Mount Vernon, having been away ten days. Subscriptions lagged and in 1787, when the Second Annual Report of the Company was issued, only £10,700 had been paid into the Treasury. Washington resigned when elected President of the United States and was

[17]Hening. *Statutes* XI, 510.
[18]*Diaries,* Vol. 2, p. 336 (note).

succeeded by Governor Thomas Johnson of Maryland, but his interest in the company continued unabated, though he was disappointed at its slow progress.

When finally in operation, flatboats loaded with the products of the Shenandoah, and even from Cumberland, were floated to Georgetown, where the boats were broken up and their lumber sold, as it was impossible to pole them back against the current. Washington knew of these difficulties, but he pinned his hopes of upstream navigation on the boat that James Rumsey had recently invented, and had exhibited to him. "Remained at Bath all day and was showed the Model of a Boat constructed by the ingenious Mr. Rumsey for ascending rapid currents by mechanism."[19]

His will bequeathed the fifty shares he held in the company to the endowment of a National University in the District of Columbia.[20] The Company was not a success, and its property was eventually acquired by the Chesapeake and Potomac Canal Company.

Another subject Washington was interested in at this time, but which caused him considerable vexation, was the Society of the Cincinnati, which was formed in 1783 by officers of the Continental Army for mutual assistance and to perpetuate the principles of liberty for which the officers had fought. Washington was elected its first President. A service of three years in the Army was a prerequisite for membership. It was proposed that separate societies be formed for each state. The French officers serving with Comte de Rochambeau and the fleet of Admiral de Grasse were eligible for membership and a French chapter was formed. The emblem of the society was a bald eagle, in gold, with an oval on its breast, in which was a representation of Cincinnatus receiving the mace at his plough; the motto of the society encircled the oval.[21] Although the object of the society seems harmless enough, it excited much animosity, particularly in New England where

[19]*Ibid.*, p. 282.
[20]Will of George Washington—*Writings,* Vol. 37, p. 280.
[21]*Diaries,* Vol. 2, p. 341 (note).

it was alleged that the limitation of membership to officers and their descendants, tended to create a separate class, apart from and superior to their fellow citizens. The first general meeting of the society took place in Philadelphia. Washington attended and submitted certain amendments to the charter, such as elimating the hereditary clause and a disclaimer of any political aims. The former recommendation was not accepted. He declined a re-election. One pleasant episode of his Presidency of the Society was the presentation of a diamond eagle by the French members. The society still exists; membership in it is coveted as a social distinction.

Lafayette had returned to France in 1781, but he longed to see Washington again and he sailed to America. Washington's *Diaries* covering the period of his visit are lost, but we know from letters to Rochambeau and Chastellux[22] that Lafayette arrived at Mount Vernon August 17, 1784. It was probably his first visit there, and we can imagine Washington's pleasure in showing him the Mansion House, his farms, the mill, the distillery. As they rode horseback or walked about they must have talked of the political happenings in France and America, of their families and friends, of plans for the future both personal and national. There were many other guests. Dinner was served in the diningroom in that bountiful style for which Mrs. Washington was noted. In the late afternoon tea was served on the portico, and a spirit of contentment pervaded the company as the shadows lengthened and the cool breezes blew from the Potomac.

After a stay of eleven days, Lafayette returned to New York City promising to come again to Mount Vernon before he left America. He went up the Hudson to Albany and at Fort Schuyler participated with the Commissioners of Congress in making a treaty with the Seneca Indians. He then visited New England and sailed from Boston for Virginia. Everywhere the Marquis went he had a hearty welcome with addresses, banquets and receptions in almost every town. On November 18th he met Washington in Richmond where

[22]*Writings,* Vol. 27, pp. 458, 459.

the Assembly voted that the Marquis and his descendants in the male line should be forever citizens of the state. Together they rode to Mount Vernon again. When the time for parting came, the General accompanied him to Annapolis where Washington placed in his hands a letter to his wife, the Marquise, and bid him an affectionate farewell. On his return home Washington wrote the following letter which was delivered to Lafayette in New York as he was about to sail for France:

Mount Vernon, December 8, 1784.

"My Dr. Marqs: The peregrination of the day in which I parted with you, ended at Marlbro': the next day, bad as it was, I got home before dinner.

"In the moment of our separation upon the road as I travelled, and every hour since, I felt all that love, respect and attachment for you, with which length of years, close connexion and your merits have inspired me. I often asked myself, as our carriages distended, whether that was the last sight, I ever should have of you? And tho' I wished to say no, my fears answered yes. I called to mind the days of my youth, and found they had long since fled to return no more; that I was now descending the hill, I had been 52 years climbing, and that tho' I was blessed with a good constitution, I was of a short lived family, and might soon expect to be entombed in the dreary mansions of my father's. These things darkened the shades and gave a gloom to the picture, consequently to my prospects of seeing you again; but I will not repine, I have had my day."[23]

The Marquis wrote in reply:

"No my beloved General, our last parting was not by any means a last interview. My whole soul revolts at the idea; and could I harbour it an instant, indeed, my dear General, it would make me miserable. I well see you will never go to France. The inexpressible pleasure of embracing you in my own house, of welcoming you in a family where your name is adored, I do not much expect to ex-

[23]*Writings,* Vol. 28, pp. 6, 7.

perience; but to you I shall return, and, within the walls of Mount Vernon, we shall speak of olden times. My firm plan is to visit now and then my friends on this side of the Atlantic; and the most beloved of all friends I ever had, or ever shall have anywhere, is too strong an inducement for me to return to him, not to think that whenever it is possible I shall renew my so pleasing visits to Mount Vernon. . . . Adieu, adieu, my dear General. It is with inexpressible pain that I feel I am going to be severed from you by the Atlantic. Everything that admiration, respect, gratitude, friendship, and filial love, can inspire, is combined in my affectionate heart to devote me most tenderly to you. In your friendship I find a delight which words cannot express. Adieu, my dear General. It is not without emotion that I write this word, although I know I shall soon visit you again. Be attentive to your health. Let me hear from you every month. Adieu, adieu."[24]

They were never to meet again. In the early stages of the French Revolution, Lafayette was its leader and its hero. He was made Commander of the National Guard of Paris. When the Bastille was stormed he sent its key to Washington where it hangs now in a glass case in the main hall of Mount Vernon. The wild, demoniac forces unloosed by the Revolution swept him aside and he was compelled to flee from France.

Washington had said in his letter to Lafayette "I am now immersed in company." He was now famous and his house was thronged with strangers, as well as his old friends and acquaintances from Alexandria and Fairfax and his own relatives. There was Elkanah Watson, of Nantes, France, who tells in his memoirs: "I was extremely oppressed by a severe cold and excessive coughing, contracted by the exposure of a harsh journey. He (Washington) pressed me to use some remedies, but I declined doing so. As usual after retiring my coughing increased. When some time had elapsed, the door of my room was gently opened, and on drawing my bed-curtains, to my utter astonishment, I beheld Washington himself,

[24]Ford, P. L. *The True George Washington*, p. 233.

standing at my bedside with a bowl of hot tea in his hand." Some of the other guests were Governor Johnson of Maryland, Mr. Duchi, "a French gentleman recommended by the Marquis de la Fayette to me," General Lincoln, Gouverneur Morris, Mr. Arnold Henry Dohrman, "a gentleman of fortune from Lisbon," Mr. James Madison, Mr. Fitzhugh from Chatham, opposite Fredericksburg, a Mr. Wooldridge, "an English Gentleman," and a Mr. Waddell, a Presbyterian minister, "together with Mr. Murray, Mr. Wilson, and Mr. Maize came here and stayed the night." Mr. Richard Bland Lee, a Mr. Brindley, "Manager of the Susquhanna Canal, and Mr. Hanes, Manager of the James River Navigation"—the list could be prolonged indefinitely. Artists came to paint pictures of Washington: Robert Edge Pine, an Englishman; Jean Antoine Houdon, the celebrated French Sculptor, "sent from Paris by Doctr. Franklin and Mr. Jefferson to take my Bust, in behalf of the State of Virginia, with three young men assistants." The bust of Washington which he modeled is generally considered the best representation we have. The completed full-length statue is now in the State Capitol in Richmond.[25]

In the midst of all this bustle and company, he got word that his mother had written his nephew George Augustine, complaining that she did not receive enough money from him, and expressing a wish to come to Mount Vernon to live. She was living in the house he had bought for her in Fredericksburg, near her daughter, Elizabeth Lewis. Mount Vernon was no place for her and he resolved to speak plainly. He sent her fifteen Guineas, and told her that while she had taken everything she wanted from his Plantation (the Ferry Farm) he had received nothing for more than twelve years and that in the same period he or his manager had sent her over three hundred pounds. As to her coming to live at Mount Vernon he wrote:

"My house is at your service, and (I) would press you most sincerely and most devoutly to accept it, but I am sure, and candor requires me to say, it will never answer your purposes in any shape

---

[25] *Diaries*, Vol. 2, p. 419.

whatsoever. For in truth it may be compared to a well resorted tavern, as scarcely any strangers who are going from north to south, or from south to north, do not spend a day or two at it. This would, were you to be an inhabitant of it, oblige you to do one of 3 things: 1st, to be always dressing to appear in company; 2d, to come into (the room) in a dishabille, or 3d, to be as it were a prisoner in your own chamber. This first you'ld not like; indeed, for a person at your time of life it would be too fatiguing. The 2d, I should not like, because those who resort here are, as I observed before, strangers and people of the first distinction. And the 3d, more than probably, would not be pleasing to either of us. Nor indeed could you be retired in any room of my house; for what with the sitting up of company, the noise and bustle of servants, and many other things, you would not be able to enjoy that calmness and serenity of mind, which in my opinion you ought now to prefer to every other consideration in life."[26]

Washington has been criticised for want of affection for his mother. It is the fact that he extended to her only one invitation to make her home at Mount Vernon, and that was while he was a bachelor on duty at Winchester and John Augustine Washington was living there. It is also the fact that in writing to Burwell Bassett in 1773 he had urged that his wife's mother, Mrs. Dandridge, "make this place her entire and absolute home."[27] That was after the death of Patsy Custis when he thought Mrs. Washington needed the consolation of her mother's presence.

In the letter just quoted, Washington advised his mother to rent her plantation, "to break up house-keeping, hire out all the rest of your servants, except a man and a maid and live with one of your children . . . as the only means by which you can be happy. The cares of a family, without anybody to assist you; the charge of an estate the profits of which depend upon wind, weather, a good overseer, an honest man, and a thousand other circumstances, cannot be right or proper at your advanced age."

---

[26]*Writings,* Vol. 29, pp. 160, 161.
[27]*Ibid.,* Vol. 3, p. 138.

She did not live with any of her children, but stayed in her own house until she died, in August 1789. Probably she was right. She was of a complaining disposition and would have been difficult to live with.

Washington "the private citizen," going about his plantation, building barns, beautifying his grounds, and showing hospitality to all who came, was ever mindful of political developments in the country. And so, in spite of his wish to remain at Mount Vernon, we shall find him again responding to his country's call.

Chapter 23

President

While at Mount Vernon in the years of his retirement after the Revolution, Washington felt strongly the inadequacy of the Articles of Confederation and the need of a more powerful central government. He wrote to Madison: "No morn ever dawned more favorable than ours did and no day was ever more clouded than the present! . . . Without some alteration in our political creed, the superstructure we have been seven years raising at the expense of so much blood and treasure, must fall. We are verging on anarchy and confusion."[1]

He was named a delegate to the Constitutional Convention which met in Philadelphia in 1787 and presided over its deliberations. By March 1789 he was convinced that there was great likelihood he would be chosen President and he paid his last visit to his mother at Fredericksburg. She died of cancer at the age of eighty-two in the following August. The electoral votes were counted. All of them were in his favor, and Charles Thomson, the venerable Secretary of the old Continental Congress, came to Mount Vernon to notify him. His diary entry (now lost but quoted by the first editor, Jared Sparks) is:

"April 16th—About ten o'clock I bade adieu to Mount Vernon, to private life, and to domestic felicity, and with a mind oppressed with more anxious and painful sensations than I have words to express, set out for New York in company with Mr. Thomson and Colo. Humphreys, with the best disposition to render service to

[1] *Writings*, Vol. 29, p. 51.

my country in obedience to its call, but with less hope of answering its expectations."[2] Martha did not at this time accompany him. His journey was celebrated with speeches, receptions, and parades in all the cities he passed through. On the Jersey shore he was met by a specially built barge manned by thirteen sea captains, and crossed the Hudson accompanied by a small fleet of decorated boats. At the Battery in New York City a salute of thirteen guns was fired in his honor. A century later, another President, Benjamin Harrison, was rowed across the river in another barge rowed by thirteen other sea captains and another salute fired in a celebration of the centennial of the first inauguration. The inauguration took place in the Federal Hall, where the two Houses of Congress were assembled. The oath was administered on the balcony over the entrance. The inaugural address was read in the Senate Chamber. Prayers were then said in St. Paul's Episcopal Church. The new government was a success from the beginning. This was due to many factors, but the factor of greatest importance was the character of the President. It was he who gave to official intercourse its dignity and distinction.

A few months after his inauguration Washington had a tumor in his thigh. Fortunately he was in a city where he could receive the best medical attention and it was removed, but the incision was slow in healing. He longed for Dr. Craik's presence. He wrote to him: "My disorder was of long and painful duration, and though now freed from the latter, the wound given by the incision is not yet closed. Persuaded as I am that the case has been treated with skill, as with as much tenderness as the nature of the complaint would admit, yet I confess I often wished for your inspection of it."[3] He went on to say that he had been confined to a lying posture on one side for six weeks and had felt "the remains of it for more than twelve." "The want of regular exercise, with the cares of office, will, I have no doubt hasten my departure for that country from whence no Traveller returns. . ." Thereafter he took abundant exer-

[2]*Diaries,* Vol. 4, p. 7.
[3]*Writings,* Vol. 30, p. 395.

cise—on horseback, in the carriage with Mrs. Washington—"walked in the afternoon"; "took a walk around the Battery"; "rid five or six miles between breakfast and dinner"; these are typical entries from his *Diaries*.

Washington made two official journeys, one to the New England states in 1789 and the other to the southern states in 1791. The reason for the first trip assigned in his diary was to "acquire knowledge of the face of the country;—the growth and agriculture thereof—and the temper and disposition of the inhabitants toward the new government." These motives were of primary importance but there was also another motive. He thought it advisable to show the presidency to the people and to stimulate public interest in the national government.

On Nov. 13, he was back in New York, "it being Mrs. Washington's night to receive visits a pretty large company of ladies and gentlemen were present."

Washington had lived on a liberal scale at Mount Vernon. There had always been plenty of guests there. Now that he was President, the demands upon him were greater than ever. He owed it to his position to entertain his official and other guests in a style befitting the first magistrate of the Republic. His receptions were held on Tuesdays and an elaborate dinner was served with wines. Mrs. Washington's receptions were on Friday, and lasted until nine o'clock in the evening. Washington did not consider himself the host when she received, but appeared as a private gentleman, conversing freely with the guests. He kept a steward and fourteen servants, whose wages were over six hundred dollars a month. He received a salary of $25,000 a year but no provision was made by Congress for a residence for him, nor did he wish it. In both New York and Philadelphia he rented expensive houses and furnished them elaborately. To meet his expenses he was obliged to sell parts of his bounty lands on the Ohio and Kanawha. Settlers were pouring across the mountains and Washington had no trouble in finding purchasers. For instance, in 1796 he sold to Captain Matthew Ritchie 2813 acres for $12,000;[4] and in 1798 he wrote Daniel McCarty he had contracted to sell a large tract on the Kanawha for $200,000 with interest at 6% until the whole sum was paid in ten years.[5] Notwithstanding his expenses Washington was our richest President before Herbert Hoover.

For all his integrity and his wisdom, he did not escape criticism, and he knew it. Early in his administration he wrote to Dr. David Stuart: "I should like to be informed, through so good a medium of the public opinion of both men and measures, and of none more than myself; not so much of what may be thought commendable parts, if any, of my conduct, as of those which are conceived to be of a different complexion. . .

"At a distance from the theatre of action truth is not always related without embellishment, and sometimes is entirely perverted from a misconception of the causes which produce the effects that are the subject of censure. 1. This leads me to think that a system which I found it indispensably necessary to adopt upon my first coming to this city, might have undergone severe strictures and have had motives very foreign from those that govern me assigned as causes therefor; I mean, returning *no* visits 2. Appointing certain days to receive them generally (not to the exclusion however of visits on any other days under particular circumstances) and 3. at first, entertaining no company, and afterwards until I was unable to entertain any at all confining it to official characters," and he went on to explain that if he had not adopted some such rules he would not have had time to transact any business nor could he have preserved the "dignity and respect that was due to the first Magistrate."[6]

Stuart wrote in reply of the jealousy felt in Virginia over the undue influence of the Eastern States; the assumption by the Federal Government of the state debts; of the fears raised by a petition of the Quakers for the abolition of slavery (Washington considered

[4]*Diaries,* Vol. 2, p. 298.
[5]*Writings,* Vol. 36, p. 439.
[6]*Ibid.,* Vol. 30, pp. 360-361.

the petition untimely). In a second letter he reported that it was felt there was too much pomp and ceremony in official receptions, but the objections were mainly to the actions of Vice President Adams. He stated: "I have been much concerned about the clamor and abuse against him. . . The Opponents to the government affect to smile at it, and consider it a verification of their prophecies about the tendency of the government. Mr. Henry's description of it, that it squinted towards monarchy, is in every mouth, and has established him in the general opinion, as a true Prophet. It has given me much pleasure to hear every part of your conduct spoke of with high approbation, and particularly your dispensing with ceremony occasionally and walking the street, while Adams is never seen but in his carriage and six."[7]

Henry's criticism stung Washington, and he replied with some heat: "For I can truly say I had rather be at Mount Vernon with a friend or two about me, than to be attended at the Seat of Government by the Officers of State and the Representatives of every Power in Europe." As to Vice President Adams, he wrote: "One of the Gentlemen whose name is mentioned in your letter, though high toned, has never, I believe, appeared with more than *two* horses in his carriage."

As to the receptions, he gave this explanation: "These visits are optional. They are made without invitation. Between the hours of three and four every Tuesday I am prepared to receive them. Gentlemen, often in great numbers, come and go, chat with each other, and act as they please. A Porter shows them into the room, and they retire from it when they please, and without ceremony. At their *first* entrance they salute me, and I them, and as many as I can talk to I do. What pomp there is in all this, I am unable to discover. Perhaps it consists in not sitting. To this two reasons are opposed; first, it is unusual: second, (which is a more substantial one) because I have no room large enough to contain a third of the chairs, which would be sufficient to admit it." His conduct, he explained, was to observe "a just medium between too much state and too

[7] *Ibid.*, p. 362 (note).

great familiarity. Similar to the above, but of more sociable kind are the visits every Friday afternoon to Mrs. Washington, where I always am. These public meetings and a dinner once a week to as many as my table will hold, with references *to* and *from* the different Departments of State and *other* Communications with *all* parts of the Union, is as much, if not more, than I am able to undergo; for I have already had within less than a year, two *severe* attacks: the last worse than the first: a third more than probable, will put me to sleep with my fathers."[8]

After he returned to New York a Committee of both houses of Congress informed him that they were ready to receive any communication he had to make. It was the same year that Louis XVI convened the States General of France. That was a pageant of color and glittering uniforms, marching through lines of Swiss Guards and French Guards, through streets lined with tapestries. Such a ceremony was not for America, but Washington decided that his first meeting with Congress should have a solemnity of its own. His diary describes it:

"According to appointment, at 11 o'clock, I set out for the City Hall in my coach, preceded by Colonel Humphreys and Majr. Jackson, in uniform, (on my two white horses) and followed by Messrs. Lear and Nelson, in my chariot, and Mr. Lewis, on horseback, following them. In their rear was the Chief Justice of the United States and Secretary of the Treasury and War Departments, in their respective carriages, and in the order they are named. At the outer door of the hall I was met by the doorkeepers of the Senate and House; and conducted to the door of the Senate Chambers; and passing from thence to the Chair—through the Senate on the right, and House of Representatives on the left, I took my seat. The gentlemen who attended me followed and took their stand behind the Senators; the whole rising as I entered. After being seated, at which time the members of both Houses also sat, I rose (as they also did) and made my speech, delivering one copy to the President of the Senate, and another to the Speaker of the House of Representatives

[8] *Ibid.,* Vol. 31, pp. 54-55.

—after which, and being a few moments seated, I retired, bowing on each side to the assembly (which stood) as I passed, and descending to the lower hall, attended as before. I returned with them to my house."[9]

After the removal of the government to Philadelphia, Washington took his southern tour, which carried him as far south as Savannah and Augusta, Georgia. As usual he noted the ladies present at the public receptions given him: "Was visited . . . by a great number of the most respectable ladies of Charleston—the first honor of the kind I had ever experienced." In the same city "went to a very elegant dancing Assembly at the Exchange, at which were 256 elegantly dressed and handsome ladies."[10] And in Savannah he went to another "dancing Assembly at which there was about 100 well dressed and handsome ladies."[11]

Washington did not want a second term. Writing to Madison, he said: "I have not been unmindful of the sentiments expressed by you . . . on the contrary I have again, and again revolved them, with thoughtful anxiety, but without being able to dispose my mind to a longer continuation in the Office I have now the honor to hold. I therefore still look forward to the fulfillment of my fondest and most ardent wishes to spend the remainder of my days (which I cannot expect will be many) in ease and tranquility."[12]

In the end the advice of Madison and others prevailed, and he acquiesced to a second term. All the electoral votes were cast for him.

His second term was to be a stormy one, the details of which can be touched on but lightly here, but one pleasant episode may be mentioned. Lafayette had been obliged to flee from the Jacobin terror in his own country. He was a prisoner of the Austrian government, confined in the castle of Olmutz. His wife, the Marquise, resolved to send their son, George Washington Lafayette, fourteen years old, to Washington, accompanied by his tutor, the Abbe

[9] *Diaries,* Vol. 4, pp. 67-68.
[10] *Ibid.,* pp. 172-173.
[11] *Ibid.,* p. 177.
[12] *Writings,* Vol. 32, p. 45.

Frestel. She wrote to Washington: "it is with the deepest and most sincere confidence that I put my dear child under the protection of the United States, which he has ever been accustomed to look upon as his second country, and which I myself have always considered as being our future home under the special protection of their President, with whose feelings towards his father I am well acquainted."[13] The letter put Washington in a quandary. He wrote to George Cabot in Boston, where young Lafayette and his tutor had landed, suggesting that he be entered as a student at Harvard College, and adding: "I will be his friend, but the manner of becoming so, considering the obnoxious light in which his father is viewed by the French Government, and my own situation, as the Executive of the U. States requires more time to consider in all its relations than I can bestow on it at present."[14] He asked Cabot to give the young gentleman "the most unequivocal assurances of my standing in the place of and becoming to him, a Father, friend, protector and supporter."

While Washington was President he felt it expedient to maintain this attitude, in public at least, but when he retired to Mount Vernon the boy became a member of his family, and he welcomed him with the tenderness of a father. The news of Lafayette's release from prison reached America in the autumn of 1797. Young Lafayette was now ready to return to his father. A revealing entry in Washington's ledger is: "By Geo. W. Fayette, gave for the purpose of getting himself such small articles of Clothing as he might not choose to ask for $100." Another item in the accounts was three hundred dollars to defray his "exps." to France.[15]

Washington gave the young man a letter to his father: "My dear Sir: This letter will, I hope and expect, be presented to you by your Son, who is highly deserving of such Parents as you and your amiable lady.

"He can relate much better than I can describe, my participation

[13]Lasteyrie du Saillant, M. A. V. (de Lafayette) *Marquise* de. Life of Madame de Lafayette.

[14]*Writings,* Vol. 34, p. 299.

[15]Ford, *True George Washington,* p. 235.

in your sufferings, my solicitude for your relief, the measures I adopted (though ineffectually) to facilitate your liberation from an unjust and cruel imprisionment, and the joy I experienced at the news of its accomplishment." The letter closed with: "If inclination or events should induce you, or any of them, to visit America, no person in it would receive you with more cordiality and affection than Mrs. Washington and myself would do, both of us being most sincerely and affectionately attached to you."[16] Lafayette and his son were to revisit the United States, but not until Washington and his wife had been in their graves nearly a quarter of a century.

Another non-controversial matter in which Washington took a deep interest in his second term was the location and laying off of the Federal City. He never called it Washington and it was not until after his death that the term came into general use. The Federal Constitution had authorized Congress to exercise exclusive jurisdiction over a district, not exceeding ten miles square, as might be ceded by particular states. Congress selected the site on the Potomac River; the States of Virginia and Maryland ceded jurisdiction and ownership to the United States, Virginia's share being about thirty-four square miles including the City of Alexandria, and the present Arlington County; and Maryland about sixty-six square miles, including the town of Georgetown. During the Revolutionary War, Washington had been unable to visit Mount Vernon except in going to and returning from the Yorktown campaign. While President he was able to make stays there between sessions of Congress. After the appointment of the Commissioners he stopped off at Georgetown to confer with them, and with the surveyors, Major Peter Charles L'Enfant and Andrew Ellicott. During his short stay at Georgetown he met the proprietors of the land embraced within the proposed city. An agreement was reached by which the proprietors conveyed their land to trustees to hold until the new city should be surveyed and laid out. For the streets they received nothing, for the land set aside for public buildings and parks the proprietors were to be paid at the rate of twenty-five pounds

[16] *Writings*, Vol. 36, pp. 40, 42.

per acre. The rest of the land was to be divided into lots, the United States to receive one-half and the proprietors the other half. The United States appropriated no money in aid of the project. The Commissioners had many difficulties to contend with, lack of materials, lack of skilled labor and lack of money.[17] The credit for the plan of the city belongs to Major L'Enfant, but although he possessed great ability, he was "perverse" (as Washington said of him), insubordinate and refused to surrender his map of the city to the Commissioners for engraving and had finally to be dismissed, with Washington's approval, and Andrew Ellicott substituted for him. The plan for the Capitol Building was drawn by Dr. William Thornton of Georgetown. Washington wrote to the Commissioners: "The Grandeur, Simplicity and Beauty of the exterior, the propriety with which the apartments are distributed; and the economy in the mass of the whole structure, will, I doubt not, give it a preference in your eyes."[18] This building was burned by the British army when it captured Washington in 1814. But Washington was aghast at the cost of the proposed President's house, £77,900. In 1798 he built two houses on lots he had purchased on North Capital St. between B and C Streets. They remained standing until about 1908 when they were torn down to increase the area of the Capitol Grounds.[19]

The troubles that beset Washington's second term arose chiefly out of the war between England and France. The excesses of the Revolution, the execution of Louis XVI and his Queen, Marie Antionette, shocked an important section of American public opinion. On the other hand, the British still retained the frontier forts in the Northwest Territory which had been ceded to the United States by the treaty of peace. The President had issued a Proclamation of Neutrality in the war between England and France, and he sent the Chief Justice of the Supreme Court, John Jay, to seek a solution of our difficulties with Great Britain. He returned with

---

[17]E. F. M. Faehtz and F. W. Pratt. *Washington in Embryo.*
[18]*Writings,* Vol. 32, p. 325.
[19]*Diaries,* Vol. 4, p. 284.

the draft of a treaty providing for the surrender of the western posts, in exchange for an agreement to pay debts due to British merchants, but was unable to secure a relaxation of the impressment of American seamen of British birth and free, unhampered trade with the British West Indies. The treaty was received in the United States with an almost universal outburst of indignation, even in Federalist Boston. Washington was dissatisfied but stood by the treaty and his influence was sufficient to secure its ratification by an exact two-thirds majority in the Senate. The formation of political parties, which was inevitable, was hastened by the dissension over the treaty. The opposition press showered insults on the President and Jay was burned in effigy. Philip Freneau, editor of the *National Gazette,* and Benjamin Franklin Bache of the *Aurora* declared in their newspapers that Washington had debauched and deceived the nation; that he showed the ostentation of an Eastern Pasha; that he had betrayed France and was the slave of England.[20]

Washington had a sensitive nature and the abuse heaped upon him must have pained him deeply. Whatever he may have felt, he expressed himself in public with moderation: "Having determined, as far as lay within the power of the executive, to keep this country in a state of neutrality, I have made my public conduct accord with the system; and whilst so acting as a public character, consistency and propriety as a private man forbid those intemperate expressions in favor of one nation or to the prejudice of another, which may have wedged themselves in, and, I will venture to add, to the embarassment of government, without producing any good to the country."[21]

The accusation of partiality to England was not the only objection to Washington's policy.

A more specious but unfair charge was that the financial measures adopted by his administration had benefited the rich at the expense of the poor. The reference was to the assumption of the State debts which were held largely by speculators. The truth was the states

---

[20]Lodge, Henry Cabot. *George Washington,* Vol. 2, p. 247.
[21]Quoted by Henry Cabot Lodge in his *George Washington,* Vol. 2, p. 248.

were now incorporated in the nation, and to dishonor their obligations would impair the national credit.

During his first administration, Washington had purposely included in his cabinet men of diverse political ideals, believing that government should be above party strife. But during his second term parties were forming. Jefferson, who had been Secretary of State, resigned and set himself to the formation of the Republican-Democratic party, which was critical of the administration. The supporters of the administration organized themselves into the Federalist party. They were led by Hamilton and Adams. Washington's policies were actually Federalist, though he did not openly ally himself with the party.

His Farewell Address underwent many, many revisions, as his letters to Hamilton, Madison and Jay show. It was a noble political valedictory. After a personal introduction stating his reasons for declining to stand for a third term, he devoted the rest of the address first to domestic and then to foreign affairs: "The Unity of Government which constitutes you one people is also now dear to you. It is justly so, for it is a main Pillar in the edifice of your real independence. . . For this you have every inducement of sympathy and interest. Citizens by birth or choice, of a common country, that country has a right to concentrate your affections. The name *American,* which belongs to you, in your national capacity, must always exalt in just pride of Patriotism, more than any appellation derived from local discriminations. With slight shades of difference, you have the same Religion, Manners, Habits and political Principles. You have in a common cause fought and triumphed together. The independence and liberty you possess are the work of joint councils and joint efforts; common dangers, sufferings and successes."

Having stated these general considerations, he went on to the danger of "The Spirit of Party" in the State: "It serves always to distract the Public Councils and enfeeble the Public Administration. It agitates the Community with ill founded jealousies and false alarms, kindles the animosity of one part against another, foments occasionally riot and insurrections. It opens the door to foreign influence and corruption, which finds a facilitated access to the government itself through the channels of party passions." These were strong words. They were addressed to the future. He was about to retire from public life. He was conscious of his rectitude. The venom of the opposition journals, the carping in Congress of a Giles, the strictures of a Monroe, could not disturb the serenity of his life, but he feared that if not moderated they might tear the nation apart. The fact was that Washington could not reconcile himself to party government. It contravened one of his deepest instincts, which was to surround himself in the administration of government with the ablest men available and work in unison for the common good. He believed that a continuance of the party strife of his second term might destroy the union so recently formed. He had the excesses of the French Revolution and its championship by its American partisans in mind. As it turned out, he was mistaken. The bond that held the states together, the centripetal forces, were strong enough to stand the strife between the followers of Hamilton and Jefferson. When Civil War came it was the result of the clash of forces deeper than the rivalries of politicians.

The English historian Lecky has well stated why a two party system is beneficial to a nation trained in self-government:

"In theory nothing could seem more absurd than a system of government in which, as it has been said, the ablest men in Parliament are divided into two classes, one side being charged with the duty of carrying on the government and the other with that of obstructing and opposing them in their task, and in which, on a vast multitude of unconnected questions, these two great bodies of very competent men, with the same facts and arguments before them, habitually go into opposite lobbies. In practice, however, parliamentary government by great parties, in countries where it is fully understood and practised, is found to be admirably efficacious in representing every variety of political opinion; in securing a constant supervision and criticism of men and measures; and in forming a safety valve through which the dangerous humours of society can expand without evil to the community."[22]

Coming to foreign affairs Washington advised: "Observe good faith and justice towds all Nations. Cultivate peace and harmony with all. . . Europe has a set of primary interests, which to us have none, or a very remote relation. Hence she must be engaged in frequent controversies, the causes of which are essentially foreign to our concerns. . . 'Tis our true policy to steer clear of permanent Alliances with any portion of the foreign world." Our isolationists seem to have forgotten that Washington added: "Taking care to always keep ourselves, by suitable establishments, or a respectably defensive posture, we may safely trust to temporary alliances for extraordinary emergencies."[23] Washington knew too well what the French alliance had meant to America, not to envisage that the future might require "temporary alliances." It is a safe conjecture that if he were alive today he would not advocate "Fortress America."

One neat way in which Washington solved a personal problem was his answer to Constantin Volney, the French scholar and revolutionist, who asked him for a general letter of introduction to be used in his travels in the United States. Considering the uncertain state of things in France he did not care to give it and he did not choose to refuse; so he wrote:

"C. Volney

needs no recommendation from

Geo. Washington."[24]

Washington's longing to return to private life and the sting he felt from the vicious attacks on his integrity, came out in a letter to Henry Knox written two days before the end of his second term: "To the wearied traveller who sees a resting place, and is bending his body to lean thereon, I now compare myself; but to be suffered to do *this* in peace, is I perceive too much, to be endured by *some*.

---

[22]Lecky, W. E. H. *The Map of Life,* pp. 124-125.
[23]"Farewell Address." *Writings,* Vol. 35, pp. 214-238.
[24]Ford, *True George Washington,* p. 306.

To misrepresent my motives; to reprobate my policies, and to weaken the confidence which has been reposed in my administration are objects which cannot be relinquished by those who will be satisfied with nothing short of a change in our political System."

John Adams was inaugurated as Washington's successor on March 4, 1797. He gave an account of the scene in a letter to his wife: "Your dearest friend never had a more trying day than yesterday. A solemn scene it was indeed, and it was made more affecting to me by the presence of the General, whose countenance was as serene and unclouded as the day. He seemed to me to enjoy a triumph over me. Methought I heard him say, 'Ay! I am fairly out and you are fairly in! See which of us will be happiest!' When the ceremony was over, he came and made me a visit, and cordially congratulated me, and wished my administration might be happy, successful and honourable. . . In the Chamber of the House of Representatives was a multitude as great as the space could contain, and I believe scarcely a dry eye but Washington's."[25]

On March 9th he left Philadelphia accompanied by Mrs. Washington, Eleanor Parke Custis, George Washington Lafayette and Felix Frestel, his tutor, and on the 15th got to Mt. Vernon in time for dinner.

[25]*Diaries*, Vol. 4, p. 253 (note).

Chapter 24

Closing Years

The Mount Vernon to which Washington retired after his Presidency was probably in a better condition than that to which he returned after the Revolution. There were several reasons for this. He had two capable managers, Whiting and Pearce. He had been able to visit the estate in the summer intervals between sessions of Congress and give it his personal supervision. He was convinced that the average farmer in Virginia paid too little attention to grazing lands. Soon after he got back to Mount Vernon he wrote: "I have had it in contemplation ever since I returned home to turn my farms into grazing principally, as fast as I can cover the fields with grass."[1]

Of the inside of the house he wrote to George Washington Parke Custis: "We are all in a litter and dirt, occasioned by joiners, masons, and painters, working in the house, all parts of which, as well as the outbuildings, I find upon examination to be exceedingly out of repairs."[2]

He described his daily life on his farms in a letter to his friend James McHenry, Secretary of War, written on May 29, 1797.

"Dear Sir: I am indebted to you for several unacknowledged letters; but ne'er mind that; go on as if you had them. You are at the source of information, and can find many things to relate; while I have nothing to say, that could either inform or amuse a Secretary of War in Philadelphia.

"I might tell him that I begin my diurnal course with the Sun;

[1]*Writings,* Vol. 35, p. 500.
[2]From Custis's *Recollection of Washington.*

that if my hirelings are not in their places at that time I send them messages expressive of my sorrow for their indisposition; then having put these wheels in motion, I examine the state of things further; and the more they are probed, the deeper I find the wounds are which my buildings have sustained by an absence and neglect of eight years; by the time I have accomplished these matters breakfast (a little after seven Oclock, about the time I presume you are taking leave of Mrs. McHenry) is ready. This over, I mount my horse and ride round my farms, which employs me until it is time to dress for dinner; at which I rarely miss seeing strange faces; come, as they say, out of respect to me. Pray, would not the word curiosity answer as well? and how different this, from having a few social friends at a cheerful board? The usual time of sitting at Table; a walk, and Tea, brings me within the dawn of Candlelight; previous to which, if not prevented by company, I resolve, that, as soon as the glimmering taper, supplies the place of the great luminary, I will retire to my writing Table and acknowledge the letters I have received; but when the lights are brought, I feel tired, and disinclined to engage in this work, conceiving that the next night will do as well: the next comes and with it the same causes for postponement, and effect, and so on.

"This will account for *your* letter remaining so long unacknowledged; and having given you the history of a day, it will serve for a year; and I am persuaded you will not require a second edition of it: but it may strike you, that in this detail no mention is made of any portion of time allotted for reading; the remark would be just, for I have not looked into a book since I came home, nor shall I be able to do it until I have discharged my Workmen: probably not before the nights grow longer; when possibly, I may be looking in doomsday book . . . ."[3]

He does not mention it, but as the evening shades lengthened, he must have enjoyed sitting on his great portico, surrounded by his guests, watching the sails of the boats passing up and down the river and on rainy days taking his exercise walking the length

[3]*Writings,* Vol. 35, pp. 455-456.

of the portico. His public career was finished. He could look back with pride and satisfaction on his accomplishments. He could have said, with the historian Edward Gibbon, that the greatest happiness of life was to be found in "that mature season in which our passions are supposed to be calmed, our duties fulfilled, our ambition satisfied, our fame and fortune established on a solid basis."

His interest in the Federal City continued unabated. Two of Mrs. Washington's granddaughters lived there—Elizabeth Custis, the wife of Thomas Law, whose house was at the corner of New Jersey Avenue and C Street S.E., and Martha Custis, the wife of Thomas Peter, whose house, on the south side of K Street, N.W., near Twenty-sixth Street, is still standing. It was not until after Washington's death that Thomas Peter built Tudor Place in Georgetown. As before noted, Washington built two large houses on North Capitol Street, more from a wish to further the development of the new city than in the expectation of profit, and he subscribed to a company which built a hotel.[4] He selected the sites on which the Capitol and the Presidential Mansion were to be erected. Other public buildings were to be near the Mansion.

Now that he was living within driving distance he could watch the laying off and grading of the streets, avenues and public reservations, and see the farm land transformed into a city, with dwelling houses scattered over it. In 1798 he and Mrs. Washington spent four days there, and "on our return home called at Mount Eagle to take our leave of the Revd Mr. Fairfax who was on the point of Embarking for England."[5] He went well provided with introductions from Washington. The short letter to Sir John Sinclair reads: "Permit me to introduce to your acquaintance and civilities my good friend and neighbor the Reverend Bryan Fairfax who is, though he has not taken upon himself the title, the Baron of Cameron.

"Ill health and advice that Sea Air might be a means of restoring his health, have induced him to take a Voyage to England. The integrity of his heart and benevolence of his mind, need only to be

[4] *Diaries,* Vol. 4, p. 286.
[5] *Ibid.,* p. 277.

known to procure his esteem, and as I can vouch for this, I shall introduce him to you as a Gentleman worthy of your attention."[6]

While in England Bryan petitioned the House of Lords to recognize his title of Lord Fairfax, Baron of Cameron, and in 1800 his claim was adjudged valid.[7] He never used the title when he returned to the United States. Washington entrusted him with a letter to Mrs. Sarah Cary Fairfax, a portion of which is here quoted:

"My dear Madam: Five and twenty years, nearly, have passed away since I have considered myself as the permanent resident at this place; or have been in a situation to endulge myself in a familiar intercourse with my friends, by letter or otherwise.

"During this period, so many important events have occurred, and such changes in men and things have taken place, as the compass of a letter would give you but an inadequate idea of. None of which events, however, nor all of them together, have been able to eradicate from my mind, the recollection of those happy moments, the happiest in my life, which I have enjoyed in your company . . . it is a matter of sore regret, when I cast my eyes towards Belvoir, which I often do, to reflect that the former Inhabitants of it, with whom we lived in such harmony and friendship, no longer reside there; and that the ruins can only be viewed as the memento of former pleasures; and permit me to add, that I have wondered often, (your nearest relations being in this Country), that you should not prefer spending the evening of your life among them rather than close the sublunary Scene in a foreign Country, numerous as your acquaintances may be, and sincere, as the friendships you may have formed . . . ."[8]

He also enclosed a letter to her from Mrs. Washington, the draft of which is in his handwriting. It is dated May 17, 1798. It is printed in Worthington C. Ford's edition of *Washington's Writings*.[9] An excerpt is here quoted:

[6]*Writings,* Vol. 36, p. 261.
[7]Neill, Edward N. *Fairfaxes of England and America,* pp. 181-182.
[8]*Writings,* Vol. 36, pp. 262, 263, 264.
[9]*Writings* . . . ed. by Ford, Vol. 13, p. 500.

"The changes which have taken place in this country, since you left it (and it is pretty much the same in all other parts of this State) are, in one word, total. In Alexandria, I do not believe there lives at this day a single family with which you had the smallest acquaintance. In our neighborhood Colo. Mason, Colo. McCarty and wife, Mr. Chichester, Mr. Lund Washington and all the Wageners, have left the stage of human life; and our visitors on the Maryland side are gone and going likewise. . . ."

Bryan Fairfax

Like his elder brother, George William, Bryan Fairfax was a lifelong friend of Washington's. A lengthy note about him is printed in the *Diaries* and is inserted here:

"Bryan Fairfax (1736-1802), first child of his father's Massachusetts wife, Deborah Clarke, and, in consequence, a half-brother of George William Fairfax, was born August 11, 1736, in Westmoreland County, Virginia. His father vested in him about 4700 acres of land in Fauquier and he was trained as a merchant, in Barbadoes. He became a lieutenant in Captain George Mercer's company of the Virginia Regiment, and while on duty experienced a religious conviction which long after carried him into holy orders. A disappointment in love caused him to resign and start North with an intention of enlisting in one of the Northern Colonies, but his brother-in-law persuaded him to return. He then became a captain in the Fairfax militia. On the death of his father, Bryan came into possession of 5500 acres of land in the vicinity of Difficult Run, Fairfax County, which his father had called 'Towlston Grange', after his birthplace in Yorkshire, England. Lord Fairfax deeded to Bryan, in 1765, the so-called 'Great Falls Manor' of 12,500 acres. On this land Matildaville, Loudoun County, was laid out in 1790. In the possession of nearly 30,000 acres, Bryan recovered from his early heart affliction and married Elizabeth, daughter of Colonel Wilson Cary, of Ceelys, and established himself at Towlston in

1759. During this period his friendship for Washington was largely developed and strengthened. His political sentiments during the dispute between the Mother Country and the colonies placed him in opposition to the Revolution and separation. In 1777 he attempted to bring about a settlement of the trouble, and on his way to New York for that purpose was arrested at Lancaster, Pennsylvania, and imprisoned. Washington immediately secured his release and allowed him to go forward into the British lines on his word of honor not to divulge anything that could be of benefit to the British. In New York he found that he could not conscientiously take the oath required by the British authorities, and he gave up his attempt to bring about an adjustment and returned to Virginia, visiting Washington, then at Valley Forge, on his way home. He lived unmolested by the State and respected by its inhabitants to the end of his life. He was one of the organizers of the Episcopalian Church in Virginia after the war. In 1789 he took orders and became minister in Fairfax and officiated at Christ Church, Alexandria, and the Falls Church. He resigned his ministerial duties in 1792 and retired to Mount Eagle. Bryan became eighth Lord Fairfax in 1793. His first wife died in 1778, and he married a second time, in 1780, Jane, daughter of James Donaldson, of Fairfax. He had numerous children."[10]

He died at Mount Eagle, near Alexandria, August 2, 1802. His house was burned about thirty years ago and a modern building bearing the same name was built on its site. His son Ferdinand (or Ferdinando) acquired the Belvoir tract as devisee of his uncle, George William Fairfax. The representative of the family now bearing the title Baron of Cameron, has returned to England to live.

Bryan Fairfax owned another estate, known as Ash Grove, on the Leesburg Pike, two miles west of Tyson's corner. Part of the house is said to have been built in 1790 and the rest added soon afterward. At the time of the Mexican War, Ash Grove, which is still standing, was owned by Capt. Henry Fairfax, grandson of Bryan. In

[10]*Diaries,* Vol. 1, pp. 130-131 (note).

1850 it was purchased by James Sherman and is still owned by the Sherman family.

Now that Washington's fame was world-wide, the guests at Mount Vernon multiplied and among them were many foreigners. Some of those noted in his diaries for 1797 and 1798 were: Capt. James Huie, a Danish merchant; Henry Pye Rich and Thomas McDonald, Englishmen, Commissioners for the liquidation of claims of British creditors, under Jay's Treaty; Vicompte d'Orleans, probably son of Louis Philippe, Duc d'Orleans; Mr. Gahn, a Swedish merchant; Mr. Delvis of Bremen; Mr. Peckmoller of Hamburg; a Spanish gentleman from Havana; Mr. Hasler, of Demerara, British Guiana; Mr. Charles W. Valangin, of London; Mr. Julian Niemcewicz, a Polish gentleman who kept a diary found many years ago; and selections describing this visit were published in the *Century Magazine*.

The visitor was charmed with everything he saw, except the slaves' quarters, but he reserved his most enthusiastic praises for Mrs. Washington and Nelly Custis. Of the former he wrote: "One of the most delightful persons one can meet. Good, sweet and exceedingly pleasant, she likes to talk and talks well of old times." Of Nelly (Eleanor) Custis, whom he calls "the divine Miss Custis," he wrote: "She was one of those celestial beings so rarely produced by nature, sometimes dreamed of by poets and painters, which one cannot see without a feeling of ecstasy."[11]

In 1798 war with France was believed imminent and President Adams appointed Washington Lieutenant-General and Commander-in-Chief of the forces to be raised for the expected conflict. Washington accepted the appointment in a long letter in which he stated among other things: "When I retired to the walks of private life, I had no idea that any event would occur that could induce me to leave them. That the pain I should feel, if it be my fate

[11]From "A Visit to Mount Vernon A Century Ago," by Julian U. Niemcewicz from THE CENTURY MAGAZINE. Copyright, 1902, The Century Company. Reprinted by permission of the publishers Appleton-Century-Crofts, Inc.

to do so, cannot easily be expressed. Yet if this Country should actually be Invaded, or such manifestations of a design to do it, as cannot be mistaken, I should be ready to render every Service in my power to repel it. . ."[12] He went on to stipulate, however, that he should not be called into the field until the army required his presence or circumstances demanded it. Fortunately war did not come, nor did Washington believe that it would come, if the country was in such a state of preparedness as to warn the existing French Government of its folly. Much of his time and correspondence had to do with the commissioning of general officers and creating a general staff. He tried to keep out of the controversies it aroused.

Benjamin H. Latrobe, the architect, visited Mount Vernon, shortly before Washington retired and described his reception:

"The President came to me. He was dressed in a plain blue coat, his hair dressed and powered. There was a reserve, but no hauteur, in his manner. . . . Dinner was served at about half past three . . . he placed me at the left hand of Mrs. Washington, Miss Custis seated at her right, and himself next to her about the middle of the table. There was very little conversation during dinner. A few jokes passed between the President and young Lafayette whom he treats more like a child than a guest. I felt a little embarrassed at the quiet reserved air that prevailed. As I drink no wine and the President drank only three glasses, the party soon returned to the Portico. . . . Coffee was brought about six oclock. . . . Breakfast was served up in the usual Virginia style, tea, coffee and cold boiled meat; and for an hour afterwards he (Washington) stood on the steps of the west door talking to the Company who were collected around him. . . . as soon as my servant came up he went to him and asked 'if he had breakfasted'. He then shook me by the hand. . . . Washington has something uncommonly commanding and majestic in his walk, his address, his figure and his countenance, His face is characterised by more intense and powerful thought than by quick and fiery conception. There is a mildness about its expression and an air of reserve in his manner covers its tone still more.

[12] *Writings*, Vol. 36, pp. 310, 311.

He is about 64 but appears some years younger, and has sufficient apparent signs to his many years. He was sometimes entirely silent for many minutes, during which time an awkwardness seemed to prevail in every one present. His answers were sometimes short and approached to moroseness. He did not, at anytime speak with any remarkable fluency. Perhaps the extreme correctness of his language which almost seemed studied produced this effect. He appeared to enjoy a humorous observation and made several himself. He laughed heartily some times and in a very good humored manner. On the morning of my departure he treated me as if had lived years in his house with ease and attention. But in general I thought there was a slight air of moroseness about him as if something had vexed him."[13]

Latrobe's visit was on July 16, 1796 as appears from his diary. Washington's diaries for the whole of that year are missing. All observers agree that Washington was not a talkative man, but the reserve that Latrobe noticed may have been heightened "by the Company who were collected around him." They were probably mostly strangers, as the conversation that Latrobe relates was about the "Establishment of a University at the Federal City." When with his friends and neighbors of Fairfax County he must have talked more freely.

Not every traveller who claimed to have visited Washington at Mount Vernon saw the mansion, much less, had a long conversation with its owner. This was the case with the English actor John Bernard, who was playing an engagement with his company at Annapolis in 1798. In a book published after Washington's death, he related that when returning from a visit to a friend living below Alexandria, he encountered an overturned chaise in which were a man and his wife who had been thrown out. At that moment another horseman galloped up. Bernard and his unknown companion removed the heavy luggage from the vehicle and managed to right it. The two "Samaritans" declined the invitation of the driver to go to Alexandria with him and take a drop of "something sociable." The stranger was "a tall, erect, well-made man, evidently advanced

[13] *Ibid.*, Vol. 35, pp. 141-142 (note).

in years, but who appeared to have retained all the vigor and elasticity resulting from a life of temperance and exercise. His dress was a blue coat buttoned to his chin, and buckskin breeches. Though the instant he took off his hat I could not avoid the recognition of familiar lineaments, which indeed I was in the habit of seeing on every sign-post and over every fireplace, still I failed to identify him, and to my surprise I found, I was an object of equal speculation in his eyes. After a moments pause he said: 'Mr. Bernard, I believe'," and he mentioned the occasion on which he had seen him play in Philadelphia. He then asked Bernard to go home with him for a couple of hours rest, and pointed out the house in the distance. At last Bernard knew to whom he was speaking. " 'Mount Vernon', I exclaimed! 'Have I the honor of addressing General Washington?' "

There is where Bernard gave himself away. The public road from Colchester to Alexandria does not pass within a mile and a half of Mount Vernon, which was not then, and is not now visible from it. It may also be noted that though Washington's diaries are complete for 1798, Bernard is not mentioned as a visitor. Having gotten himself inside Mount Vernon, Bernard had no difficulty in inventing a plausible conversation on negro slavery, a subject on which Washington's views were well known; on the state of the fine arts in America, and the causes of their backwardness.

Other remarks he claims Washington made seem to the present writer most improbable. He credits his host as regarding "the happiness of America but as the first link in a series of universal victories; for his full faith in the power of those results of civil liberty which he saw all around him led him to forsee that it would erelong, prevail in other countries, and that the social millenium of Europe would usher in the political."[14] With the memory of the Jacobin terror and the confiscation of the estates of Lafayette and other French friends fresh in his mind, Washington was not likely to take such a rosy view of the social millenium. Looking back now we can see that the French Revolution was, on the whole, productive

[14]Lodge, *George Washington,* Vol. 2, pp. 276-277, 338-339.

of great good to France and to Europe; but to Washington its cruelties and the uprooting of a social order shocked his conservative mind.

This account has been taken from Henry Cabot Lodge's *George Washington*. The senator gives full credence to Bernard's story. In justice to him it should be recalled that when he visited Mount Vernon practically all travellers from the Northern States came by steamboat and he knew nothing of the public roads in its vicinity.

Frederic Harrison, an English author who visited the United States in 1901, wrote:

"Of all that I saw in America, I look back with most emotion to my visit to Mount Vernon, the home and burial-place of George Washington. I saw it on a lovely spring day, amidst thousands of pilgrims, in the Inauguration week. On a finely-wooded bluff, rising above the grand Potomac river, stands the plain but spacious wooden house of the Founder of the Republic. It has been preserved and partly restored with perfect taste, the original furniture, pictures, and ornaments supplemented by fit contemporary pieces. It enables one perfectly to conjure up an image of the homely, large, and generous life of the President before the war called him to the field, and after he had retired from all cares of state. We fancy him sitting under the spacious eastern portico, with its eight tall columns, looking out over the broad landscape of forest and river, or lying in his last sleep in the simple bed, with its dimity coverlet, and then laid to rest in the rural tomb below the house, which he ordered himself, and in which his descendants have insisted on keeping his remains. . . . It has been frequently attempted to remove from Mount Vernon, his home, the sarcophagus in which Washington lies, in order to place it under the dome of the Capitol. But as yet it has been wisely decided to do nothing which can impair the unique legend which has gathered round the memory of the western Cincinnatus."[15]

Sickness was a perpetual threat to Washington. He noted in his diary of August 20, 1798: "No account kept of the weather, etc.

[15]Harrison, Frederic. *Memories and Thoughts,* pp. 193-194.

from hence to the end of the Month, on acct of my Sickness, which commenced with a fever on the 19th and lasted until the 24th which left me debilitated."[16] A note by the editor states: "Probably an attack of malarial fever, as it yielded to Dr. Craik's treatment with 'Jesuits bark' as Quinine was then called."

In September 1799 Washington received notice of the death of his youngest brother, Charles, from Colonel Burgess Ball who had married Charles' daughter, Frances. After expressing his regret, Washington wrote: "I was the *first* and am now the *last* of my father's Children by the second marriage who remain; when I shall be called upon to follow them, is known only to the giver of life. When the moment comes I shall endeavor to obey it with a good grace."[17]

On the seventh of December 1799 Washington dined at Lord Fairfax's home at Mount Eagle, and on the eleventh he entertained his last guests: "Lord Fairfax, his Son Thomas, and daughter, Mrs. Warner Washington and son and Mr. Jno. Herbert dined here and returned after dinner."[18] It is pleasant to know that the last persons he entertained were relatives and intimate friends.

The last words written by Washington were probably the entries in his diary of Dec. 13, 1799; they relate to the snow that was then falling.[19]

" 'On Thursday, December 12th, the General rode out to his farms about ten o'clock, and did not return till past three. Soon after he went out, the weather became very bad, rain, hail and snow falling alternately, with a cold wind. When he came in . . . his neck appeared to be wet, and the snow was hanging upon his hair. He came to dinner (which had been waiting for him) without changing his dress. In the evening he appeared to be as well as usual.' *(Tobias Lear's account)*. The next day a heavy snow prevented him from riding out as usual. He complained of a sore throat".[20] "In the

[16]*Diaries,* Vol. 4, p. 283.
[17]*Writings,* Vol. 37, p. 372.
[18]*Diaries,* Vol. 4, p. 319.
[19]*Ibid.,* p. 320.
[20]*Ibid.,* Vol. 4, p. 320 (note).

evening the papers were brought from the post office, and the family remained in the parlor until nine o'clock when Mrs. Washington went up to Mrs. Lewis's room. After that he (Lear) and the General read. Washington was quite hoarse; and when he left as Lear supposed for the night, the latter observed to the General that he had better take something for his cold. Washington replied, 'No, you know I never take anything for a cold—let it go as it came'."[21]

"Between two and three o'clock Saturday morning (December 14) he woke Mrs. Washington and told her he was ill. He could scarcely speak, but would not allow her to get up for fear of her catching cold. Tobias Lear immediately sent for Dr. Craik. At Washington's request Albin Rawlins (an employee on the estate), with much hesitancy, bled him. About one half a pint of blood was taken." Dr. Craik arrived about nine o'clock in the morning. Dr. Gustavus Brown of Port Tobacco, Maryland and Dr. Elisha Cullen Dick of Alexandria arrived about three P.M., and various remedies —hot applications, foot baths, gargle, etc. were tried," but to no effect. It was decided to bleed him again. Dr. Dick protested, saying "he needs all his strength; bleeding will diminish it." Washington was aware by this time that he was dying. He said: "I find that I am going," and smiling added, that it was "the debt we must all pay," he looked to the event with perfect resignation. As his pain increased, he said to Doctor Craik: "Doctor, I die hard, but I am not afraid to go. I believed from my first attack that I should not survive it." Later with great difficulty he said: "Do not let my body be put in the vault until I have been dead three days." His last words were: " 'Tis well."

"About ten minutes after ten, Tobias Lear, who sat by the bedside holding Washington's hand, called softly to Dr. Craik, who sat by the fire absorbed in grief. The Doctor recognizing at once that the end was at hand, came to the bedside and placed his hand gently and reverently over Washington's eyes. When he removed his hand the eyes were closed forever. Dr. Dick stepped over to the

---

[21]Custis, G. W. P. *Recollections,* p. 473 note (based on account of Tobias Lear, source of all accounts).

fire place and cut the cord which operated the pendulum of the small clock which stood on the mantel. The hands stood at twenty minutes after ten."[22] Mrs. Washington, who was sitting at the foot of the bed, asked in a firm voice: "Is he gone?" Lear signalled that he was dead. Again she spoke: "All is now over, I shall soon follow him. I have no more trials to pass through."[23] Washington's body was placed on the portico. The funeral was fixed for Wednesday, the 18th of December. The *Alexandria Times* gave an account of the public grief: "From the time of his death to the time of his interment the bells continued to toll, the shipping in the harbor wore their colors at half mast high and every public expression of grief was observed. On Wednesday the inhabitants of the town, of the county and the adjacent parts of Virginia and Maryland proceeded to Mount Vernon to perform the last offices to the body of their illustrious neighbor. All the military within a considerable distance and three Masonic lodges were present."[24]

Tobias Lear, states in his diary: "Troops, horse and foot, Music, playing a solemn dirge. . . The General's horse, with his saddle, holster and pistols, led by two grooms in black. The body born by the Freemasons and Officers." The principal mourners were Mrs. Stuart and Mrs. Law, Miss Nancy and Sally Stuart; Miss Fairfax and Miss Dennison, Mr. Law and Mr. Peter, Mr. Lear and Dr. Craik, Lord Fairfax and Fernando Fairfax, Lodge No. 39 and the Corporation of Alexandria. The pall holders were Colonels Little, Payne, Gilpin, Ramsay and Marsteller. Colonel Blackburn preceded the corpse. Colonel DeNeale marched with the military. The burial service was read by the Rev. Thomas Davis, Rector of Christ Church, Alexandria. The Rev. James Muir, pastor of the Presbyterian Church of Alexandria, Dr. Addison, an Episcopal clergyman from across the river in Maryland, also attended the service. The Masonic ritual was then recited and the coffin placed inside the vault.

[22]William Buckner McGroarty. "The Death of Washington," *Virginia Magazine of History and Biography,* April 1946.

[23]This account is based mainly on Tobias Lear's *Letters and Recollections of George Washington.*

[24]W. H. Snowden. *Old Historic Landmarks,* p. 45.

Martha Washington had directed a door to be made for the vault instead of sealing it because it would be necessary soon to open it again. She never slept afterward in the room in which Washington died, but occupied a small room on the third floor above their former bedroom. She remained in the mansion until her death in 1802 and was attended in her last illness by Dr. Craik.

As to the method of treatment used by Washington's physicians, Senator Lodge has this interesting note.

"In response to an inquiry as to the modern treatment of this disease, Dr. F. H. Hooper of Boston, well known as an authority on diseases of the throat, writes me: 'Washington's physicians are not to be criticised for their treatment, for they acted according to their best light and knowledge. To treat such a case in such a manner in the year 1889 would be little short of criminal. At the present time the physicians would use the laryngoscope and *look* and *see* what the trouble was. (The laryngoscope has only been used since 1857.) In this disease the function most interfered with is breathing. The one thing which saves a patient in this disease is a *timely tracheotomy*. (I doubt if tracheotomy had ever been performed in Virginia in Washington's time.) Washington ought to have been tracheotomized, or rather that is the way cases are saved today. No one would think of antimony, calomel, or bleeding now. The point is to let in the air, and not to let out the blood. After tracheotomy has been performed, the oedema and swelling of the larynx subside in three to six days. The tracheotomy tube is then removed, and respiration goes on again through the natural channels.' "[25]

Washington's will contained a clause stating that "the family vault at Mount Vernon requiring repairs, being improperly situated besides, I desire that a new one of brick, and upon a larger Scale may be built . . . on the ground which is marked out." A note by the editor of the *Writings* states: "the new vault (the present one), was built in 1830-31 by Lawrence Lewis and George Washington Parke Custis. They were the then surviving executors of the will.

[25]Lodge, *George Washington,* Vol. 2. p. 296.

The schedule attached to Washington's will shows that he owned nearly 50,000 acres, exclusive of his share in the Dismal Swamp partnership which proved to be worthless. About 37,000 of this 50,000 acres was situated on the Ohio River, the Great Kanawha and in Kentucky. He had sold much of his western holdings in his lifetime. To this total should be added the Mount Vernon estate which comprised, according to his estimate, 8077 acres. Besides, the will enumerates improved lots in Alexandria, Bath, the Federal City and an unimproved lot in Winchester.

At his death his estate must have been worth nearly a million dollars, which made him one of the richest Americans of his day, and his fortune had been honestly earned. His success was in large measure due to his foresight in acquiring rich bottom lands and holding them until they could be sold at a handsome profit.[26]

Washington was not a demonstrative man. He was born and grew up in a society with courtly and stately manners which repressed the outward expression of deep feeling, but he was capable of warm affections. He was denied children, but the love he would have given to his own issue, he gave to his wife's children and grandchildren. He felt the death of little Patsy Custis almost as deeply as her mother. "The Sweet Innocent Girl entered into a more happy and peaceful abode than any she has met with in the afflicted Path she hitherto has trod." His love for Eleanor Custis and his satisfaction in her marriage with his loved nephew, Lawrence Lewis, brightened his closing days. His best loved brother was John Augustine (Jack, he called him), whom he styled "the intimate companion of my youth and the friend of my ripened age." When he heard of his death in 1787, he called him his "beloved brother" and he bequeathed Mount Vernon to his son Bushrod.

He was equally fond of his nephew, George Augustine Washington, son of his brother Charles. When he found this nephew was in love with Frances Bassett, he advised their speedy marriage, and employed him as an estate manager. When he was threatened

[26]A full account of Washington's estate is given in E. E. Prussing's *Estate of George Washington, Deceased.*

with tuberculosis, Washington supplied him with money to travel in search of health, and when he died, wrote to his widow: "To you who so well know the affectionate regard I had for our departed friend, it is unnecessary to describe the sorrow with which I was afflicted at the news of his death." In his will he left his River Farm to George Augustine's children.

His letters show his affection for some of his friends, George William Fairfax and his wife, Bryan Fairfax, Dr. Craik, Lafayette, Chastellux and others.

He was sincerely attached to some of his employees and dependents; to Milly Posey, sending her his "affectionate regards" during the Revolution when he had scant time for anything but the war. When his servant and overseer, John Alton, died he called him "an old and faithful servant who had lived with me 30 odd years." The day after Alton's death he noted in his diary the death of another old servant, the wife of Thomas Bishop, "who had lived with me an equal number of years." Bishop had been Braddock's servant, whom he commended to Washington when dying. He lived with Washington forty years. Washington's affection for his favorite slave, William (Billy) Lee, has been described. But though friendly and affectionate, he knew how to maintain his dignity. There is a story that General Henry Lee (whom Washington certainly counted among his intimate friends) once boasted that he would show his familiarity with him, and coming up from behind, slapped him on the back. Washington turned on him with a thunderous "Sir," which put Lee in his place.

Washington's religious opinions have been much discussed. There is no question, however, that he was a fairly regular attendant at Pohick Church before the Revolution, at Christ Church, Alexandria, thereafter, and at Episcopal Churches in New York and Philadelphia while President.

Bishop Meade reports that the Reverend Lee Massey, rector of Pohick Church from about 1767 until after 1777, wrote, "I never knew so constant an attendant at church as Washington. His behaviour in the house of God was ever so reverential that it produced the happiest effects on my congregation and greatly assisted me in my pulpit labours. No company ever kept him from church."[27]

But as Mr. Massey had retired from the ministry before Washington returned to Mount Vernon after the Revolution, his testimony, if wholly accurate, covers only a few years, seven or eight at the most. There seems to be doubt whether he partook of communion after the Revolution. Eleanor Custis, writing of the time he was President, stated that "on communion Sundays he left the church with me, after the blessing, and returned home, and we sent the carriage back for my grandmother."

That he was a Theist there can be no doubt. He usually called God the Author of the Universe, the Supreme Being or Providence and he believed in a Divine Revelation. He believed that American independence was due to Divine intervention. Considering all that he had been through in the war, that was natural. He detested religious controversy, and none of his letters, as far as the writer has found, deal with strictly religious subjects. Dogmatic Christianity left him unmoved. In his Farewell Address, he wrote: "Observe good faith and justice tow'ds all Nations, Cultivate peace and harmony with all. Religion and morality enjoin this conduct. . . Can it be that Providence has not connected the permanent felicity of a Nation with its virtue?"

Perhaps the best account of Washington's religion was given by Madison. Jared Sparks, who published the writings of Washington, visited President Madison at Montpelier in 1830. Excerpts from his Journal are reprinted in the *Virginia Magazine of History and Biography,* April 1952. He reports: "Mr. Madison does not suppose that Washington ever attended to the arguments for Christianity and for the different systems of religion, or in fact that he had formed definite opinions on the subject. But he took things as he found them existing and was constant in his observances of worship according to the received forms of the Episcopal Church in which he was brought up."

In the debate over the disestablishment of the Episcopal Church

[27]Meade, William. *Old Churches, Ministers, and Families of Virginia,* Vol. 2, p. 247.

in Virginia, the question of taxing the members of each denomination for the support of its ministers was mooted and Washington stated his views in a letter to George Mason:

"Altho, no man's sentiments are more opposed to *any kind* of restraint upon religious principles than mine are; yet I must confess, that I am not amongst the number of those who are so much alarmed at the thoughts of making people pay towards the support of that which they profess, if of the denomination of Christians; or declare themselves Jews, Mahomitans or otherwise, and thereby obtain proper relief. As the matter now stands, I wish an assessment had never been agitated, and as it has gone so far, that the Bill, could die an easy death; because I think it will be productive of more quiet to the State, than by enacting it into a Law; which, in my opinion, would be impolitic, admitting there is a decided majority for it, to the disquiet of a respectable minority. In the first case the matter will soon subside; in the latter, it will rankle and perhaps convulse, the State. . ."[28]

Although Washington favored what today would be called "State aid" to religious organizations, he sensed the fact that the measure would be controversial and he feared it would "convulse" the State.

The separation of church and state was embodied in the first of the ten amendments to the Constitution, popularly known as the "Bill of Rights," and adopted concurrently with the Constitution. In the United States where there are so many religious sects, the system works well and there are few, if any, who would wish to change it. Washington's idea of State support of religious bodies has been carried out with apparent success in other countries. In most democratic countries independence of the church in spiritual matters has become a settled principle, but it has been considered desirable and even necessary that the state contribute financial assistance to the maintenance of religion. In Canada, the government contributes to the Protestant and Catholic churches. In Norway, Sweden, Denmark, Holland and Belgium the State gives financial aid to religion. In England, the church is established, and though

[28]*Writings,* Vol. 28, p. 285.

it no longer represents the majority of the English people, all but a handful support the principle of establishment. In France, both Catholic and Protestant churches received state aid until the separation of state and church shortly after the beginning of the twentieth century, and then Alsace was exempted. Recently the State has declared the Cathedrals "national monuments." In Italy, the hostility of the Vatican led Cavour to enunciate the doctrine of a "free church in a free state." The one statesmanlike act of Mussolini was his settlement of the "Roman Question."

This digression has been thought necessary to explain Washington's position. The Church had been disestablished; the glebes of its clergy confiscated. The Tory sympathies of some of its clergy and their close connection with the Church of England—all had made it unpopular. Its ruin seemed inevitable. The Baptists were seeking its extermination.

Nothing is more true than the often-repeated statement that character is of more importance in winning success in life than intelligence. Washington is the supreme example. This is not to say that he lacked intelligence. His early education was defective, except perhaps in Mathematics, but no reader of his correspondence can doubt his wide and varied practical intelligence. It was the consciousness of his want of a formal education that made him so willing to contribute to the education of his nephews and other deserving young men. He was therefore "honored and greatly affected" when in 1788 he was elected Chancellor of the College of William and Mary. His real education was his companionship with his half brothers, particularly Lawrence, and the Fairfax family. But it was his character that made him a man of mark. Responsibility came to him when still a boy, and at twenty-one he was carrying on his shoulders the burden of the defense of his native colony. When called to a wider field in the Revolutionary War, it was his steadfastness in disaster that prevented the dissolution of the Continental Army in its retreat across New Jersey and in the terrible winter at Valley Forge. It was shown in his patience with Congress. Having accepted the position of Commander-in-Chief, no criticism, no complaint, no indifference, no cabal, no treachery could force him to resign. He must finish his task; he must win independence for his country, and then return to his estate in Virginia.

It was much the same in his second term as President. He was a proud, sensitive man and resented what he considered slanderous attacks upon his conduct.

He wrote to General Henry Lee:

"But in what will abuse terminate? The result, as it affects myself, I care not: for I have consolation within that no earthly efforts can deprive me of, and that is, that neither ambition nor interested motives have influenced my conduct."

He was peculiarly sensitive to any accusation of nepotism, so when his nephew, Bushrod Washington, applied for appointment to a federal judgeship, he replied:

"You cannot doubt my wishes to see you appointed to any office of honor or emolument in the new government, to the duties of which you are competent; but however deserving you may be of the one you have suggested, your standing at the bar would not justify my nomination of you to the Federal district Court in preference of some of the oldest, and most esteemed General Court Lawyers in your own State, who are desirous of this appointment. My political conduct in nominations, even if I was uninfluenced by principle, must be exceedingly circumspect and proof against just criticism, for the eyes of Argus are upon me, and no slip will pass unnoticed that can be improved into a supposed partiality for friends or relations."

As a young officer he was ambitious, and resented any infringement upon his authority as colonel of the Virginia militia regiment. He journeyed all the way to Boston to have his authority over a certain Captain Dagworthy confirmed by Governor Shirley. Earlier he had declined to enter Braddock's army until the General sent him a pressing invitation to serve as his aide. After his marriage military ambition subsided and he was content to represent his county as a Burgess. His subsequent services as General and President were not of his seeking. They were almost forced upon him. In these capacities he sought advice from his associates and subordinates and frequently accepted their judgment in preference to his own.

In reporting the surrender of Cornwallis to Congress he gave generous praise to Rochambeau, DeGrasse and their officers, to the Engineers and the artillery of both armies, to the emulating spirit of the American Army, but of the part he had played in planning and executing the campaign, there was not a word.

He was a modest man, frequently distrustful of his own judgment. He was slow in making up his mind. His character impressed the French generals who served with him in the war. When peace was re-established with England, he received many tributes of respect and admiration from representative Englishmen. His greatness was universally recognized in his lifetime, but probably no tribute gave him greater satisfaction than the one received from Colonel John Fitzgerald and Dr. James Craik of Alexandria on March 13, 1797 as he returned to his native state to become once more a private citizen: "A number of the Inhabitants of this town and its vicinity wish to have the pleasure of meeting you on your entrance into the State and escorting you to Mt. Vernon. As they flatter themselves that this token of their sincere affection and esteem will not meet your disapprobation, they have dispatched the bearer to request you will let them know at what time you will probably cross the ferry (from Georgetown) that they may regulate themselves accordingly."

Jefferson had been unsympathetic to many of Washington's policies while President, but after his death, he paid him this noble tribute: "His integrity was most pure, his justice the most inflexible I have ever known; no motives of interest, or consanguinity, or friendship, or hatred being able to bias his decision. He was indeed in every sense of the word, a wise, a good and a great man."

Chapter 25

The End of an Era

An English gentleman travelling in Virginia shortly after the Revolution named some of the estates he saw on the Potomac: "beginning at Alexandria a little below the falls: On the Virginia side, Mr. Alexander's, General Washington's, Colonel Martin's, Colonel Fairfaxes, Mr. Lawton's near the mouth of Occoquan, Colonel Mason's, Mr. Lee's near the mouth of Quantico, Mr. Brent's (house burnt by the enemy during the war), Mr. Mercer, Mr. Fitzhugh, Mr. Alexander, of Boyd's Hole and all Chotank, Colonel Frank Thornton of Machodock, Mrs. Blair, Mr. McCarty, Col. Phil Lee of Nominy; . . . The situations and gentleman's sites on this river are beyond comparison or description beautiful. Every advantage, every elegance, every charm that bountiful nature can bestow is heaped with liberality and even profusion on the delightful banks of this most noble and superlatively grand river."[1]

Fithian, who was in Westmoreland County just before the Revolution, describes a wealthy educated society with its old-fashioned stateliness and grace, living on the banks of the Potomac and Rappahannock, with parties and long visits to each other's houses. And Chastellux in 1781 notes that the country through which he passed in his visit to and from Monticello was one of the finest in lower Virginia. He saw "many well cultivated estates and handsome houses" on the Pamunkey, the Appomattox and the James Rivers.

He mentions and describes briefly the Bowling (Bolling) house near Petersburg, Battersea (built by Colonel John Banister), Col. Cary's (Ampthill); Randolph houses on the Appomattox, Mr.

[1]Smyth, J. F. D. *Tours in the U. S.*, Vol. 2, p. 145.

Meade's and Westover on the James. The latter he says "surpasses all other houses in the magnificance of the buildings, the beauty of its situation and the pleasures of society." It was then the home of Mrs. Byrd, widow of the third William Byrd.

The wealth of the Pre-revolutionary Virginia aristocracy was based upon cheap and abundant land, cheap labor (African slavery) and a steady market for its tobacco. The war destroyed its tobacco market, and the connections with the Scotch and English tobacco merchants were never renewed. The Jeffersonian legislation abolishing entails and primogeniture broke up the great estates. The flood of irredeemable currency issued during the Revolution caused wild inflation which lasted until Congress assumed payment of Continental and state debts in 1790. This inflation affected all classes, but bore harder on the poor than on the rich.

The temper of the emerging society was hostile to both the aristocracy and the established church. The fertility of the soil was, if not destroyed, much impaired. Thousands were deserting Virginia for the virgin soil of Kentucky, Tennessee, and tributaries of the Mississippi. No wonder the value of Virginia farm land declined. Writing to Daniel McCarty in 1797 about a proposed purchase of the latter's Sugarland Run land in Northwestern Fairfax, Washington said: "If I mistake not lands here are not only at a stand, but on a decline." That was but the beginning. In the early nineteenth century many planters sold their ancestral estates in the tidewater for what they could get, and carried their slaves, their belongings, their cattle, their farm implements, to the then western lands and began life anew. This emigration did not seriously affect the Piedmont, the Shenandoah Valley or the southwestern part of the state. It did, however, affect and temporarily almost destroy, " a region roughly speaking half the size of England and once pre-eminently the England of the New World, where the manners and customs, the sports and even the prejudices of the mother country were reproduced with a fidelity that in colonial days was almost pathetic, and the traces of which are even yet not wholly extinct."[2]

[2]A. G. Bradley. *Sketches from Old Virginia,* pp. 109, 110.

What happened to Mount Vernon was happening all over the tidewater. John Randolph of Roanoke, writing in 1814 to Francis Scott Key, spoke of a visit to Cawsons, his old home, and said: "The days of my boyhood seemed to be renewed, but at the end of my journey I found desolation and stillness as of death—the fires of hospitality long since quenched—the parish church associated with my earliest and tenderest recollections, tumbling to pieces, not more from natural decay than from sacrilegious violence. What a spectacle does our lower country present? Deserted and dismantled country houses, once seats of cheerfulness and plenty, and the temples of the Most High ruinous and desolate, 'frowning in portentous silence upon the land'. The very mansions of the dead have not escaped violence. Shattered fragments of armorial bearings and epitaphs on sculptured stone attest the piety and vanity of the past and the brutality of the present age."

Randolph's biographer, Hugh A. Garland, mentions some of these estates near Cawsons. "Mayfield, Burlington, Mansfield, Olive Hill, Violet Hill, Roslin, all on the same river; many in sight and none more than two miles distant. These were the residences of gentlemen of ample fortune, of liberal education, polished manners, refined hospitality and devoted patriotism. They have all since passed into other hands. Some have gone down entirely and the wild pine and broomsedge have made such steady encroachments that a wilderness has grown up in place of fruitful fields."

The change was inevitable. The old plantation life of large estates had its virtues. It fostered independence of spirit, love of home and family. It solved the problem of living happily for the fortunate upper classes, and in colonial times there is little evidence of discontent among the other less fortunate classes. Transition from a lower social level to a higher one was relatively easy—marriage, talents, increase of land holdings, election to local magistracies; these sufficed to transform the descendants of many who came to Virginia as indentured servants into the lower gentry, who were welcomed at Mount Vernon, West's Grove and Gunston Hall. The portraits of the eighteenth century worthies show the unlined faces of men who were contented with life as they found it. Washington's life as a planter, vestryman, and burgess left happy memories to which in later years he looked back with nostalgia. George Mason in his will recommended to his sons, "from my own experience in life to prefer the happiness of independence and a private station," on their estates to any other mode of life.

But the old order that molded the character of Virginia's most famous soldiers and statemen was doomed. It was based upon class distinctions and African slavery: it was the rule of the privileged few over the many. A King Carter ruling a thousand dependents, a George Mason ruling five hundred and a George Washington ruling scarcely less, became an anomaly in a republic where birth and inherited wealth counted for little.

The Jeffersonian and later the Jacksonian Democracy broke the power of the educated classes which in church and state had dominated political and social life of what has been called "the golden age of Virginia." For good or for ill, such class consciousness had become a hindrance to the Virginia of the Republic, and what remained of that old society perished in the cataclysm of the Civil War.

And there were other causes at work to make the great estates of the past unprofitable. When agriculture recovered after the abolition of slavery, the owner of a hundred or two hundred acres, by the aid of labor-saving machinery and the use of agricultural fertilizers, found he could farm his land with a modicum of hired help, at a fair profit. Farm products became more diversified. North of the James River the culture of tobacco as a money crop has almost ceased, though it flourishes in the adjoining counties of Maryland. The sandy soil of the tidewater is well suited to growth of vegetables for which the nearby cities afford a market. Factories for canning tomatoes are fairly numerous in the counties near the Chesapeake Bay. Washington felt his neighbors did not appreciate the value of grazing lands and he resolved to devote a good portion of his farm land to that use as soon as he could cover his fields with grass. His death prevented carrying out his plans. A chief industry in Fairfax

County today is cattle raising and dairying. It has the advantage it could not have in Washington's day—a neighboring metropolitan city to take its milk, cream and butter.

The Virginia of today cherishes her past, but her life, in city and country, is almost the opposite of what it was in the eighteenth century. But there still stand on the banks of her rivers over forty colonial churches and several hundred country homes, precious memorials of a vanished age.

Sources Consulted

Before listing the sources consulted in this study, a brief note is given about the editors and collectors who have done such valuable service in making Washington's writings available.

Jared Sparks

Jared Sparks was born in 1789 and died in 1866. He was President of Harvard College from 1849 to 1853. During the years 1834 to 1837 he published the *Writings of George Washington* in twelve volumes, containing about 2500 letters and documents.

Washington had bequeathed to his nephew, Bushrod Washington, "all the papers in my possession which relate to my Civil and Military Administration of the affairs of this Country . . . and such of my private papers as are worth preserving." Bushrod Washington gave away many valuable papers, some of which have been found and purchased, or reproduced by the United States government; but many have been lost.

In preparation for his edition Sparks visited Mount Vernon, but found he needed more supplemental data than was available there, and persuaded Bushrod to let him take the manuscripts to Cambridge, Massachusetts. Bushrod died while the manuscripts were in Sparks' possession, and by his will the ownership of the collection passed to his nephew, George Corbin Washington. The United States purchased the manuscripts and many books belonging to the Mount Vernon library in 1834 and 1849 for $25,000 and $20,000.

Sparks' method of editing and the many changes he made in the text of the letters have been severely criticised. However, his work included valuable letters and extracts from Washington's *Diaries* which are now lost.

Worthington C. Ford

Worthington C. Ford, chief of the Manuscript Division of the Library of Congress from 1889 to 1893, published a new edition of Washington's letters in fourteen volumes, omitting some letters published by Sparks and adding about eight hundred letters not previously published. He corrected many of Sparks' inaccuracies, and his work remained the standard edition in use by all historians until the *Writings* edited by Fitzpatrick appeared.

Dr. Joseph M. Toner

Dr. Joseph M. Toner was an eminent physician in the City of Washington and a member of the Washington School Board. An elementary school building there bears his name. Though he wrote no book about George Washington he was an indefatigable collector of information about him. Dr. Fitzpatrick said of him, "His accumulations are large in quantity and include a vast number of transcripts, the originals of which are no longer available . . . no serious study of the available Washingtoniana can be made without the investigator becoming deeply impressed with the tremendous and valuable work done by Dr. Toner." The Toner Collection is now in the Library of Congress.

John C. Fitzpatrick

John C. Fitzpatrick was born in 1876, and died in 1940. He entered the service of the Library of Congress in 1897; became assistant chief of the Division of Manuscripts in 1912. In 1928, he resigned to devote himself to the study of the manuscripts relating to George Washington. He had edited the *Diaries of George Washington,* which were published in 1925 under the auspices of the Mount Vernon Ladies Association of the Union. In 1927 he published *George Washington, Colonial Traveller, 1732-1775,* tracing Washington's journeys until the beginning of the Revolutionary War. He was also the author of *George Washington, Day by Day,* and of a *Life of Washington.*

He edited several volumes of the Continental Congress. His labors gained him many honorary degrees and membership in various historical societies, including the American Catholic Historical Association, of which he was president. His crowning honor was his appointment as editor of the *Writings of George Washington,* published by the United States Bicentennial Commission of the Two Hundredth Anniversary of the Birth of George Washington. He gave the last years of his life to this work, which was practically completed before his death. His primary interest was the original sources, rather than the use of them as a basis for secondary books.

Land Records

Fairfax County, Virginia
- Deed Books.
- Will Books.

Northern Neck Land Grants. Liber C.
- These manuscript volumes are preserved in the State Capitol in Richmond.

Prince William County, Virginia.
- Deed Books.
- Will Books.

Bibliography

Armes, Ethel. *Stratford Hall; The Great House of the Lees.* Richmond, Garrett and Massie, Inc., 1936. 575 pp.

Baedeker, Karl. *Great Britain; handbook for travellers.* Leipsic, Karl Baedeker, publisher, 1901. 600 pp. Colchester, England.

Bradley, A. G. *Sketches from Old Virginia.* London, Macmillan and Co., Ltd., 1897. 284 pp.

Bridenbaugh, Carl. "Baths and Watering Places of Colonial America," *William and Mary Quarterly,* 3rd ser., v. 3, no. 4, April, 1946, pp. 151-181.

Brydon, George Maclaren. *Virginia's Mother Church and the Political Conditions under which it grew.* v. 2. The Story of the Anglican Church and the Development of Religion in Virginia, 1727-1814. Philadelphia, Church Historical Soc., 1952. 688 pp.

Burnaby, Andrew. *Burnaby's Travels through North America.* Reprinted from the 3rd ed. of 1798 . . . N. Y., A. Wessels Company, 1904. 265 pp.

Callahan, Charles H. *Washington, the Man and the Mason. . .* Pub. under the auspices of the Memorial Temple Committee of the George Washington Masonic National Memorial Association. Washington, D. C., Press of Gibson Bros., 1933. 366 pp.

Chastellux, François Jean, Marquis de. *Travels in North America, in the years 1780-81-82.* New York, 1928.

Colles, Christopher. *Survey of the Roads of the United States of America.* A. D. 1789.

"The author was an engineer, inventor, and promoter of internal improvements. He was deeply interested in road building and during the late eighties made a personal tour of the existing road system. The maps in the volume are actually based on surveys made by American Army Engineers, Robert Erskine and Simeon DeWitt, under the direction of General George Washington. In scope, this first Blue Book of American Roads covers the States of New York, Connecticut, New Jersey, Pennsylvania, Maryland, and Virginia."—From Exhibit card in the Library of Congress.

Cooke, John Esten. *Virginia; a history of the people.* Boston, Houghton Mifflin Co., c. 1911. 535 pp.

Custis, George Washington Parke. *Recollections and Private Memoirs of Washington.* Philadelphia, J. W. Bradley, 1861. 644 pp.

Davis, Deering, and others. *Alexandria Houses,* 1750-1830. By Deering Davis, Stephen P. Dorsey & Ralph Cole Hall. Special Article by Nancy McClelland. New York, Architectural Book Publishing Co., Inc., 1946. 128 pp.; illus.

Dodge, Harrison Howell. *Mount Vernon; Its Owner and Its Story. . .* Including His Personal Recollections after Continuous Service since 1885 as Resident Custodian. . . Philadelphia, J. B. Lippincott Co., 1932: 232 pp.; illus.

Duhamel, James F. *Belvoir.* Columbia Hist. Soc. of Washington, D. C. *Records,* v. 35-36, p. 149. 1935.

Eckenrode, H. J. *The Story of the Campaign and Siege of Yorktown.* Washington, Govt. Print. Off., 1931. 54 pp. (U. S. Congress, 71st, 3d session. Senate Doc. no. 318.)

Encyclopaedia Britannica. 11th edition.
Article on John Stuart Mill and others.

Eubank, H. Ragland. *Touring Historyland; The Authentic Guide Book of Historic Northern Neck of Virginia; The Land of George Washington and Robert E. Lee.* Issued by The Northern Neck Association, Colonial Beach, Virginia. Richmond, Va., Whittet & Shepperson, 1934. 108 pp.

Faehtz, Ernest F. M., comp. *Washington in Embryo; or, The National Capital from 1791 to 1800. . . .* Prepared with the special assistance of Brainard H. Warner, by E. F. M. Faehtz and F. W. Pratt. Washington, D. C., 1874. 78 pp.; maps.

Fithian, Philip Vickers. *Journal & Letters of Philip Vickers Fithian, 1773-1774.* Williamsburg, Virginia, Colonial Williamsburg, Inc., 1943. 323 pp. (Williamsburg Restoration Historical Studies, No. 30.)

Fithian, Philip Vickers. *Philip Vickers Fithian: Journal,* 1775-1776, written on the Virginia-Pennsylvania Frontier and in the Army around New York. Princeton University Press, 1934. 279 pp. This is volume 2. Volume 1 was published in 1900 by the Princeton Historical Society, and covers 1767-1774.

Fitzpatrick, John C. *George Washington: Colonial Traveller,* 1732-1775. Indianapolis, Bobbs-Merrill Co., 1927. 416 pp.; map.

Fitzpatrick, John C. *George Washington Himself; a Commonsense Biography, Written from His Manuscripts.* Indianapolis, Bobbs-Merrill Co., 1933. 544 pp.

Fleet, Beverley. "John Washington Settles in Virginia." *Virginia Magazine of History and Biography,* v. 53, no. 2, April, 1945, pp. 124-126.

Ford, Paul Leicester. *The True George Washington.* 8th ed. Philadelphia, J. B. Lippincott Co., 1900. 319 pp.

Ford, Worthington Chauncey, ed. *Wills of George Washington and His Immediate Ancestors.* Brooklyn, N. Y., Historical Printing Club, 1891. 210 pp.

Freeman, Douglas Southall. *George Washington; A Biography.* New York, C. Scribner's Sons, 1948-1954. v. 1-6.

Freeman, Douglas Southall. *Lee's Lieutenants.* New York, Charles Scribner's Sons, 1942-1944. 3 v.

Freeman, Douglas Southall. *R. E. Lee; A Biography.* New York, C. Scribner's Sons, 1933-1935. 4 vols.

Garden Club of Virginia. *Homes and Gardens in Old Virginia.* Edited by Frances Archer Christian and Susanne Williams Massie. Richmond, Garrett and Massie, Inc., 1931 and 1950. 1950 edition revised by Virginia Christian Claiborne, Ella Williams Smith, and Caroline Pickrell Strudwick.

Garland, Hugh A. *The Life of John Randolph of Roanoke.* New York, D. Appleton & Company, 1850, 2 v.

George Washington's Grist Mill. An unpaged pamphlet distributed at the restored mill.

Goolrick, John T. *Fredericksburg and the Cavalier Country; America's Most Historic Section, Its Homes: Its People and Romances.* Richmond, Garrett & Massie, 1935. 92 pp.; illus.

Gray, Arthur P. "Washington's Burgess Route." *Virginia Magazine of History and Biography,* v. 46, no. 4, October 1938, pp. 299-315; map.

Gray, Arthur P. "The White House—Washington's Marriage Place." *Virginia Magazine of History and Biography,* v. 42, July, 1934, pp. 229-240; illus.

Groome, H. C. *Fauquier during the Proprietorship; a Chronicle of the Coloniza-*

tion and Organization of a Northern Neck County. Richmond, Old Dominion Press, 1927. 255 pp.

Hamilton, Stanislaw Murray, ed. *Letters to Washington, and Accompanying Papers;* published by the Society of the Colonial Dames of America. Boston, Houghton Mifflin Co., 1898-1902. 5 v.

Harrison, Fairfax. *Landmarks of Old Prince William; a Study of Origins in Northern Virginia.* Richmond, The Old Dominion Press, 1924. 2 v. continuously paged.

Harrison, Fairfax. "The Proprietors of the Northern Neck; Chapters of Culpeper Genealogy." *Virginia Magazine of History and Biography,* v. 33, no. 2, 3, 4, April, July, Oct. 1925, pp. 113-153, 223-267, 333-358; v. 34, no. 1, Jan. 1926, pp. 19-64.

Harrison, Frederic. *Memories and Thoughts.* New York, Macmillan Co., 1906. 409 pp.

Hartwell, Henry, Blair, James, and Chilton, Edward. *The Present State of Virginia, and the College.* Williamsburg, Virginia, Colonial Williamsburg, Inc., 1940. 105 pp.; illus. (Williamsburg Restoration Historical Studies, No. 1.)

Haworth, Paul Leland. *George Washington, Country Gentleman; Being an Account of His Home Life and Agricultural Activities.* Indianapolis, Bobbs-Merrill Co., 1925. 336 pp.

Haycock, Robert Lee. "Career of Col. Charles Broadwater, Fairfax County, Va." *Virginia Magazine of History and Biography,* v. 47, no. 3, July, 1939, pp. 234-238.

Hayden, Horace E. *Virginia Genealogies.* Reprinted, Washington, D. C. The Rare Book Shop, 1931. 758 pp.

Howe, James Lewis. "George Washington Custis Lee." *Virginia Magazine of History and Biography,* vol. 47, no. 4, pp. 315-327. Oct. 1940.

Hening, William Waller, comp. *The Statutes at Large; Being a Collection of all the Laws of Virginia, from the First Session of the Legislature, in the Year 1619.* Published Pursuant to an Act of the General Assembly of Virginia, Passed on the Fifth Day of February, One Thousand Eight Hundred and Eight.

Hopkins, Griffith M. *Map of the Vicinity of Washington, D. C.* Philadelphia, G. M. Hopkins, 1894. Folded, colored maps giving names of home owners and acreage.

Hoyt, William D. "Selfportrait. Eliza Custis, 1808." *Virginia Magazine of History and Biography,* v. 53, no. 2, April, 1945, pp. 89-100.

Jackson, Cordelia. *Edward Washington and His Kin.* Washington, D. C., Mimeoform Press, 1934. 24 pp.

Jefferson, Thomas. *Notes on the State of Virginia.* Philadelphia, H. C. Carey & I. Lea, 1825. 344 pp.

Kabler, Dorothy H. *The Story of Gadsby's Tavern.* Alexandria, Va., Newell-Cole Co., Printers, 1952. 71 pp.

Kibler, J. Luther. *Sketches of One Hundred and Thirty-Three Historic Virginia Landmarks from Cape Henry to Richmond.* Richmond, Garrett & Massie, Inc., 1929. 141 pp.; illus.

Lanman, Charles. Biographical Annals of the Civil Government of the United States, during Its First Century. Washington, J. Anglim, 1876. 676 pp.

Lasteyrie du Saillant, Marie Antoinette Virginie. *Life of Madame de Lafayette . . .* translated from the French by Louis de Lasteyrie. Paris, Léon Techener, 1872. 456 pp.

Lecky, William Edward Hartpole. *The Map of Life; Conduct and Character.* New York, Longmans, Green and Co., 1899. 353 pp.

Lewis, Charles. *Journal of Captain Charles Lewis of Fredericksburg, Virginia, When in the Service of the Colony of Virginia, in the Year 1755.* Privately printed, 1925(?), 23 pp.

Lindsey, Mary. *Historic Homes and Landmarks of Alexandria, Virginia.* Alexandria, Virginia, Printed by Newell-Cole Co., Inc., c. 1947. 56 pp.; illus.

Lodge, Henry Cabot. *George Washington.* Boston, Houghton Mifflin Co., 1889. 2 v.

McGroarty, William Buckner. "The Death of Washington." *Virginia Magazine of History and Biography,* v. 54, no. 2, April, 1946, pp. 152-156.

McGroarty, William Buckner. "Elizabeth Washington of Hayfield." *Virginia Magazine of History and Biography,* v. 33, no. 2, April, 1925, pp. 154-165.

Martin, Lawrence, ed. *George Washington Atlas.* Washington, D. C., U. S. George Washington Bicentennial Commission, 1932. 50 plates; 85 maps.

Meade, William. *Old Churches, Ministers and Families of Virginia.* Philadelphia, J. B. Lippincott Co., 1900. 2 v.

Moore, Gay Montague. *Seaport in Virginia; George Washington's Alexandria.* Richmond, Virginia, Garrett and Massie, Inc., 1949. 274 pp.; illus.

Moore, R. Walton. *Dr. James Craik, Chief Physician and Surgeon of the Continental Army.* Address by Hon. R. Walton Moore of Virginia, delivered at the Unveiling of a Monument to the Memory of Dr. James Craik . . . in the Churchyard of the Old Presbyterian Meeting House in Alexandria, Va., on October 14, 1928. Washington, U. S. Govt. Print. Off., 1929. 8 pp. (Printed in the Congressional Record, Februray 22, 1929.)

Moore, R. Walton. *Some Work of George Washington as a Statesman in His Home County.* Speech of Hon. R. Walton Moore of Virginia in the House of Representatives, February 22, 1930. Washington, U. S. Govt. Print. Off., 1930. 12 pp.

Neill, Edward D. *The Fairfaxes of England and America in the Seventeenth and Eighteenth Centuries . . .* Albany, N. Y., Joel Munsell, 1868. 234 pp.

Niemcewicz, Julian. "Visit to Mount Vernon a Century Ago." *Century Magazine,* v. 63, Feb., 1902, pp. 510-522.

Niles, Blair. *Martha's Husband; an Informal Portrait of George Washington.* New York, McGraw-Hill Book Co., Inc., c. 1951. 307 pp.; illus.

Norwood, Henry. "A Voyage to Virginia." In *Virginia Reader; a Treasury of Writings* (Ed. by Francis Coleman Rosenberger. New York, E. P. Dutton & Co., 1948.), pp. 116-171. "A little known account of an exciting voyage to Virginia in 1649."

Palmer, Lucy Jane Brent, comp. "Charles Brent of Stafford County, Virginia, and Some of His Descendants," *Virginia Magazine of History and Biography,* v. 34, no. 2, April, 1926, pp. 180-183. Cites Overwharton Parish Register.

Petit Larousse Illustré; Nouveau Dictionnaire Encyclopédique . . . Paris, Librairie Larousse, 1913. 1664 pp. Chastellux (*le marquis* François Jean *de*), p. 1222.

Prince William; the Story of Its People and Its Places. Compiled by Workers of the Writers Program of the Work Projects Administration in the State of Virginia. Richmond, Va., Whittet & Shepperson, 1941. 261 pp. (American Guide Series) "Copyright 1941 The Bethlehem Good Housekeeping Club, Manassas, Va."

Proctor, "CC". (Mary Lucile Proctor). "After-Dinner Anecdotes of James Madison; Excerpts from Jared Sparks' Journal for 1829-31." *Virginia Magazine of History and Biography,* v. 60, no. 2, April, 1952, pp. 255-265.

Prussing, Eugene E. *The Estate of George Washington, Deceased.* Boston, Little, Brown, and Co., 1927. 512 pp.

Rowland, Kate Mason. *The Life of George Mason,* 1725-1792. New York, G. P. Putnam's Sons, 1892. 2 v.

Showalter, William Joseph. "The Travels of George Washington; Dramatic Episodes in His Career as the First Geographer of The United States." *National Geographic Magazine,* v. 61, no. 1, January, 1932, pp. 1-63. Illustrated and contains a folded map of the travels of George Washington.

Slaughter, Philip. *The History of Truro Parish in Virginia. . .* Ed. with notes and addenda by Edward L. Goodwin. Philadelphia, George W. Jacobs & Co., 1908. 164 pp. Quotes entries from the *Truro Parish Vestry Book.*

Smith, Goldwin. *The United States; an Outline of Political History, 1492-1871.* New York, Macmillan and Co., 1893. 312 pp.

Smyth, John Ferdinand Dalziel. *Tours in the United States of America.* London, For G. Robinson, 1784. 2 v.

Snowden, W. H. *Some Old Historic Landmarks of Virginia and Maryland.* Philadelphia, J. B. Lippincott Co., 1894. 71 pp.; illus.

Snowden, W. H. *Some Old Historic Landmarks of Virginia and Maryland.* 3rd ed. Alexandria, Va., Printed by G. H. Ramey & Son, 1902. 122 pp.; illus.

Stetson, Charles W. *Four Mile Run Land Grants.* Washington, D. C., Mimeoform Press, 1935. 142 pp.; illus.

Terrett et al., v. Taylor et al. 9 Cranch. U. S. Supreme Court Reports 43. 1815.

Torrence, Clayton. "A Virginia Lady of Quality and Her Possessions—Mrs. Mildred Willis, of Fredericksburg." *Virginia Magazine of History and Biography,* v. 56, no. 1, January, 1948, pp. 42-56.

Tyler, J. E. "Colonel George Mercer's Papers." *Virginia Magazine of History and Biography,* v. 60, no. 3, July, 1952, pp. 405-420.

U. S. Army. *The Engineer Center, Fort Belvoir, Virginia.* Fort Belvoir, Va., 1952. 28 pp. (Information Pamphlet).

U. S. George Washington Bicentennial Commission. *Family Relationships of George Washington.* Washington, D. C., U. S. Govt. Print. Off., 1931. 20 pp.

U. S. National Park Service. *George Washington Birthplace National Monument.* Washington, D. C., 1941. (Unpaged Folder.)

Virginia: a Guide to the Old Dominion. Compiled by the Workers of the Writers' Program of the Work Projects Administration in the State of Virginia. New York, Oxford University Press, 1940. 699 pp. (Amer. Guide Ser.) Cited as Virginia Guide.

Wall, Charles C. "Notes on the Early History of Mount Vernon." *William and Mary Quarterly,* 3rd ser., v. 2, no. 2, April, 1945, pp. 173-190; illus.

Washington, George. *The Diaries of George Washington,* 1748-1799, edited by

John C. Fitzpatrick. Published for the Mount Vernon Ladies' Association of the Union. Boston, Houghton Mifflin Co., 1925. 4 v.

Washington, George. *The Writings of George Washington;* collected and ed. by Worthington Chauncey Ford. New York, G. P. Putnam's Sons, 1889-93. 14 v.

Washington, George. *The Writings of George Washington from the Original Manuscript Sources 1745-1799;* prepared under the Direction of the United States George Washington Bicentennial Commission and Published by Authority of Congress; John C. Fitzpatrick, editor. Washington, U. S. Govt. Print. Off., 1931-44. 39 v.

Waterman, Thomas Tileston. *The Mansions of Virginia,* 1706-1776. Chapel Hill, The University of North Carolina Press, 1946. 456 pp.; illus.

Wayland, John W. "Washington West of the Blue Ridge." *Virginia Magazine of History and Biography,* v. 48, no. 3, July, 1940, pp. 193-201.

West Virginia; a Guide to the Mountain State. Compiled by Workers of the Writer's Program of the Work Projects Administration in the State of West Virginia. New York, Oxford Univ. Press, 1941. 559 pp. (Amer. Guide Ser.). Cited as West Virginia Guide. "Sponsored by the Conservation Commission of West Virginia."

Whitlock, Brand. *La Fayette.* New York, D. Appleton and Co., 1930. 2 v.; illus.

Wilstach, Paul. *Mount Vernon; Washington's Home and the Nation's Shrine.* Indianapolis, Bobbs-Merrill Co., c. 1916. 301 pp.; illus.

Woodlawn Plantation, Mount Vernon, Virginia. A folder distributed at Woodlawn, which is administered by The National Trust for Historic Preservation.

Index

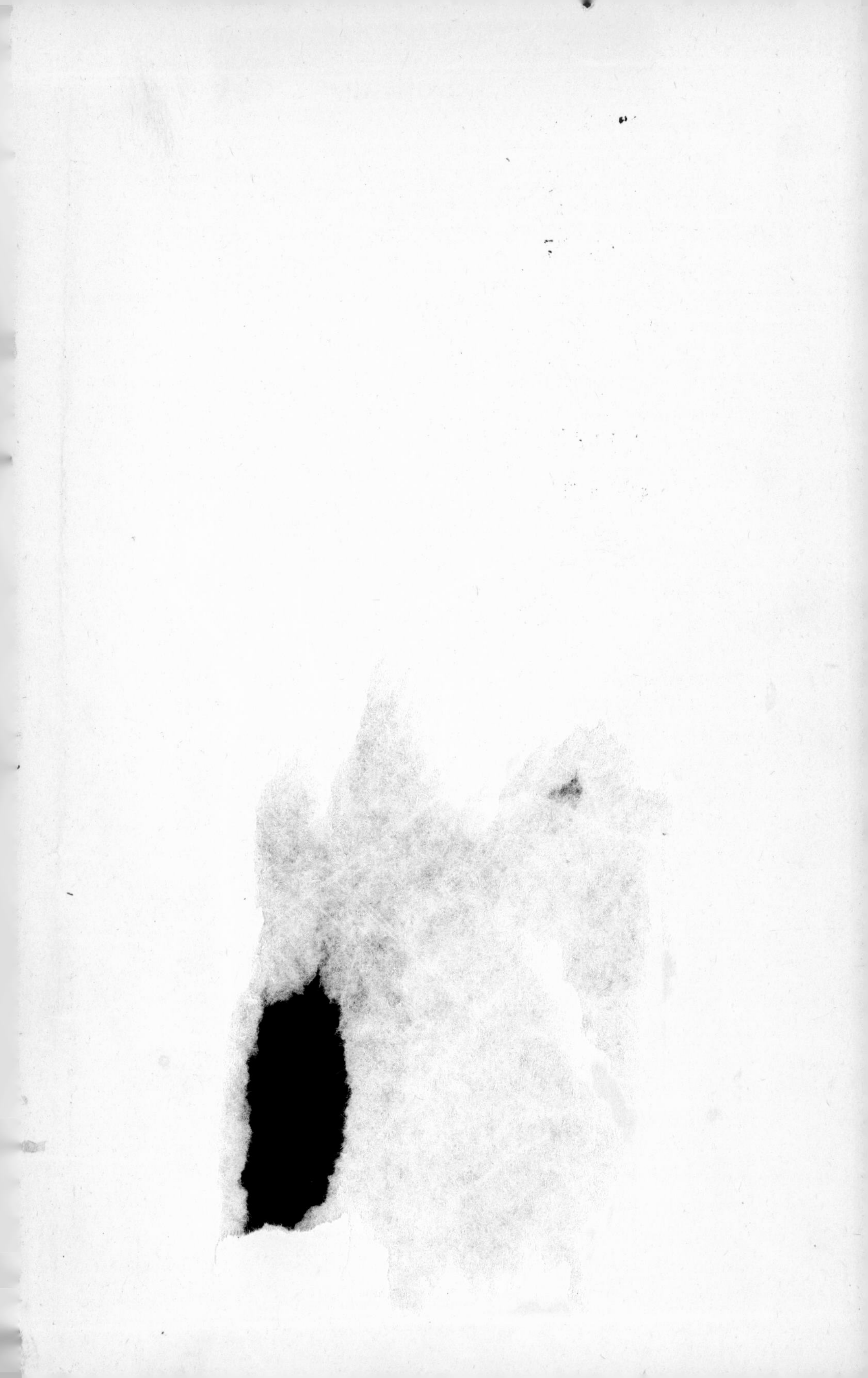

References

A Within these lines one or two medium farms might be formed independent
land is capable of high improvement into Meadow being low; part of it is alread
to be so: requiring to be drained.—There are no houses on it.

B Great part within these lines is in Wood, but there is a sufficiency of ground
middle sized farm, with a house thereon; and a most beautiful Site for a Gentle

C Possesses the same advantage.—The whole of it is cleared of the Wood but ha

D Is cleared land, and might be added to River farm;—or if that farm shoul
of the smaller ones—affording pleasant sites for houses on the River.

E The use of this farm is given to a relation.

No. 7
No. 6
Dogue
No. 5
Run
No. 2
No. 3
No. 4
No. 1
A
B
part of No. 4
Part of No. 4
Meadow 42 acres
No. 3
No. 5
Union
No. 6
Farm
No. 2
No. 1
part of No. 1
No. 7
Part of No. 1
Mudd
No. 2
No. 3
No. 4
Mansion
Far